How Did We Get Into This Mess?

How Did We Get Into This Mess?

Politics, Equality, Nature

George Monbiot

VERSO

London • New York

First published by Verso 2016
© George Monbiot 2016

Many of the articles reprinted here appeared first in the *Guardian*

3 5 7 9 10 8 6 4

Verso
UK: 6 Meard Street, London W1F 0EG
US: 20 Jay Street, Suite 1010, Brooklyn, NY 11201
versobooks.com

Verso is the imprint of New Left Books

ISBN-13: 978-1-78478-362-4
eISBN-13: 978-1-78478-361-7 (US)
eISBN-13: 978-1-78478-363-1 (UK)

British Library Cataloguing in Publication Data
A catalogue record for this book is available from the British Library

Library of Congress Cataloging-in-Publication Data

Names: Monbiot, George, 1963– author.
Title: How did we get into this mess? : politics, equality, nature / George
Monbiot.
Description: London ; Brooklyn, NY : Verso, 2016.
Identifiers: LCCN 2015050747| ISBN 9781784783624 (hardback) | ISBN
9781784783617 (E-ISBN : US)
Subjects: LCSH: Social history– 21st century. | World politics– 21st century.
| Economic history– 21st century. | Corporations– Political activity. |
Business and politics. | Environmental degradation. | Globalization. |
BISAC: POLITICAL SCIENCE / Political Freedom & Security / Civil Rights. |
SCIENCE / Environmental Science. | NATURE / Ecosystems & Habitats /
General.
Classification: LCC HN18.3 .M66 2016 | DDC 301.09/051– dc23
LC record available at http://lccn.loc.gov/2015050747

Typeset in Fournier MT by Hewer Text Ltd, Edinburgh
Printed in the US by Maple Press

To Rebecca, Hanna and Martha

Contents

Introduction   1

Part 1: There Is Such a Thing as Society

1. Falling Apart   9
2. Deviant and Proud   14
3. Work-Force   19
4. Addicted to Comfort   23
5. Dead Zone   27
6. Help Addicts, but Lock Up the
      Casual Users of Cocaine   32

Part 2: Lost Youth

7. Rewild the Child   39
8. The Child Inside   43
9. Amputating Life Close to Its Base   48
10. 'Bug Splats'   53

11. Kin Hell   58
12. The Sacrificial Caste   62
13. A Modest Proposal for Tackling Youth   67
14. Pro-Death   72

Part 3: The Wild Life

15. Everything Is Connected   79
16. Civilisation Is Boring   88
17. End of an Era   99
18. The Population Myth   103
19. The Dawning   108

Part 4: Feeding Frenzy

20. Sheepwrecked   119
21. Ripping Apart the Fabric of the Nation   123
22. Drowning in Money   130
23. Small Is Bountiful   139

Part 5: Energy Vampires

24. Leave It in the Ground   147
25. Applauding Themselves to Death   152
26. The Grime behind the Crime   160
27. Going Critical   164
28. Power Crazed   169

Part 6: Riches and Ruins

29. The Impossibility of Growth   175
30. Curb Your Malthusiasm   179

31. Kleptoremuneration   184
32. The Self-Attribution Fallacy   188
33. The Lairds of Learning   193
34. The Man Who Wants to Northern Rock the Planet   198
35. The Gift of Death   203

Part 7: Dance with the One Who Brung You

36. How the Billionaires Broke the System   209
37. Plutocracy's Boot Boys   213
38. How Did We Get Into This Mess?   217
39. Going Naked   222

Part 8: Out of Sight, Out of Mind

40. The Holocaust We Will Not See   227
41. The Empire Strikes Back   232
42. Unremitting Pain   236
43. Bomb Everyone   241

Part 9: Holding Us Down

44. A Global Ban on Leftwing Politics   249
45. Innocent until Proved Dead   254
46. The Paranoia Squad   258
47. Union with the Devil   263

Part 10: Finding Our Place

48. Someone Else's Story   271
49. Highland Spring   275

50. A Telling Silence   280
51. The Values of Everything   285

Acknowledgements   291
Notes   293
Index   333

Introduction

In *Capital in the Twenty-First Century*, Thomas Piketty argues that no government programme could be sustained without an 'apparatus of justification'.[1] Without the corporate press, without spin doctors and lobbyists and think tanks, the unnecessary programmes of austerity that several governments have imposed would be politically impossible. Current levels of inequality would be considered intolerable. The destruction of the living world would be the occasion of constant protest. This apparatus of justification, or infrastructure of persuasion, and the justifying narratives it generates allow the rich to seize much of our common wealth, to trample the rights of workers and to treat the planet as their dustbin. Ideas, not armies or even banks, run the world. Ideas determine whether human creativity works for society or against it.

Ever since Andrew Carnegie, John D. Rockefeller and Thomas Edison financed the publication of Herbert Spencer's works in the late nineteenth century,[2] which argued, among other propositions, that millionaires stand at the top of a *scala natura* established by natural selection, with which we would be foolish to interfere, and that profound economic inequalities are both natural and necessary, global oligarchs have invested heavily in the infrastructure of persuasion. The newspapers they own and the think tanks they fund seek the best minds money can buy to produce brilliant and persuasive arguments in defence of the elite.

For every independent voice with a national platform, there are one hundred working on behalf of plutocratic power. Of course, this role is not specified in their contracts. I doubt that many people ask themselves before writing a column or a position paper, 'How can I best serve the interests of my billionaire proprietor today?' But it does not take long to discover which positions and arguments secure your advancement, and which compromise it. In the media, proprietors appoint editors in their own image; editors tend to hire and promote the journalists whose views they find congenial.

The oligarchs spread their money wide. Some, for example, fund a large number of think tanks, creating the impression that their demands express a pre-existing consensus; that hundreds of thinkers have come to the same view independently. They use their power to browbeat and marginalise the few outlets they do not control: witness the global assault on public service broadcasting.

So few are the countervailing voices, and so thoroughly have they been excluded from most of the media, including the public broadcasters (now locked in a permanent state of terror and anticipatory compliance as they await the next assaults on their budgets), that the dominant forms of power remain almost unchallenged.

Take, for example, the ideology that now governs our lives. Not only is it seldom challenged; it is seldom even identified. As a result, no one seems to know what to call it. Neoliberalism? Market fundamentalism? Laissez-faire economics? Though it is a clear and consistent belief system, though it is the ideology to which most governments and major opposition parties subscribe, and though it determines everything from the distribution of wealth to the treatment of the living planet, it has no standard or widely recognised name.

Everyone knows, or thinks they know, what communism and anarchism mean, though both are now endangered species. But mention the dominant ideology in conversation – whatever you choose to call it – and most people will look at you blankly. Even if they have previously heard the term you use, they are unlikely to be able to define it. What greater power can there be than to operate namelessly?

So pervasive has neoliberalism become that we seldom even recognise it as an ideology. We appear to accept the neoliberal proposition that this utopian, millenarian faith (which holds that the free market, unimpeded by government intervention, will answer all human needs) is nothing more than a description of a neutral, natural force – a kind of biological law, like Darwin's theory of evolution.

In reality, the free market is a political construction, that often has to be imposed through violence, such as Suharto's massacres in Indonesia, Pinochet's coup in Chile and the suppression of protests against structural adjustment and austerity all over the world.[3] Far from being a neutral forum, the market is dominated by powerful agents – corporations and oligarchs – who use their position to demand special treatment: contracts, handouts, tax breaks, treaties, the crushing of resistance and other political favours. They extend their power beyond their trading relationships through their ownership of the media and their funding and control of political parties.

Freedom of the kind championed by neoliberals means freedom from competing interests. It means freedom from the demands of social justice, from environmental constraints, from collective bargaining and from the taxation that funds public services. It means, in sum, freedom from democracy. The negative freedom enjoyed by corporations and billionaires (freedom to be or to act without interference from others; as defined by Isaiah Berlin in his essay *Two Concepts of Liberty* [4]) intrudes upon the negative freedom the rest of us enjoy. As a result, the great flowering of freedom that has enhanced so many lives since the end of the Second World War is now at risk.

The freedom of the elite from democratic restraint limits other people's freedom from hunger, poverty and brutal conditions of employment. It limits free access to health and education; freedom from industrial injuries; freedom from pollution, addiction, loan sharks and confidence tricksters. Freedom for the financial sector means speculative chaos, economic crises and bailouts for which the rest of us must pay.

The crushing of protest and the promotion of corporate power (by instruments such as the proposed Transatlantic Trade and Investment Partnership) are just two forms of the extreme government intervention required to create a system which claims to be free from government intervention. Another example is the vast infrastructure of law and coercion needed to commodify land, labour and money, none of which fall organically into a market economy.[5] Another is the invention of limited liability, which permits companies to shed and socialise their losses. Neoliberalism, far from revealing biological laws, describes a system that creates its own reality.

All this remains largely invisible to citizens: unnamed, unexamined and shrouded by the mysteries of faith. The anonymity of neoliberalism is not only an expression of power; it is a source of power. You can judge the openness and pluralism of a society by the extent to which its dominant forces are identified. On this measure, ours is in poor political health.

So the work on which I have spent most of my adult life, which is sometimes characterised by people who deliver more tangible goods and services as pointless, even sybaritic, could in fact be quite useful. While those who write and speak for a living produce neither food nor medicine, generate little in the way of money or employment, dig no wells and build no bridges, it is arguable that without their influence, the efforts of those whose achievements are more visible might be vitiated.

Without countervailing voices, naming and challenging power, political freedom withers and dies. Without countervailing voices, a better world can never materialise. Without countervailing voices, wells will still be dug and bridges will still be built, but only for the few. Food will still be grown, but it will not reach the mouths of the poor.[6] New medicines will be developed, but they will be inaccessible to many of those in need. Think of how different political environments create radically different health systems – and health outcomes – in countries with comparable levels of economic activity. When captured by certain ideologies, most forms of productivity and genius, which could otherwise be harnessed for good, can be mobilised to harm.

The social utility of the more obviously productive professions is dependent on the ideological framework in which they operate, a framework shaped by competing voices. Voices that are independent of plutocratic power, that are able to articulate interests and perspectives at variance with its demands, are among the few means by which its capture of productive activity might be impeded.

This is not to suggest that essayists and pundits, journalists and commentators, however independent and persuasive they may be, can change the world by themselves. Progressive change requires mass mobilisation. But, by identifying and challenging power, by discovering its failings and proposing alternatives, by showing the world as it is rather than as the apparatus of justification would wish people to see it, we can, I believe, play a helpful part in this mobilisation, alongside politicians, protesters, social entrepreneurs, pressure groups and a host of other agents of change. This, at least, is the conviction that enables me to keep writing.

Part 1

There Is Such a Thing as Society

1

Falling Apart

What do we call the age we live in? It's no longer the information age. The collapse of popular education movements left a void filled by marketing and conspiracy theories. Like the Stone Age, Iron Age and space age, the digital age says plenty about our artefacts, but little about society. The Anthropocene, in which humans exert a major impact on the biosphere, fails to distinguish this century from the previous twenty. What clear social change marks out our time from those that precede it? To me it's obvious. This is the Age of Loneliness.

Thomas Hobbes could not have been more wrong when he claimed that in the state of nature, before authority arose to keep us in check, we were engaged in a war 'of every man against every man'. We were social creatures from the start, mammalian bees, who depended entirely on each other. The hominids of East Africa could not have survived one night alone. We are shaped, to a greater extent than almost any other species, by contact with others. The age we are entering, in which we exist apart, is unlike any that has gone before.

In the past few years, we have seen loneliness become an epidemic among young adults.[1] Now we learn that it is just as great an affliction for older people. A study by Independent Age shows that severe loneliness in England blights the lives of 700,000 men and 1.1 million women over fifty,[2] and is rising with astonishing speed.

Ebola is unlikely ever to kill as many people as the disease of loneliness. Social isolation is as potent a cause of early death as smoking fifteen cigarettes a day, while loneliness, research suggests, is twice as deadly as obesity.[3] Dementia, high blood pressure, alcoholism and accidents – all these, like depression, paranoia, anxiety and suicide, become more prevalent when connections are cut.[4] We cannot cope alone.

Yes, factories have closed, people travel by car instead of by bus, use YouTube rather than go to the cinema. But these shifts alone fail to explain the speed of our social collapse. These structural changes have been accompanied by a life-denying ideology, which enforces and celebrates our social isolation. The war of every man against every man – competition and individualism, in other words – is the religion of our time, justified by a mythology of lone rangers, sole traders, self-starters, self-made men and women, going it alone. For the most social of creatures, who cannot prosper without love, there is now no such thing as society, only heroic individualism. What counts is to win. The rest is collateral damage.

British children no longer aspire to be train drivers or nurses. More than a fifth now say they 'just want to be rich' – wealth and fame being the sole ambitions of 40 per cent of those surveyed.[5] A government study in June 2014 revealed that Britain is the loneliness capital of Europe.[6] We are less likely than other Europeans to have close friends or to know our neighbours. Who can be surprised, when everywhere we are urged to fight like stray dogs over a dustbin?

We have changed our language to reflect this shift. Our most cutting insult is 'loser'. We no longer talk about people. Now we call them individuals. So pervasive has this alienating, atomising term become that even the charities fighting loneliness use it to describe the bipedal entities formerly known as human beings.[7] We can scarcely complete a sentence without getting personal. Personally speaking (to distinguish myself from a ventriloquist's dummy), I prefer personal friends to the impersonal variety and personal belongings to the kind that don't belong to me. Though that's just my personal preference, otherwise known as my preference.

One of the tragic outcomes of loneliness is that people turn to their televisions for consolation: two-fifths of older people now report that the one-eyed god is their principal company.[8] This self-medication enhances the disease. Research by economists at the University of Milan suggests that television helps to drive competitive aspiration.[9] It strongly reinforces the income–happiness paradox: the fact that, as national incomes rise, happiness does not rise with them. Aspiration, which increases with income, ensures that the point of arrival, of sustained satisfaction, retreats before us.

The researchers found that those who watch a lot of television derive less satisfaction from a given level of income than those who watch only a little. Television speeds up the hedonic treadmill, forcing us to strive even harder to sustain the same level of satisfaction. You have only to think of the wall-to-wall auctions on daytime TV, *Dragon's Den*, *The Apprentice* and the myriad forms of career-making competition the medium celebrates, the generalised obsession with fame and wealth, the pervasive sense, in watching it, that life is somewhere other than where you are, to see why this might be.

So what's the point? What do we gain from this war of all against all? Competition drives growth, but growth no longer makes us wealthier. New figures show that while the income of company directors has risen by more than a fifth, wages for the workforce as a whole have fallen in real terms over the past year.[10] The bosses now earn – sorry, I mean take – 120 times more than the average full-time worker. (In 2000, it was forty-seven times.) And even if competition did make us richer, it would make us no happier, as the satisfaction derived from a rise in income would be undermined by the aspirational impacts of competition.

The top 1 per cent now own 48 per cent of global wealth,[11] but even they aren't happy. A survey by Boston College of people with an average net worth of $78 million found that they too are assailed by anxiety, dissatisfaction and loneliness.[12] Many of them reported feeling financially insecure: to reach safe ground, they believed, they would need, on average, about 25 per cent more money. (And if they got it? They'd doubtless need another 25 per cent.) One respondent said he wouldn't get there until he had $1 billion in the bank.

For this we have ripped the natural world apart, degraded our conditions of life, surrendered our freedoms and prospects of contentment to a compulsive, atomising, joyless hedonism, in which, having consumed all else, we start to prey upon ourselves. For this we have destroyed the essence of humanity: our connectedness.

Yes, there are palliatives, clever and delightful schemes like Men in Sheds and Walking Football developed by charities for isolated older people.[13] But if we are to break this cycle and come together once more, we must confront the world-eating, flesh-eating system into which we have been forced.

Hobbes's pre-social condition was a myth. But we are now entering a post-social condition our ancestors would have believed impossible. Our lives are becoming nasty, brutish and long.

14 October 2014

2

Deviant and Proud

To be at peace with a troubled world: this is not a reasonable aim. It can be achieved only through a disavowal of what surrounds you. To be at peace with yourself within a troubled world: that, by contrast, is an honourable aspiration. This essay is for those who feel at odds with life. It calls on you not to be ashamed.

I was prompted to write it by a remarkable book, by a Belgian professor of psychoanalysis, Paul Verhaeghe.[1] *What about Me?: The Struggle for Identity in a Market-Based Society* is one of those books that, by making connections between apparently distinct phenomena, permits sudden new insights into what is happening to us and why.

We are social animals, Verhaeghe argues, and our identity is shaped by the norms and values we absorb from other people. Every society defines and shapes its own normality – and its own abnormality – according to dominant narratives, and seeks either to make people comply or to exclude them if they don't.

Today the dominant narrative is that of market fundamentalism, widely known in Europe as neoliberalism. The
story it tells is that the market can resolve almost all social,
economic and political problems. The less the state regu-
lates and taxes us, the better off we will be. Public services
should be privatised, public spending should be cut and
business should be freed from social control. In countries
such as the UK and the US, this story has shaped our norms
and values for around thirty-five years, since Thatcher and
Reagan came to power. It's rapidly colonising the rest of
the world.

Verhaeghe points out that neoliberalism draws on the
ancient Greek idea that our ethics are innate (and
governed by a state of nature it calls the market) and on
the Christian idea that humankind is inherently selfish
and acquisitive. Rather than seeking to suppress these
characteristics, neoliberalism celebrates them: it claims
that unrestricted competition, driven by self-interest,
leads to innovation and economic growth, enhancing the
welfare of all.

At the heart of this story is the notion of merit.
Untrammelled competition rewards people who have talent,
who work hard and who innovate. It breaks down hier-
archies and creates a world of opportunity and mobility. The
reality is rather different. Even at the beginning of the
process, when markets are first deregulated, we do not start
with equal opportunities. Some people are a long way down
the track before the starting gun is fired. This is how the
Russian oligarchs managed to acquire such wealth when the
Soviet Union broke up. They weren't, on the whole, the
most talented, hard-working or innovative people, but those

with the fewest scruples, the most thugs and the best contacts, often in the KGB.

Even when outcomes are based on talent and hard work, they don't stay that way for long. Once the first generation of liberated entrepreneurs has made its money, the initial meritocracy is replaced by a new elite, who insulate their children from competition by inheritance and the best education money can buy. Where market fundamentalism has been most fiercely applied – in countries like the US and UK – social mobility has greatly declined.[2]

If neoliberalism were anything other than a self-serving con, whose gurus and think tanks were financed from the beginning by some of the richest people on earth (the American tycoons Coors, Olin, Scaife, Pew and others), its apostles would have demanded, as a precondition for a society based on merit, that no one should start life with the unfair advantage of inherited wealth or economically determined education. But they never believed in their own doctrine. Enterprise, as a result, quickly gave way to rent.

All this is ignored, and success or failure in the market economy is ascribed solely to individual effort. The rich are the new righteous, the poor are the new deviants, who have failed both economically and morally, and are now classified as social parasites.

The market was meant to emancipate us, offering autonomy and freedom. Instead it has delivered atomisation and loneliness. The workplace has been overwhelmed by a mad, Kafkaesque infrastructure of assessments, monitoring, measuring, surveillance and audits, centrally directed and rigidly planned, whose purpose is to reward the winners and punish the losers. It destroys autonomy, enterprise, innovation and loyalty, and breeds frustration, envy and fear. Through a magnificent paradox, it has led to the revival of a grand old Soviet tradition, known in Russian as *tufta*. It means the falsification of statistics to meet the diktats of unaccountable power.

The same forces afflict those who can't find work. They must now contend, alongside the other humiliations of unemployment, with a whole new level of snooping and monitoring. All this, Verhaeghe points out, is fundamental to the neoliberal model, which everywhere insists on comparison, evaluation and quantification. We find ourselves technically free but powerless. Whether in work or out of work, we must live by the same rules or perish. All the major political parties promote them, so we have no political power either. In the name of autonomy and freedom we have ended up controlled by a grinding, faceless bureaucracy.

These shifts have been accompanied, Verhaeghe writes, by a spectacular rise in certain psychiatric conditions: self-harm, eating disorders, depression and personality disorders. Performance anxiety and social phobia are rising fast; both of them reflect a fear of other people, who are perceived as both evaluators and competitors, the only roles for society that market fundamentalism admits. Depression and loneliness plague us. The infantilising diktats of the workplace destroy our self-respect. Those who end up at the bottom of the pile are assailed by guilt and shame. The self-attribution fallacy cuts both ways: just as we congratulate ourselves for our successes, we blame ourselves for our failures, even if we had little to do with them.

So if you don't fit in; if you feel at odds with the world; if your identity is troubled and frayed; if you feel lost and ashamed, it could be because you have retained the human values you were supposed to have discarded. You are a deviant. Be proud.

5 August 2014

3
Work-Force

Perhaps because the alternative is hideous to contemplate, we persuade ourselves that those who wield power know what they are doing. The belief in a guiding intelligence is hard to shake.

We know that our conditions of life are deteriorating. Most young people have little prospect of owning a home, or even of renting a decent one. Interesting jobs are sliced up, through digital Taylorism, into portions of meaningless drudgery.[1] The natural world, whose wonders enhance our lives, and upon which our survival depends, is being rubbed out with horrible speed. Those to whom we look for guardianship, in government and among the economic elite, do not arrest this decline; they accelerate it.

The political system that delivers these outcomes is sustained by aspiration: the faith that if we try hard enough, we could join the elite, even as living standards decline and social immobility becomes almost set in stone. But to what are we aspiring? A life that is better than our own, or worse?

In June 2015, a note from an analyst at Barclays Global
Power and Utilities in New York was leaked.[2] It addressed
students about to begin a summer internship, and offered a
glimpse of the toxic culture into which they are inducted.

> I wanted to introduce you to the 10 Power Commandments . . . For
> nine weeks you will live and die by these . . . We expect you to be the
> last ones to leave every night, no matter what . . . I recommend
> bringing a pillow to the office – it makes sleeping under your desk a
> lot more comfortable . . . the internship really is a 9-week commit-
> ment at the desk . . . an intern asked our staffer for a weekend off for
> a family reunion – he was told he could go. He was also asked to
> hand in his Blackberry and pack up his desk . . . Play time is over and
> it's time to buckle up.

Play time is over, but did it ever begin? If these students have
the kind of parents featured in the *Financial Times*, perhaps not.
The article marked a new form of employment: the nursery
consultant.[3] These people, who charge £290 an hour, must find
a nursery that will put their clients' toddlers on the right track to
an elite university. They spoke of parents who have already
decided that their six-month-old son will go to Cambridge then
Deutsche Bank, or whose two-year-old daughter 'had a tutor
for two afternoons a week (to keep on top of maths and literacy)
as well as weekly phonics and reading classes, drama, piano,
beginner French and swimming'. They were considering
adding Mandarin and Spanish. 'The little girl was so exhausted
and on edge she was terrified of opening her mouth.'

In New York, playdate coaches, charging $450 an hour,
train small children in the social skills that might help secure
their admission to the most prestigious private schools. They

are taught to hide traits that could suggest they're on the autistic spectrum, which might reduce their chances of selection.

From infancy to employment, this is a life-denying, love-denying mindset, informed not by joy or contentment, but by an ambition that is both desperate and pointless, for it cannot compensate for what it displaces: childhood, family life, the joys of summer, meaningful and productive work, a sense of arrival, living in the moment. For the sake of this toxic culture, the economy is repurposed; the social contract is rewritten; the elite is released from tax, regulation and the other restraints imposed by democracy.

Where the elite goes, we are induced to follow. As if the assessment regimes were too lax, last year the education secretary announced a new test for four-year-olds. A primary school in Cambridge has just taken the obvious next step: it is now streaming four-year-olds into classes according to perceived ability.[4] The Education and Adoption Bill, announced in the Queen's Speech, will turn the screw even tighter. Will this help children, or hurt them?

Who knows? Governments used to survey the prevalence of children's mental health issues every five years, but this ended in 2004. Imagine publishing no figures since 2004 on, say, childhood cancer, and you begin to understand the extent to which successive governments have chosen to avoid this issue. If aspirational pressure is not enhancing our well-being but damaging it, those in power don't want to know.

But there are hints. Mental health beds for children in England increased by 50 per cent between 1999 and 2014, but still failed to meet demand.[5] Children suffering mental health crises are being dumped in adult wards or even left in police cells because of the lack of provision (put yourself in their position and imagine the impact).[6]

The number of young people admitted to hospital because of self-harm has risen by 68 per cent in ten years, while the number of young patients with eating disorders has almost doubled in three years.[7] Without good data, we don't have a clear picture of what the causes might be, but it's worth noting that in the past year, according to the charity YoungMinds, the number of children receiving counselling for exam stress has tripled.[8]

An international survey of children's well-being found that the United Kingdom, where such pressures are peculiarly intense, ranked thirteenth out of fifteen countries for children's life satisfaction, thirteenth for agreement with the statement 'I like going to school', fourteenth for children's satisfaction with their bodies and fifteenth for self-confidence. So all that pressure and cramming and exhortation – that worked, didn't it?

In the cause of self-advancement, we are urged to sacrifice our leisure, our pleasures, our time with partners and children, to climb over the bodies of our rivals and to set ourselves against the common interests of humankind. And then? We discover that we have achieved no greater satisfaction than that with which we began. In 1653, Izaak Walton described the fate of 'poor-rich men', who 'spend all their time first in getting, and next in anxious care to keep it; men that are condemned to be rich, and then always busie or discontented'.[9] Today this fate is confused with salvation.

Finish your homework, pass your exams, spend your twenties avoiding daylight, and you too could live like the elite. But who in their right mind would want to?

9 June 2015

4

Addicted to Comfort

The question has changed a little since Rousseau's day, but the mystery remains.[1] Why, when most of us enjoy greater freedom than any preceding generations except the previous two or three – freedom from tyranny, freedom from slavery, freedom from hunger – do we act as if we don't?

I'm prompted to ask by the discovery that the most illiberal and oppressive instrument proposed by any recent government – injunctions to prevent nuisance and annoyance in the Anti-Social Behaviour Bill – has been attacked by Labour not because it is draconian but because it is not draconian enough.[2] The measure was decisively rejected by the Lords.[3] But in March 2014, the bill was passed into law.

Why do we tolerate a politics that offers no effective choice? That operates largely at the behest of millionaire funders, corporate power and a bullying media? Why, in an age in which people are no longer tortured and executed for criticising those in power, have we failed to create viable alternatives?

In the US Congress, for the first time, a majority of members are millionaires.[4] As the representatives become richer, the laws they pass ensure that they exercise ever less power over the rich and ever more power over the poor. Yet, as the Center for Responsive Politics notes, 'There's been no change in our appetite to elect affluent politicians to represent our concerns in Washington.'[5]

We appear to possess an almost limitless ability to sit back and watch as political life is seized by plutocrats, as the biosphere is trashed, as public services are killed or given to corporations, as workers are dragooned into zero-hour contracts. Though there are a few wonderful exceptions, on the whole protest is muted and alternatives are shrugged away without examination. How did we acquire this superhuman passivity?

The question is not confined to politics. Almost universally we now seem content to lead a proxy life, a counterlife, of vicarious, illusory relationships, of second-hand pleasures, of atomisation without individuation. Those who possess some disposable income are extraordinarily free, by comparison with almost all our great-grandparents, but we tend to act as if we have been placed under house arrest. With the amount most of us spend on home entertainment, we could probably buy a horse and play buzkashi every weekend. But we would rather stare at an illuminated box, watching other people jumping up and down and screaming. Our political constraint is one aspect of a wider inhibition, a wider failure to be free.

I'm not talking about think tank freedoms here: the freedom of billionaires not to pay their taxes, of corporations to pollute the atmosphere or induce children to smoke, of landlords to exploit their tenants. We should respect the prohibitive decencies we owe to others. But there are plenty of freedoms we can exercise without diminishing other people's.

Had our ancestors been asked to predict what would happen in an age of widespread prosperity in which most religious and cultural proscriptions had lost their power, how many would have guessed that our favourite activities would not be fiery political meetings, masked orgies, philosophical debates, hunting wild boar or surfing monstrous waves but shopping and watching other people pretending to enjoy themselves? How many would have foreseen a national conversation – in public and in private – that revolves around the three Rs: renovation, recipes and resorts? How many would have guessed that people possessed of unimaginable wealth and leisure and liberty would spend their time shopping for onion goggles and wheatgrass juicers? Man was born free, and he is everywhere in chain stores.

A few years ago, a friend explained how depressed he had become while trying to find a stimulating partner through online dating sites. He kept stumbling across the same phrase, used verbatim by dozens of the women he looked up: 'I like nothing better than a night in on the sofa with a glass of red and a good DVD.' The horror he felt arose not so much from the preference as from its repetition: 'the failure to grasp the possibilities of self-differentiation.'

I wrote to him recently to see if anything had changed. Yes: he has now tumbled into the vortex that dismayed him. He dated eighteen women in 2013, seeking 'the short sharp hit which keeps you coming back despite the fact that the experience taken as a whole does not add up to anything worth having. My life . . . is beginning to dance to the

Internet rhythm of desire satiated immediately and thinly.' In seeking someone who was not trapped on the hedonic treadmill, he became trapped on the hedonic treadmill.

Could it be this – the immediate satisfaction of desire, the readiness with which we can find comfort – that deprives us of greater freedoms? Does extreme comfort deaden the will to be free?

If so, it is a habit learnt early and learnt hard. When children are housebound, we cannot expect them to develop an instinct for freedom that is intimately associated with being outdoors. We cannot expect them to reach for more challenging freedoms if they have no experience of fear and cold and hunger and exhaustion. Perhaps freedom from want has paradoxically deprived us of other freedoms. The freedom which makes so many new pleasures available vitiates the desire to enjoy them.

Alexis de Tocqueville made a similar point about democracy: it threatens to enclose each of us 'entirely in the solitude of his own heart'.[6] The freedoms it grants us destroy the desire to combine and to organise. To judge by our reluctance to create sustained alternatives, we wish neither to belong nor to deviate.

It is not hard to see how our elective impotence leads before long to tyranny. Without coherent popular movements, which are required to prevent opposition parties from falling into the clutches of millionaires and corporate lobbyists, almost any government would be tempted to engineer a nominally democratic police state. Freedom of all kinds is something we must use or lose. But we seem to have forgotten what it means.

20 January 2014

5

Dead Zone

*This essay was widely credited with altering the bill it discusses.
Until it was published, the impending legislation had scarcely
been discussed beyond Parliament.*

Until the late nineteenth century, much of our city space
was owned by private landlords. Squares were gated,
streets were controlled by turnpikes.[1] The great unwashed,
many of whom had been expelled from the countryside by
Acts of enclosure, were also excluded from desirable parts
of town.

Social reformers and democratic movements tore down
the barriers, and public space became a right, not a privilege.
But social exclusion follows inequality as night follows day,
and now, with little public debate, our city centres are again
being privatised or semi-privatised. They are being turned
by the companies that run them into soulless, cheerless,
pasteurised piazzas, in which plastic policemen harry anyone
loitering without intent to shop.

Street life in these places is reduced to a trance-world of consumerism, of conformity and atomisation, in which nothing unpredictable or disconcerting happens, a world made safe for selling mountains of pointless junk to tranquilised shoppers. Spontaneous gatherings of any other kind – unruly, exuberant, open-ended, oppositional – are banned. Young, homeless and eccentric people are, in the eyes of those upholding this dead-eyed, sanitised version of public order, guilty until proven innocent.

Now this dreary ethos is creeping into places which are not, ostensibly, owned or controlled by corporations. It is enforced less by gates and barriers (though plenty of these are reappearing) than by legal instruments, used to exclude or control the ever-widening class of undesirables.

The existing rules are bad enough. Introduced by the 1998 Crime and Disorder Act, anti-social behaviour orders (ASBOs) have criminalised an apparently endless range of activities, subjecting thousands – mostly young and poor – to bespoke laws.[2] They have been used to enforce a kind of caste prohibition: personalised rules, which prevent the untouchables from intruding into the lives of others.

You get an ASBO for behaving in a manner deemed by a magistrate as likely to cause harassment, alarm or distress to other people. Under this injunction, the proscribed behaviour becomes a criminal offence. ASBOs have been granted which forbid the carrying of condoms by a prostitute, homeless alcoholics from possessing alcohol in a public place, a young man from walking down any road other than his own, children from playing football in the street.[3] They were used to ban peaceful protests against the Olympic clearances.[4]

Inevitably, over half the people subject to ASBOs break

them. As Liberty says, these injunctions 'set the young, vulnerable or mentally ill up to fail', and fast-track them into the criminal justice system.[5] They allow the courts to imprison people for offences which are not otherwise imprisonable. One homeless young man was sentenced to five years in jail for begging: an offence for which no custodial sentence exists.[6] ASBOs permit the police and courts to create their own laws and their own penal codes.

When the Anti-Social Behaviour, Crime and Policing Bill was first put before parliament, in 2013, it was scarcely debated, inside or out. Hardly anyone seemed aware of what was about to hit us.[7]

The bill permits injunctions against anyone of ten years old or above who 'has engaged or threatens to engage in conduct capable of causing nuisance or annoyance to any person'.[8] It replaces ASBOs with IPNAs (Injunctions to Prevent Nuisance and Annoyance), which not only forbid certain forms of behaviour, but also force the recipient to discharge positive obligations.[9] In other words, they can impose a kind of community service on people who have committed no crime, which could, the law proposes, remain in force for the rest of their lives.

The bill also introduces Public Space Protection Orders, which can prevent either everybody or particular kinds of people from doing certain things in certain places. It creates new dispersal powers, which can be used by the police to exclude people from an area (there is no size limit), whether or not they have done anything wrong.

While, as a result of a successful legal challenge, ASBOs can be granted only if a court is satisfied 'beyond reasonable doubt' that anti-social behaviour took place, IPNAs can be granted 'on the balance of probabilities'. Breaching them will not be classed as a criminal offence, but can still carry a custodial sentence: without committing a crime, you can be imprisoned for up to two years. Children, who cannot currently be detained for contempt of court, will be subject to an inspiring new range of punishments for breaking an IPNA, including three months in a young offenders' centre.

Lord Macdonald, formerly the director of public prosecutions, points out, 'It is difficult to imagine a broader concept than causing "nuisance" or "annoyance". The phrase is apt to catch a vast range of everyday behaviours to an extent that may have serious implications for the rule of law.'[10] Protesters, buskers, preachers: all, he argues, could end up with IPNAs.

The Home Office minister, Norman Baker, once a defender of civil liberties, now the architect of the most oppressive bill pushed through any recent parliament, claimed that the amendments he offered in December 2012 would 'reassure people that basic liberties will not be affected'.[11] But Liberty describes them as 'a little bit of window-dressing: nothing substantial has changed'.[12]

The new injunctions and the new dispersal orders create a system in which the authorities can prevent anyone from doing more or less anything. But they won't be deployed against just anyone. Advertisers, who cause plenty of nuisance and annoyance, have nothing to fear; nor do opera lovers hogging the pavements of Covent Garden. Annoyance and nuisance are what young people cause; they are inflicted by oddballs, the underclass, those who dispute the claims of power.

These laws will be used to stamp out plurality and difference, to douse the exuberance of youth, to pursue children for the crime of being young and together in a public place, to help turn this nation into a money-making monoculture, controlled, homogenised, lifeless, strifeless and bland. For a government which represents the old and the rich, that must sound like paradise.

6 January 2014

6

Help Addicts, but Lock Up the Casual Users of Cocaine

It looked like the first drop of rain in the desert of drugs policy. Antonio Maria Costa, executive director of the UN Office on Drugs and Crime, said what millions of liberal-minded people have been waiting to hear, 'Law enforcement should shift its focus from drug users to drug traffickers . . . people who take drugs need medical help, not criminal retribution.'[1] Drugs production should remain illegal, possession and use should be decriminalised. Hurray? Not at all.

I believe that informed adults should be allowed to inflict whatever suffering they wish – on themselves. But we are not entitled to harm other people. I know people who drink Fairtrade tea and coffee, shop locally and take cocaine at parties. They are revolting hypocrites.

Every year, cocaine causes some 20,000 deaths in Colombia and displaces several hundred thousand people from their homes.[2] Children are blown up by landmines, indigenous people are enslaved, villagers are tortured and killed, rainforests are razed.[3] You'd probably cause less human suffering if instead of discreetly retiring to the toilet at a media drinks party you went into the street and mugged someone. But the counter-cultural association appears to insulate people from ethical questions. If commissioning murder, torture, slavery, civil war, corruption and deforestation is not a crime, what is?

I am talking about elective drug use, not addiction. I cannot find comparative figures for the United Kingdom, but in the United States casual users of cocaine outnumber addicts by around twelve to one.[4] I agree that addicts should be helped, not prosecuted. I would like to see a revival of the British programme that was killed by a tabloid witch-hunt in 1971: until then all heroin addicts were entitled to clean, legal supplies administered by doctors.[5] Cocaine addicts should be offered residential detox. But while cocaine remains illegal, casual users should remain subject to criminal law. Decriminalisation of the products of crime expands the market for this criminal trade.

We have a choice of two consistent policies. The first is to sustain global prohibition, while helping addicts and prosecuting casual users. This means that the drugs trade will remain the preserve of criminal gangs. It will keep spreading crime and instability around the world, and ensure that narcotics are still cut with contaminants. As Nick Davies argued during his investigation of drugs policy for the *Guardian*, major seizures raise the price of drugs.[6] Demand among addicts is inelastic, so higher prices mean that they must find more money to buy them. The more drugs the police capture and destroy, the more robberies and muggings addicts will commit.

The other possible policy is to legalise and regulate the global trade. This would undercut the criminal networks and guarantee unadulterated supplies to consumers. There might even be a market for certified Fairtrade cocaine.

Mr Costa's report begins by rejecting this option. If it did otherwise, he would no longer be executive director of the UN Office on Drugs and Crime. The report argues that, 'Any reduction in the cost of drug control . . . will be offset by much higher expenditure on public health (due to the surge of drug consumption).'[7] It admits that tobacco and alcohol kill more people than illegal drugs, but claims that this is only because fewer illegal drugs are consumed.[8] Strangely however, it fails to supply any evidence to support the claim that narcotics are dangerous. Nor does it distinguish between the effects of the drugs themselves and the effects of the adulteration and disease caused by their prohibition.

Why not? Perhaps because the evidence would torpedo the rest of the report. The largest study on cocaine ever undertaken, completed by the World Health Organisation in 1995,[9] reports:

Health problems from the use of legal substances, particularly alcohol and tobacco, are greater than health problems from cocaine use. Few experts describe cocaine as invariably harmful to health. Cocaine-related problems are widely perceived to be more common and more severe for intensive, high-dosage users and very rare and much less severe for occasional, low-dosage users . . . occasional cocaine use does not typically lead to severe or even minor physical or social problems.[10]

This study was suppressed by the WHO after threats of an economic embargo by the Clinton government. Drugs policy in most nations is a matter of religion, not science.

The same goes for heroin. The biggest study of opiate use ever conducted (at Philadelphia General Hospital) found that addicts suffered no physical harm, even though some of them had been taking heroin for twenty years.[11] The devastating health effects of heroin use are caused by adulterants and the lifestyles of people forced to live outside the law. Like cocaine, heroin is addictive, but unlike cocaine the only consequence of its addiction appears to be . . . addiction.

Costa's half-measure, in other words, gives us the worst of both worlds: more murder, more destruction, more muggings, more adulteration. Another way of putting it is this: you will, if Mr Costa's proposal is adopted, be permitted without fear of prosecution to inject yourself with heroin cut with drain cleaner and brick dust, sold illegally and soaked in blood, but not with clean and legal supplies.

His report does raise one good argument, however. At present the Class A drugs trade is concentrated in the rich nations. If it were legalised, we could cope. The use of drugs is likely to rise, but governments could use the extra taxes to help people tackle addiction. But because the wholesale price would collapse with legalisation, these drugs would for the first time become widely available in poorer nations, which are easier for companies to exploit (as tobacco and alcohol firms have found) and which are less able to regulate, raise taxes or pick up the pieces. The widespread use of cocaine or heroin in the poor world could cause serious social problems: I've seen, for example, how a weaker drug – khat – seems to dominate life in Somali-speaking regions of Africa. 'The universal ban on illicit drugs', the UN argues, 'provides a great deal of protection to developing countries.'[12]

So Mr Costa's office has produced a study comparing the

global costs of prohibition with the global costs of legalisation, allowing us to see whether the current policy (murder, corruption, war, adulteration) causes less misery than the alternative (widespread addiction in poorer nations). The hell it has. Even to raise the possibility of such research would be to invite the testerics in Congress to shut off the UN's funding. The drugs charity Transform has addressed this question, but only for the UK, where the results are clear-cut: prohibition is the worse option.[13] As far as I can discover, no one has attempted a global study. Until that happens, Mr Costa's opinions on this issue are worth as much as mine or anyone else's: nothing at all.

30 June 2009

Part 2
Lost Youth

7

Rewild the Child

What is the best way to knacker a child's education? Force him or her to spend too long in the classroom.

An overview of research into outdoor education by King's College London found that children who spend time learning in natural environments 'perform better in reading, mathematics, science and social studies'.[1] Exploring the natural world 'makes other school subjects rich and relevant and gets apathetic students excited about learning'.

Fieldwork in the countryside, a British study finds, improves long-term memory.[2] Dozens of papers report sharp improvements in attention when children are exposed to wildlife and the great outdoors. Teenaged girls taken on a three-week canoeing trip in the US remained, even eighteen months later, more determined, more prepared to speak out and show leadership and more inclined to challenge conventional notions of femininity.[3]

Studies of the programmes run by the Wilderness Foundation UK, which takes troubled teenagers into the mountains, found that their self-control, self-awareness and behaviour all improved.[4] Ofsted, the schools inspection service, reports that getting children out of the classroom raises 'standards, motivation, personal development and behaviour'.[5]

Recently, I saw the evidence for myself. With the adventure learning charity WideHorizons, I spent two days taking a group of ten-year-olds from a deprived borough in London rockpooling and roaming the woods in mid-Wales. Many of them had never been to the countryside before and had never seen the sea.

I was nervous before I met them. I feared that our differences might set us apart. I thought they might be bored and indifferent. But my fears evaporated as soon as we reached the rockpools.

Within a few minutes, I had them picking up crabs and poking anemones. When I showed them that they could eat live prawns out of the net they were horrified, but curiosity and bravado conquered disgust, and one after another they tried them.

Raw prawns are as sweet as grapes: some of the children were soon shovelling them into their mouths. I don't think there was anyone in the group who managed not to fall into the water. But no one complained.

In the woods the next day we paddled in a stream, rolled down a hill, ate blackberries, tasted mushrooms, had helicopter races with sycamore keys, explored an ants' nest, broke sticks and collected acorns. Most had never done any of these things before, but they needed no encouragement: the exhilaration with which they explored the living world seemed instinctive. I realised just how little contact they'd had when I discovered that none of them had seen a nettle or knew what happens if you touch it.

But what hit me hardest was this. One boy stood out: he had remarkable powers of observation and intuition. When I mentioned this to his teacher, her reply astonished me: 'I must tell him. It's not something he will have heard before.' When a child as bright and engaged as this is struggling at school, the problem lies not with the child but with the education system. We foster and reward a narrow set of skills.

The governments of this country accept the case for outdoor learning. In 2006, the departments for children and schools, culture and the environment signed a manifesto which says the following: 'We strongly support the educational case for learning outside the classroom. If all young people were given these opportunities we believe it would make a significant contribution to raising achievement.'[6] In 2011, the Conservative government published a White Paper proposing 'action to get more children learning outdoors, removing barriers and increasing schools' abilities to teach outdoors'.[7]

So what happened? Massive cuts. The BBC reports that 95 per cent of outdoor education centres have had their entire local authority funding cut.[8] Instead of being encouraged to observe and explore and think and develop, children are being treated like geese in a foie gras farm. Confined to the classroom, stuffed with rules and facts, dragooned into endless tests: there could scarcely be a better formula for ensuring that they become bored and disaffected.[9]

When children are demonised by the newspapers, they are often described as feral. But feral is what children should be: it means released from captivity or domestication. Those who live in crowded flats, surrounded by concrete, mown grass and other people's property, cannot escape their captivity without breaking the law. Games and explorations that are seen as healthy in the countryside are criminalised in the cities. Children who have never visited the countryside – 50 per cent in the UK according to WideHorizons – live under constant restraint.[10]

Why shouldn't every child spend a week in the country-side every term? Why shouldn't everyone be allowed to develop the kind of skills the children I met were learning: rock climbing, gorge scrambling, caving, night walking, ropework and natural history? Getting wet and tired and filthy and cold, immersing yourself, metaphorically and literally, in the natural world: surely by these means you discover more about yourself and the world around you than you do during three months in a classroom. What kind of government would deprive children of this experience?

7 October 2013

8

The Child Inside

Where do the children play? Where can they run around unsupervised? On most of the housing estates I visit, the answer is hardly anywhere.

A community not built around children is no community at all. A place that functions socially is one in which they are drawn to play outdoors. As Jay Griffiths argues in her magnificent, heartrending book *Kith*, children fill the 'unoccupied territories', the spaces not controlled by tidy-minded adults, 'the commons of mud, moss, roots and grass'.[1] But such places are being purged from the land and their lives. 'Today's children are enclosed in school and home, enclosed in cars to shuttle between them, enclosed by fear, by surveillance and poverty and enclosed in rigid schedules of time.' Since the 1970s, the area in which children roam without adults has decreased by almost 90 per cent.[2] 'Childhood is losing its commons.'

Given all that we know about the physical and psychological impacts of this confinement, you would expect the authorities to ensure that the remaining 10 per cent of their diminished range is designed to draw children out of their homes. Yet almost everywhere they are designed out. Housing estates are built on the playing fields and rough patches children used to inhabit, and offer almost nothing in return.

In the Coalition government's master plan for England – the national planning policy framework – children are mentioned only twice: In both occasions in a catalogue of housing types.[3] In Parliament's review of these plans, they aren't mentioned at all.[4] Young people, around whom our lives should revolve, have been airbrushed from the planning system.

I spent Monday wandering the new and newish developments on the east side of Northampton. I chose this area because the estates here are spacious and mostly built for families. In other words, there is no possible excuse for excluding young people.

In the places built ten or twenty years ago, there's plenty of shared space, but almost all of it is allocated to cars. Grass is confined to the roundabouts or to coffin-like gardens, in which you can't turn a cartwheel without hitting the fence. I came across one exception: a street with wide grass verges. But they sloped towards the road: dangerous and useless, a perfect waste of space.

This land of missed opportunities, designed by people without a spark of joy in their hearts, reifies the idea that there is no such thing as society. Had you set out to ensure that children are neither seen nor heard, you could not have done a better job. On the last day of the holidays, which was warm and dry, across four estates I saw only one child.

By comparison, the Cherry Orchard estate just completed by Bellway Homes is a children's paradise. But only by comparison. Next to the primary school, with plenty of three- and four-bedroom houses, it is designed to appeal to young families. But while plenty of thought has gone into the homes, it seems to me that almost none has gone into their surroundings.

In the middle of the development, where a village green might have been, there's a strange grassy sump, surrounded by a low fence. It's an empty balancing pond, to catch water during exceptional floods. Remove the fence, plant it with trees, throw in some rocks and logs, and you'd have a rough and mossy playground. But no such thing was in the plans.

Other shared spaces in the estate have the charming ambience of a prison yard: paved and surrounded by garden fences almost nine feet high.

There were a few children outdoors, but they seemed pressed to the edges, sitting in doorways or leaning on the fences. Children don't buy houses, so who cares?

Throughout the country, they become prisoners of bad design, and so do adults.[5] Without safe and engaging places in which they can come together, no tribe forms. So parents must play the games that children would otherwise play among themselves, and everyone is bored to tears.

The exclusion of children arises from the same pathology that denies us decent housing. In the name of market freedom, the volume house-builders, sitting on their land banks, are free to preside over speculative chaos, while we are free to buy dog kennels priced like palaces in placeless estates designed so badly that community is dead on arrival. Millions, given the chance, might want to design and build their own homes, but almost no plots are available, as the big builders have seized them.

In Scotland, the government is considering compulsory sale orders, which would pull down prices: essential when the speculative price of land has risen from 2 per cent of the cost of a home in the 1930s to 70 per cent today.[6] A national housing land corporation would assemble the sites and supply the infrastructure, then sell plots to community groups, housing associations and people who want to build their own. It goes far beyond England's feeble community right-to-build measures, which lack the muscular facilitation that only public authorities can provide.[7] But still not far enough.

What if people were entitled to buy an option for a plot on a new estate, which they would then help to plan? Not just the houses, but the entire estate would be built for and by those who would live there. The council or land corporation would specify the number and type of homes, then the future residents, including people on the social housing waiting list, would design the layout. Their children would help to create the public spaces. Communities would start to form even before people moved in, and the estates would doubtless look nothing like those built today.

To the Westminster government, this probably sounds like communism. But as countries elsewhere in Europe have found, we don't need volume house-builders, except to construct high-rises.[8] They do not assist the provision of decent, affordable homes. They impede it. What is good for them is bad for us.

Bellway, its brochure reveals, asked children at the neighbouring primary school to paint a picture of a cherry orchard, and displayed the winning entries in its show home. 'Why not pop over to say hello, view our wonderful development and sneak a peek?' That's the role the children were given: helping the company to sell the houses it had already built. Why can't we shape the places that shape our lives?

6 January 2015

9

Amputating Life Close to Its Base

To seek enlightenment, intellectual or spiritual; to do good; to love and be loved; to create and to teach: these are the highest purposes of humankind. If there is meaning in life, it lies here.

Those who graduate from the leading universities have more opportunity than most to find such purpose. So why do so many end up in pointless and destructive jobs? Finance, management consultancy, advertising, public relations, lobbying: these and other useless occupations consume thousands of the brightest students. To take such jobs at graduation, as many do every year, is to amputate life close to its base.

I watched it happen to my peers. People who had spent the preceding years laying out exultant visions of a better world, of the grand creative projects they planned, of adventure and discovery, were suddenly sucked into the mouths of corporations dangling money like anglerfish. At first they said they would do it for a year or two, 'until I pay off my debts'. Soon afterwards they added: '. . . and my mortgage'. Then it became, 'I just want to make enough not to worry any more.' A few years later, 'I'm doing it for my family.' Now, in middle age, they reply, 'What, that? That was just a student fantasy.'

Why did they not escape, when they perceived that they were being dragged away from their dreams? I have come to see the obscene hours some new recruits must work – sometimes fifteen or sixteen a day – as a form of reorientation, of brainwashing. You are deprived of the time, sleep and energy you need to see past the place into which you have been plunged. You lose your bearings, your attachments to the world you inhabited before, and become immersed in the culture that surrounds you. Two years of this and many are lost for life.

Employment by the City has declined since the financial crash. Among the universities I surveyed with the excellent researcher John Sheil, the proportion of graduates taking jobs in finance and management consultancy ranges from 5 per cent at Edinburgh to 13 per cent at Oxford, 16 per cent at Cambridge, 28 per cent at the London School of Economics and 60 per cent at the London Business School.[1] But to judge by the number of applications and the rigour of the selection process, these businesses still harvest many of the smartest graduates.

Recruitment begins with lovebombing of the kind that cults use. They sponsor sports teams and debating societies, throw parties, offer meals and drinks, send handwritten letters, use student ambassadors to offer friendship and support. They persuade undergraduates that even if they don't see themselves as consultants or bankers (few do), these jobs are stepping stones to the careers they really want. They make the initial application easy, and respond immediately and enthusiastically to signs of interest. They offer security and recognition when people are most uncertain and fearful about their future. And there's the flash of the king's shilling: the paid internships, the golden hellos, the promise of stupendous salaries within a couple of years. Entrapment is a refined science.

We have but one life. However much money we make, we cannot buy it back. As far as self-direction, autonomy and social utility are concerned, many of those who enter these industries and never re-emerge might as well have dropped dead at graduation. They lost it all with one false step, taken at a unique moment of freedom.

John Sheil and I sent questions to eight of the universities with the highest average graduate salaries: Oxford, Cambridge, Imperial, the LSE, the London Business School, Warwick, Sheffield and Edinburgh. We asked whether they seek to counter these lavish recruitment drives and defend students from the love blitz. With one remarkable exception, their responses ranged from feeble to dismal. Most offered no evidence of any prior interest in these questions. Where we expected deep deliberation to have taken place, we found instead an intellectual vacuum.

They cited their duty of impartiality, which, they believe, prevents them from seeking to influence students' choices, and explained that there were plenty of other careers on offer. But they appear to have confused impartiality with passivity. Passivity in the face of unequal forces is anything but impartial. Impartiality demands an active attempt to create balance, to resist power, to tell the dark side of the celestial tale being pummelled into the minds of undergraduates by the richest City cults.

Oxford University asked us, 'Isn't it preferable that [the City] recruits bright, critical thinkers and socially engaged graduates who are smart enough to hold their employers to account when possible?' Oh blimey. This is a version of the most desperate excuse my college friends attempted: 'I'll reform them from within.' This magical thinking betrays a profound misconception about the nature and purpose of such employers. They respond to profit, the regulatory environment, the demands of shareholders, not to the consciences of their staff. We all know how they treat whistleblowers.[2] Why should 'bright, critical thinkers and socially engaged graduates' be despatched on this kamikaze mission? I believe these universities are failing in their duty of care.

The hero of this story is Gordon Chesterman, head of the careers service at Cambridge, and the only person we spoke to who appears to have given some thought to these questions. He told me his service tries to counter the influence of the richest employers. It sends out regular emails telling students, 'If you don't want to become a banker, you're not a failure', and runs an event called 'But I Don't Want to Work in the City.' It imposes a fee on rich recruiters and uses the money to pay the train fares of non-profits. He expressed anger about being forced by the government to provide data on graduate starting salaries. 'I think it's a very blunt and inappropriate means [of comparison], that rings alarm bells in my mind.'

Elsewhere, at this vulnerable, mutable, pivotal moment, undergraduates must rely on their own wavering resolve to resist peer pressure, the herd instinct, the allure of money, flattery, prestige and security. Students, rebel against these soul-suckers! Follow your dreams, however hard it may be, however uncertain success might seem.

3 June 2015

10
'Bug Splats'

'Mere words cannot match the depths of your sorrow, nor can they heal your wounded hearts . . . These tragedies must end. And to end them, we must change.'[1] Every parent can connect with what Barack Obama said about the 2012 murder of twenty children in Newtown, Connecticut. There can scarcely be a person on earth with access to the media who is untouched by the grief of the people of that town.

It must follow that what applies to the children murdered there by a deranged young man also applies to the children murdered in Pakistan by a sombre American president. These children are just as important, just as real, just as deserving of the world's concern. Yet there are no presidential speeches or presidential tears for them; no pictures on the front pages of the world's newspapers; no interviews with grieving relatives; no minute analysis of what happened and why.

If the victims of Mr Obama's drone strikes are mentioned by the state at all, they are discussed in terms which suggest that they are less than human. The people who operate the drones, *Rolling Stone* magazine reports, describe their casualties as 'bug splats', 'since viewing the body through a grainy-green video image gives the sense of an insect being crushed'.[2] Or they are reduced to vegetation: justifying the drone war, Obama's counter-terrorism adviser Bruce Riedel explained that, 'You've got to mow the lawn all the time. The minute you stop mowing, the grass is going to grow back.'[3]

Like Bush's government in Iraq, Barack Obama's administration neither documents nor acknowledges the civilian casualties of the CIA's drone strikes in north-west Pakistan. But a report by the law schools at Stanford and New York universities suggests that during the first three years of his time in office, the 259 strikes for which he is ultimately responsible killed between 297 and 569 civilians, of whom 64 were children.[4] These are figures extracted from credible reports: there may be more which have not been fully documented.

The wider effects on the children of the region have been devastating. Many have been withdrawn from school because of fears that large gatherings of any kind are being targeted. There have been several strikes on schools since George W. Bush launched the drone programme that Obama has expanded so enthusiastically: one of Bush's blunders killed sixty-nine children.[5]

The study reports that children scream in terror when they hear the sound of a drone. A local psychologist says that their fear and the horrors they witness is causing permanent mental scarring. Children wounded in drone attacks told the researchers that they are too traumatised to go back to school and have abandoned hopes of the careers they might have had: their dreams as well as their bodies have been broken.[6]

Obama does not kill children deliberately. But their deaths are an inevitable outcome of the way his drones are deployed. We don't know what emotional effect these deaths might have on him, as neither he nor his officials will discuss the matter: almost everything to do with the CIA's extra-judicial killings in Pakistan is kept secret. But you get the impression that no one in the administration is losing much sleep over it.

Two days before the murders in Newtown, Obama's press secretary was asked about women and children being killed by drones in Yemen and Pakistan. He refused to answer, on the grounds that such matters are 'classified'.[7] Instead, he directed the journalist to a speech by John Brennan, Obama's counter-terrorism assistant. Brennan insists that 'Al-Qaida's killing of innocents, mostly Muslim men, women and children, has badly tarnished its appeal and image in the eyes of Muslims.'[8] He appears unable to see that the drone war has done the same for the United States. To Brennan the people of north-west Pakistan are neither insects nor grass: his targets are a 'cancerous tumour', the rest of society 'the tissue around it'. Beware of anyone who describes a human being as something other than a human being.

Yes, he conceded, there is occasionally a little 'collateral damage', but the US takes 'extraordinary care [to] ensure precision and avoid the loss of innocent life'. It will act only if there's 'an actual ongoing threat' to American lives.[9] This is cock and bull with bells on.

The 'signature strike' doctrine developed under Obama, which has no discernible basis in law, merely looks for patterns.[10] A pattern could consist of a party of unknown men carrying guns (which scarcely distinguishes them from the rest of the male population of north-west Pakistan), or a group of unknown people who look as if they might be plotting something. This is how wedding and funeral parties get wiped out; this is why forty elders discussing royalties from a chromite mine were blown up in March 2011.[11] It is one of the reasons why children continue to be killed.

Obama has scarcely mentioned the drone programme and has said nothing about its killing of children. The only statement I can find is a brief and vague response during a video conference in January 2011.[12] The killings have been left to others to justify. In October 2012, the Democratic cheerleader Joe Klein claimed on MSNBC, 'The bottom line in the end is whose four-year-old gets killed? What we're doing is limiting the possibility that four-year-olds here will get killed by indiscriminate acts of terror.'[13] As the estimable Glenn Greenwald has pointed out, killing four-year-olds is what terrorists do.[14] It doesn't prevent retaliatory murders; it encourages them, as grief and revenge are often accomplices.

Most of the world's media, which has rightly commemorated the children of Newtown, either ignores Obama's murders or accepts the official version that all those killed are 'militants'. The children of north-west Pakistan, it seems, are not like our children. They have no names, no pictures, no memorials of candles and flowers and teddy bears. They belong to the other: to the non-human world of bugs and grass and tissue.

'Are we', Obama asked, 'prepared to say that such violence visited on our children year after year after year is somehow the price of our freedom?'[15] It's a valid question. He should apply it to the violence he is visiting on the children of Pakistan.

17 December 2012

11
Kin Hell

'Throughout history and in virtually all human societies marriage has always been the union of a man and a woman.' So says the Coalition for Marriage, whose petition against same-sex unions in the UK has so far attracted 500,000 signatures.[1] It's a familiar claim, and it is wrong. Dozens of societies, across many centuries, have recognised same-sex marriage.[2] In a few cases, before the fourteenth century, it was even celebrated in church.

This is an example of a widespread phenomenon: myth-making by cultural conservatives about past relationships. Scarcely challenged, family values campaigners have been able to construct a history that is almost entirely false.

The unbiblical and ahistorical nature of the modern Christian cult of the nuclear family is a rare marvel to behold. Those who promote it are followers of a man born out of wedlock and allegedly sired by someone other than his mother's partner. Jesus insisted, 'If any man come to me, and hate not his father, and mother, and wife, and children, and brethren, and sisters ... he cannot be my disciple.'[3] He issued no such injunction against homosexuality: the threat he perceived was heterosexual and familial love, which competed with the love of God.

This theme was aggressively pursued by the church for some 1,500 years. In his classic book *A World of Their Own Making*, Professor John Gillis points out that until the Reformation the state of holiness was not matrimony but lifelong chastity.[4] There were no married saints in the early Mediaeval church. Godly families in this world were established not by men and women, united in bestial matrimony, but by the holy orders, whose members were the brothers or brides of Christ. Like most monotheistic religions (which developed among nomadic peoples), Christianity placed little value on the home.[5] A Christian's true home belonged to another realm, and until he reached it, through death, he was considered an exile from the family of God.

The Reformation preachers created a new ideal of social organisation – the godly household – but this bore little relation to the nuclear family. By their mid-teens, often much earlier, Gillis tells us, 'Virtually all young people lived and worked in another dwelling for shorter or longer periods.' Across much of Europe, the majority belonged – as servants, apprentices and labourers – to houses other than those of their biological parents. The poor, by and large, did not form households; they joined them.

The father of the house, who described and treated his charges as his children, typically was unrelated to most of them. Family, prior to the nineteenth century, meant everyone who lived in the house. What the Reformation sanctified was the proto-industrial labour force, working and sleeping under one roof.[6]

The belief that sex outside marriage was rare in previous centuries is also unfounded. The majority, too poor to marry formally, Gillis writes, 'Could love as they liked as long as they were discreet about it.' Prior to the nineteenth century, those who intended to marry began to sleep together as soon as they had made their spousals (declared their intentions). This practice was sanctioned on the grounds that it allowed couples to discover whether or not they were compatible: if they were not, they could break it off. Premarital pregnancy was common and often uncontroversial, as long as provision was made for the children.[7]

The nuclear family, as idealised today, was an invention of the Victorians, but it bore little relation to the family life we are told to emulate. Its development was driven by economic rather than spiritual needs, as the Industrial Revolution made manufacturing in the household inviable. Much as the Victorians might have extolled their families, 'it was simply assumed that men would have their extramarital affairs and women would also find intimacy, even passion, outside marriage', and often with other women.[8] Gillis links the twentieth century's attempt to find intimacy and passion only within marriage – and the impossible expectations this raises – to the rise in the rate of divorce.

Children's lives were characteristically wretched: farmed out to wet nurses, sometimes put to work in factories and mines, beaten, neglected, often abandoned as infants. In his book *A History of Childhood*, Colin Heywood reports that, 'The scale of abandonment in certain towns was simply staggering', reaching one-third or a half of all the children born in some European cities.[9] Street gangs of feral youths caused as much moral panic in late nineteenth-century England as they do today.

Conservatives often hark back to the golden age of the 1950s. But in the 1950s, John Gillis shows, people of the same persuasion believed they had suffered a great moral decline since the early twentieth century. In the early twentieth century, people fetishised the family lives of the Victorians. The Victorians invented this nostalgia, looking back with longing to imagined family lives before the Industrial Revolution.

In the *Telegraph*, Cristina Odone maintains that, 'Anyone who wants to improve lives in this country knows that the traditional family is key.'[10] But the tradition she invokes is imaginary. Far from this being, as cultural conservatives assert, a period of unique moral depravity, family life and the raising of children is, for most people, now surely better in the West than at any time in the past 1,000 years.

The conservatives' supposedly moral concerns turn out to be nothing but an example of the age-old custom of first idealising and then sanctifying one's own culture. The past they invoke is fabricated from their own anxieties and obsessions. It has nothing to offer us.

14 May 2012

12

The Sacrificial Caste

Texas is a largely Christian state that appears to believe in neither forgiveness nor redemption. Much of its vengeful justice is visited upon children. Police now patrol the schools, arresting and charging pupils as young as six for breaches of discipline.[1]

Among the villainies for which they have been apprehended are throwing paper aeroplanes, using perfume in class, cheeking the teacher, wearing the wrong clothes and arriving late for school. A twelve-year-old boy with attention deficit disorder was imprisoned for turning over a desk; six years later, he's still inside. Children convicted of these enormities – 300,000 such tickets were issued by Texas police in 2010 – acquire a criminal record. This makes them ineligible for federal aid at university and for much subsequent employment.

Yet most of them have committed no recognised crime. As one of the judges who hears their cases explained to the *Guardian*, 'If any adult did it it's not going to be a violation.'[2]

On the other hand, no charges have been brought against a Texas judge called William Adams. Last year, a video was released which showed him beating the living daylights out of his daughter with a leather belt.[3] The attack was so savage that when I watched it I nearly threw up. Adams cannot be prosecuted because the beating took place eight years ago. But even if it had happened yesterday, he might not have been charged, as he could have claimed that he was disciplining his child. In both cases the law permits people to do things to children that they could not do to adults.

Before we start feeling too superior, we should remember that systematic injustice towards children is common to many nations. Consider these cases, all from the past few decades: the theft of babies and forced adoptions in Spain; the teenage girls pressed into slavery in Ireland's Magdalene laundries; the sexual abuse in its industrial schools; similar institutional abuse, also by Catholic priests, in many parts of the world; buggery and beatings in Welsh children's homes; the British children told, wrongly, that they were orphans and exported to Australia, Canada and other Commonwealth countries; the assaults by staff in privately run child jails.[4] It seems to me that such abuses have three common characteristics.

The first is that the countries in which they occur appear to possess a sacrificial caste of children, whose rights can be denied and whose interests can be disregarded with impunity. The second is that these countries have a powerful resistance towards confronting and addressing this injustice: discussing it often amounts to a taboo. (These two traits were chillingly dramatised in Kazuo Ishiguro's novel *Never*

Let Me Go.) The third is that systematic abuse becomes widely acknowledged only after determined people – such as Margaret Humphreys (the child migrants) and Alison Taylor (the Welsh care homes) – spend years trying to force it into the open in the face of official denial.

So I want to try once more to begin a discussion about an issue we still refuse to examine: early boarding. It is as British as warm beer, green suburbs and pointless foreign wars. Despite or because of that we won't talk about it. Those on the right will not defend these children, as they will not criticise private schools. Those on the left won't defend them, as they see them as privileged and therefore undeserving of concern. But children's needs are universal; they know no such distinctions.

The UK Boarding Schools website lists eighteen schools which take boarders from the age of eight, and thirty-eight which take them from the age of seven. I expect such places have improved over the past forty years; they could scarcely have got worse. Children are likely to have more contact with home; though one school I phoned told me that some of its pupils still see their parents only in the holidays.[5] But the nature of boarding is only one of the forces that can harm these children. The other is the fact of boarding.

In a paper published in the *British Journal of Psychotherapy*, Dr Joy Schaverien identifies a set of symptoms common among early boarders that she calls Boarding School Syndrome.[6] Her research suggests that the act of separation, regardless of what might follow it, 'can cause profound developmental damage', as 'early rupture with home has a lasting influence on attachment patterns'.

When a child is brought up at home, the family adapts to accommodate it: growing up involves a constant negotiation between parents and children. But an institution cannot rebuild itself around one child. Instead, the child must adapt to the system. Combined with the sudden and then repeated loss of parents, siblings, pets and toys, this causes the child to shut itself off from the need for intimacy. This can cause major problems in adulthood: depression, an inability to talk about or understand emotions, the urge to escape from or to destroy intimate relationships. These symptoms mostly affect early boarders: those who start when they are older are less likely to be harmed.[7]

It should be obvious that this system could also inflict wider damage. A repressed, traumatised elite, unable to connect emotionally with others, is a danger to society: look at the men who oversaw the First World War.

Over the past few days, I have phoned the education department, the Boarding Schools Association and the head teachers of several schools to ask them a simple question: how did they decide that seven or eight was an appropriate age for children to start boarding? In every case the answer was the same: they didn't. This, they all told me, is just the way it has always been done. No inquiry, no committee, no board, no ethics council has, as far as they know, ever examined this question. Very young children are being sent away from home in a complete vacuum of professional advice. Compare this with the ethical agonising over whether or not children should be taken into care and you encounter the class prejudice common to all British governments: the upper classes require no oversight.

So yes, rage against Texas and its monstrosities, and wonder at the cruel, authoritarian system a nominal democracy can produce. But remember that this is not the only place in which governments endorse the damage done to children.

16 January 2012

13

A Modest Proposal for Tackling Youth

They have proved to be an effective means of dealing with the epidemic of youth on our streets. But now that acoustic dispersal devices are likely to be banned, how will we tackle one of this country's most distressing and pervasive crimes: being young in a public place?

Acoustic deterrence was, until recently, used only to repel rats, mice and cockroaches. But thanks to an invention by the former British Aerospace engineer Howard Stapleton it is now just as effective at discouraging human vermin.[1] The Mosquito™ youth dispersal device, manufactured by Compound Security Systems, produces a loud, high-pitched whine that can be heard strongly only by children and teenagers, and not at all by people over twenty-five. It allows councils to keep children out of public places, making them safe for law-abiding citizens. It enables shopkeepers to determine who should and should not be permitted to use the streets. It ensures that society is not subjected, among other intrusions, to the unpleasant and distressing noises that youths are inclined to make.

A survey by the *Guardian* shows that 25 per cent of local authorities in the UK use or have used these machines in their attempts to discourage the youthwave.[2] Altogether, 3,500 Mosquitos™ have been sold here, far more than in any other country.[3] The product's success is one of many signs of the enlightened attitudes to the menace of childhood which distinguish the United Kingdom from less civilised parts of the world. But last week the bleeding hearts in the Council of Europe's parliamentary assembly unanimously recommended that acoustic deterrents be banned from public places, on the preposterous grounds that they discriminate against young people and deny their right to free assembly.[4]

In a blatant attempt at emotional blackmail, the council's parliament contends that, as well as causing distress to teenagers whether they are wearing hooded tops or not, these devices cause 'dramatic reactions' in many younger children, particularly babies, who often 'cry or shout out and cover their ears, to the surprise of their parents, who, unaware of the noise, do not know why'. Nor, it says, do we yet know what impact high-frequency noise has on unborn children.

Really, who cares?

This is just the sort of Eurotrash we have come to expect from the fat cats of Strasbourg. Happily their decision is not binding, but it can be only a matter of time before the pressure on our legislators – especially high-pitched whining from do-gooders such as the Children's Rights Alliance for England – becomes intolerable, and they cave in to the forces of political correctness.[5]

What this will mean is that the police, councils and owners of property will be deprived of an essential weapon in the fight against youth. Youth statistics might be improving, but there are still far too many occasions on which young people venture out of their homes, sometimes in concert. It is true that the police have specific, if limited, powers to deal with individual cases. Admittedly the United Kingdom has one of the world's most enlightened policies on the age of criminal responsibility. Children can be tried and imprisoned here at the age of ten. This is four years younger than in China, whose government is notoriously soft on crime, and six years younger than in the pinko, wet-blanket state of Texas.[6] Admittedly, we have more child prisoners than any other country in Europe,[7] and behaviour laws, such as ASBOs, extra-judicial fines, house arrest for excluded children,[8] £5,000 fines for the parents of anti-social toddlers,[9] that dictatorships can only dream of.

But while these measures offer society some protection against actual offences, they do nothing to address the general issue of young people in our midst. Worse, they attempt to draw a distinction between criminals and teen-agers. As everyone over the age of forty knows, this distinction is a false one. Now that the Mosquito™ is likely to be excluded from the armoury, now that police officers may no longer respond to the incidence of youth with a simple cuff round the ear, or a falling down the stairs or out of a police station window, how will Britain deal with this menace?

The authorities have been seeking creative solutions, but none meets the challenge we face. Some councils have imported an idea pioneered in Australia whose purpose is to disperse teenagers from public places: playing the songs of Barry Manilow over their loudspeaker systems.[10] The problem with the Manilow Method is that it is too blunt an instrument, as it disperses everyone except the hard of hearing.

Youth curfews, introduced by the Crime and Disorder Act 1998,[11] and dispersal orders, brought into effect by the Anti-Social Behaviour Act 2003,[12] go some of the way towards tackling the problem, but they require the active involvement of the police, and apply only where and when they have been implemented. There is as yet no universal provision against those who insist, often in active collaboration with others, on being young people in public view.

I have a modest proposal for dealing with this problem. While forestalling sterner measures, which might otherwise be deployed to address the troubling existence of youth, it enables good citizens to go about their lives at liberty. It also prevents young people from getting into trouble and ending up in the worst situation of all: the horror and humiliation of prison, where their golden years are blighted and they fall into the clutches of people ready to exploit them.

I propose that from school age onwards, young people should, for the good of themselves and society, be kept in a safe, secure environment, under supervision and out of situations that might tempt them into trouble. Each would be given a small room, simple but comfortable, which in some cases they might share with another. They would be permitted one hour of exercise a day in a purpose-built yard offering appropriate facilities.

Besides schooling, occupations would be designed to keep them busy and happy, and prevent them from engaging in the kind of group activities the citizens of this country deplore. These pastimes might include assembling bags of the kind used for postal deliveries. They would also be offered the opportunity to pursue vocational qualifications, particularly in the subsurface fossil fuel extraction and smoke duct cleansing industries.

This firm but fair treatment programme will consolidate the policies the last government introduced in a piecemeal and incoherent fashion; reverse the disastrous social experiment of the past hundred years, which unleashed the youth-wave onto our streets; and make devices such as the Mosquito™ redundant, useful as they are in the current legislative vacuum. It will ensure that the youth class ceases to blight the lives of law-abiding owners of property.

Juvenile citizens would be restrained from engaging with society until they have learnt to shoulder the burden of respect and responsibility this entails. By this means we will rear the young people we all want to see: happy, well-adjusted, out of sight and out of mind.

28 June 2010

14
Pro-Death

Who carries the greatest responsibility for the deaths of unborn children in this country? I accuse the leader of the Catholic Church in England and Wales, His Eminence Cardinal Cormac Murphy-O'Connor. I charge that he is partly to blame for our abnormally high abortion rate.

Let me begin with a point of agreement. 'Whatever our religious creed or political conviction', Murphy-O'Connor writes, the level of abortion in the UK 'can only be a source of distress and profound anguish for us all'.[1] Quite so. But why has it climbed so high? Is it because of the rising tide of liberalism? The absence of abstinence? Strange as it may seem, the evidence suggests the opposite.

In February 2008, the Cardinal sacked the board of a hospital in north London.[2] It had permitted a GP's surgery to move onto the site and the doctors there, horror of horrors, were helping women with family planning. Though it is partly funded by the NHS, St John and St Elizabeth's is a Catholic hospital, which forbids doctors from prescribing contraceptives or referring women for abortions. The cardinal says he wants the hospital to provide medical help that is 'truly in the interests of human persons'.[3]

Murphy-O'Connor has denounced contraception and abortion many times before. That's what he is there for: the primary purpose of most religions is to control women. But while we may disagree with his position, we seldom question either its consistency or its results. It's time we started. The most effective means of preventing the deaths of unborn children is to promote contraception.

In the history of most countries which acquire access to modern medical technology, there is a period during which the rates of contraception and abortion rise simultaneously. Christian fundamentalists suggest that the two trends are related, and attribute them to what Pope Benedict XVI calls 'a secularist and relativist mentality'.[4] In fact it's a sign of demographic transition. As societies become more prosperous and women acquire better opportunities, they seek smaller families. During the early years of transition, contraceptives are often hard to obtain and poorly understood, so women will also use abortion to limit the number of children they have. But, as a study published in the journal *International Family Planning Perspectives* shows, once the birth rate has stabilised, the use of contraceptives continues to increase and the rate of abortion falls. In this case one trend causes the other: 'rising contraceptive use results in reduced abortion incidence'.[5] The rate of abortion falls once 80 per cent of the population is using effective contraception.[6]

A study published in the *Lancet* shows that between 1995 and 2003 the global rate of induced abortions fell from 35 per 1,000 women each year to 29.[7] This period coincides with the rise of the 'globalized secular culture' the Pope laments.[8] When you look at the broken-down figures, it becomes clear that (except in the countries of the former Soviet Union) the incidence of abortion is highest in conservative and religious societies. In the largely secular nations of Western Europe, the average rate is twelve abortions per 1,000 women. In the more religious Southern European countries, the average rate is eighteen. In the United States, where church attendance is still higher, there are twenty-three abortions for every 1,000 women,[9] the highest level in the rich world. In Central and South America, where the Catholic Church holds greatest sway, the rates are twenty-five and thirty-three respectively. In the very conservative societies of East Africa, it's thirty-nine.[10] One abnormal outlier is the UK: our rate is six points higher than those of our Western European neighbours.[11]

I am not suggesting a sole causal relationship here: the figures also reflect the regions' changing demographics. But it's clear that religious conviction does little to reduce the abortion rate and plenty to increase it. The highest rates of all – forty-four per 1,000 – occur in the former Soviet Union. Under communism, contraceptives were almost impossible to obtain. But, thanks to better access to contraception, this is also where the fastest decline is taking place: in 1995 the rate was twice as high. There has been a small rise in the level of abortions in Western Europe, attributed by the Guttmacher Institute in the US to 'immigration of people with low levels of contraceptive awareness'.[12] The explanation, in other words, is consistent: more contraception means less abortion.

There is also a clear relationship between sex education and falling rates of unintended pregnancy. A report by the United

Nations agency UNICEF notes that in the Netherlands, which has the world's lowest abortion rate, a sharp reduction in unwanted teenage pregnancies was caused by 'the combination of a relatively inclusive society with more open attitudes towards sex and sex education, including contraception'.[13] In the US and UK, by contrast, which have the highest teenage pregnancy rates in the developed world, 'contraceptive advice and services may be formally available, but in a "closed" atmosphere of embarrassment and secrecy'.[14]

A paper published by the *British Medical Journal* assessed four programmes seeking to persuade teenagers in the UK to abstain from sex. It found that they 'were associated with an increase in number of pregnancies among partners of young male participants'.[15] This shouldn't be surprising. Teenagers will have sex whatever the grown-ups say, and those who are the least familiar with contraceptives are the most likely to become pregnant. The more effectively religious leaders and conservative newspapers anathemise contraception, sex education and premarital sex, the higher the abortion rate will be. Institutions like the Catholic church help to sustain our appalling level of unwanted pregnancies.

But while the Catholic church causes plenty of suffering in the rich nations, this doesn't compare to the misery inflicted on the poor. Chillingly, as the *Lancet* paper shows, there is no relationship between the legality and the incidence of abortion. Women who have no access to contraceptives will try to terminate unwanted pregnancies whatever the consequences might be. A report by the World Health Organisation shows that almost half the world's abortions are unauthorised and unsafe.[16] In eastern Africa and Latin America, where religious conservatives ensure that terminations remain illegal, they account for almost all abortions. Methods include drinking turpentine or bleach, shoving sticks or coat hangers into the uterus[17] and pummelling the abdomen, which often causes the uterus to burst, killing the patient.[18] The WHO estimates that between 65,000 and 70,000 women die as a result of illegal abortions every year, while 5 million suffer severe complications. These effects, the organisation says, 'are the visible consequences of restrictive legal codes.'[19] I hope David Cameron, who has announced that he wants to place restrictions on legal terminations in the UK, knows what the alternatives look like.[20]

When Pope Benedict XVI told bishops in Kenya, the global epicentre of this crisis, that they should defend traditional family values 'at all costs' against agencies offering safe abortions,[21] or when he travelled to Brazil to denounce the government's contraceptive programme,[22] he condemned women to death. When George Bush blocked US aid for family planning charities that promote safe abortions, he ensured, paradoxically, that contraceptives would be replaced with backstreet foeticide.[23] Such people spread misery, disease and death. And they call themselves pro-life.

26 February 2008

Part 3
The Wild Life

15

Everything Is Connected

I can hear you muttering already: he's completely lost it this time. He's written 2,000 words on whale poo. I admit that at first it might be hard to see the relevance to your life. But I hope that by the time you have finished you will have become as obsessed with marine faecal plumes as I am. What greater incentive could there be to read on?

In truth it's not just about whale poo, though that is an important component. It's about the remarkable connectivity, on this small and spherical planet, of living processes. Nothing human beings do, and nothing that takes place in the natural world, occurs in isolation.

When I was a student, back in the days when mammoths roamed the Earth, ecologists tended to believe that the character of living systems was largely determined by abiotic factors. This means influences such as local climate, geology or the availability of nutrients. But it now seems that this belief arose from the study of depleted ecosystems. The rules they derived now appear to have described not the world in its natural state, but the world of our creation. We now know that living systems which retain their large carnivores and large herbivores often behave in radically different ways from those which have lost them.

Large carnivores can transform both the populations and the behaviour of large herbivores. In turn this can change the nature and structure of the plant community, which in turn affects processes such as soil erosion, river movements and carbon storage. The availability of nutrients, the physical geography of the land, even the composition of the atmosphere: all now turn out to be affected by animals. Living systems exert far more powerful impacts on the planet and its processes than we suspected.

I'm talking about trophic cascades: ecological processes that tumble from the top of an ecosystem to the bottom. (Trophic means relating to food and feeding.) It turns out that many living processes work from the top down, rather than the bottom up.

Trophic cascades have often been detected in places in which large carnivores still exist or have been reintroduced. But what has been discovered so far is likely to underestimate their natural prevalence. For what we now describe as 'top predators' are often – from the perspective of palaeoecology – nothing of the kind.

Species such as wolves and lynx, for example, would be more accurately described as mesopredators: belonging to the second rank. They would once have had to contend with lions, hyaenas, scimitar cats, sabretooths, bear dogs and other such monsters, throughout their ranges. Even the giant lions and giant sabretooths that lived in North America until the first humans arrived could not unequivocally be considered the kings of the jungle. The short-faced bear, which stood thirteen feet in its hind socks, appears to have been a specialist scavenger: specialising in driving giant lions and giant sabretooths off their prey.[1]

One hypothesis which might help to explain the sudden disappearance from many parts of the world of the mega-fauna, following the first arrival of human beings, is that we triggered trophic cascades of destruction.

For example, before humans reached Australia, the continent teemed with great beasts. There was a spiny anteater the size of a pig; a giant herbivore a bit like a wombat, which weighed two tonnes; a marsupial tapir as big as a horse; a ten-foot kangaroo; a marsupial lion with opposable thumbs and a stronger bite than any other known mammal, which I believe was a specialist predator of giant kangaroos;[2] a horned tortoise eight feet long; a monitor lizard bigger than the Nile crocodile. Most of them, and many other marvellous creatures, disappeared between 40,000 and 50,000 years ago. At roughly the same time, the dense rainforests which covered much of that continent began to be replaced by the grass and scrubby trees which populate much of the Outback today.

One paper suggests that the first humans in Australia hunted some of the large animals to extinction, and that this caused the destruction of the rainforests, which in turn wiped out much of the remaining fauna.[3] How? It postulates that when the giant herbivores disappeared, the leaves and twigs that would otherwise have been browsed began to build up on the forest floor, creating a fuel supply that allowed wild-fires to rage unhindered through the rainforests. This cata-lysed the shift to grass and scrub.

In Europe, ecologists are beginning to wake up to the fact that our ecosystems were and remain shaped by elephants, rhinos, hippos and the other great beasts that lived here during the last interglacial period, when the climate was similar to today's.[4] You can still see evidence of co-evolution with elephants and rhinos in the way that our deciduous trees respond to attack.

In other words, the natural world is even more fascinating and complex than we had imagined. And we are only just beginning to understand just how rich and strange ecological processes might be.

I promised whale poo, and whale poo you shall have. Studies in the 1970s proposed that the great reduction in the large whales of the southern oceans would lead to an increase in the population of krill, their major prey. It never materialised. Instead there has been a long-term decline.[5] How could that be true? It now turns out that whales maintain the populations of the animals they eat.

They often feed at depth, but they seldom defecate there, because when they dive the stress this exerts on the body requires the shutdown of some of its functions. So they perform their ablutions when they come up to breathe. What they are doing, in other words, is transporting nutrients from the depths, including waters too dark for photosynthesis to occur, into the photic zone, where plants can live.

In the southern oceans, iron is a limiting nutrient, without which the plant plankton at the bottom of the food chain cannot reproduce and grow. By producing their poonamis – sorry, faecal plumes – in the surface waters, the whales fertilise the plant plankton on which the krill and fish depend.[6] This effect, known as the 'whale pump', has been hypothesised

for several years.[7] But now there is some experimental evidence
to support it. A team of scientists at the University of Tasmania
collected some pygmy blue whale poo (who knew that marine
biology was so rich with possibility?) and grew plankton in
water containing varying concentrations of it.[8] They found
that the richer the mix, the greater the productivity. No
surprises there.

Separate research, in the Gulf of Maine, estimates that
whales and seals, by defecating at the surface and recycling
nutrients there, would, before their numbers were reduced
by hunting, have been responsible for releasing three times
as much nitrogen into those waters as the sea absorbed
directly from the atmosphere.[9] The volume of plant plankton has declined across much of the world over the past
century, probably as a result of rising global temperatures.
But the decline appears to have been steepest where whales
and seals have been most heavily hunted.[10] The fishermen
who have insisted that predators such as seals should be
killed might have been reducing, not enhancing, their catch.

But it doesn't end there. Plant plankton, when they die,
slowly descend into the abyss, taking with them the carbon
they have absorbed from the atmosphere. It is hard to quan-
tify, but when they were at their historical populations,
whales are likely to have made a small but significant contribution to the removal of carbon dioxide from the atmosphere. The recovery of the great whales, which were reduced
by between two-thirds and 90 per cent, but whose numbers
are slowly climbing again in some parts of the oceans, could
be seen as a benign form of geo-engineering.[11]

This should not be the only, or even the main, reason why
we should wish them to return, but the way in which whales

change the composition of the atmosphere provides yet another refutation of the idea that we can manipulate the living world with simple, predictable results.

With the Sustainable Human team – an online platform that shares content relating to crises that afflict civilisation and the Earth we live on – I produced a video about trophic cascades featuring the whale pump.[12] Another – about the unexpected impact of wolves in Yellowstone National Park – has been watched 20 million times.[13] The belief that people cannot handle complexity is a myth. There is a tremendous public appetite to understand the world in all its fascinating detail.

But I haven't finished with the whales yet. One research paper proposes that as the great whales declined, killer whales, some of which would have specialised in feeding on them, switched their diet to animals such as seals and sea lions.[14] This is likely to have had major effects on fish populations.

But now, in the Aleutian archipelago, the reduction of seals by human hunters appears to have caused the killer whales to switch their diet again, in this case to sea otters. A large part of the diet of sea otters consists of sea urchins. As the otters have declined, the number of urchins has risen, to the point that in some places they have grazed the vast kelp forests that once thronged the coastal waters of the western seaboard of the Americas until almost nothing remains. Not only has this caused the collapse of the coastal ecosystem, but it has also caused the release of more carbon dioxide into the atmosphere, as the carbon stored in the kelp has been oxidised.[15]

And even that is not the end of the story. It now seems that whaling may have been a leading cause of the decline of the

Californian condor. Condors appear to have specialised in scavenging the carcasses of stranded whales. As whales were destroyed, the condors were deprived of a major food source, and were forced to feed on dead terrestrial animals. Some of these carcasses are of animals that die after being shot and then lost by human hunters. The ingestion of lead from bullets and shot has been one of the reasons for the condors' fragile grip on existence.

Who would have guessed that the impacts of whaling would cascade through so many living systems?

(Incidentally, until humans arrived in the Americas, the condor was one of the smaller scavenging birds. The North American roc (*Aiolornis incredibilis*) had a wingspan of sixteen feet and a hooked bill the length of a man's foot. No skull of another predatory bird, the Argentine roc (*Argentavis magnificens*) has yet been found, but the available bones suggest that its wings were twenty-six feet across and that it weighed twelve stone.)

And it's not just whales. When plant plankton are attacked by the small animals that eat them, some of them release a chemical called dimethyl sulphide. This compound attracts predators that feed on the animals eating the plants. It appears that the tube-nosed birds, such as albatrosses, fulmars, shearwaters and petrels, which have a highly developed sense of smell, can detect dimethyl sulphide, and use its presence to find their prey. Not only might this help to protect the plant plankton from some of the animals grazing on them, but by defecating in the feeding zone, the birds help to fertilise the plants that brought them there.[16]

There's one more twist. Dimethyl sulphide seems to have a powerful role in the formation of clouds at sea. Because the sea has a dark surface, and clouds are white, the greater the cloud cover, the more sunlight is reflected back into space. So as plant plankton are attacked, they might help to cool the planet.

There are similar effects on land. Before serious conservation efforts began in the 1960s, wildebeest numbers in the Serengeti fell from about 1.2 million to 300,000. The result was similar to the hypothesised mechanism for the destruction of much of the Australian rainforest. As dry grass and other vegetation that the wildebeest would otherwise have eaten accumulated, wildfires ravaged around 80 per cent of the Serengeti every year.[17]

As wildebeest numbers have recovered, the frequency of fires has fallen and more dung is incorporated into the soil. The Serengeti has been transformed from a net carbon source to a net carbon sink: a shift equivalent to the entire current emissions of carbon dioxide from burning fossil fuels in East Africa.[18]

But it's important not to generalise from one example. In other parts of the world, grazing animals can increase the production of greenhouse gases. Domestic livestock are a major cause of global warming. So are some wild herbivores. As moose numbers in Canada have risen, partly due to the destruction of their predators by people, through a series of complicated impacts on both vegetation and soil they have sharply reduced the storage of carbon in the boreal forests. One estimate suggests that the difference in carbon storage between high and low moose numbers is the equivalent of between 42 and 95 per cent of the carbon dioxide Canada produces through the burning of fossil fuels. Allowing wolves to return to their historical levels could make a massive difference to Canada's greenhouse gas emissions.[19]

Nor should we imagine that wolves and whales and wildebeest and plant plankton and sea otters alone can prevent the climate breakdown that the unchecked consumption of fossil fuels will cause. Annual plant growth cannot match the burning of fossil fuels, which mobilises the stored remains of many centuries of accumulated plant carbon every year. But these first inklings of the unexpected impacts of our destruction should provide yet another reason for treating the living planet gently. Everything is connected.

I would hate to see the protection of wildlife reduced to a calculation about greenhouse gases. For me, there are powerful intrinsic reasons for defending the natural world: because it is wonderful; because it enriches and enchants our lives; because to understand how these magnificent and complex systems work is to wander into an enchanted kingdom.

But the little we now know of trophic cascades and the unexpected complexities they reveal, which doubtless presages a much deeper and richer understanding in the years to come, enhances for me the awe with which I contemplate our world of wonders. It makes me all the more determined to protect it from destruction.

12 December 2014

16

Civilisation Is Boring

'One of the penalties of an ecological education is that one lives alone in a world of wounds', the pioneering conservationist Aldo Leopold wrote. 'An ecologist must either harden his shell and make believe that the consequences of science are none of his business, or he must be the doctor who sees the marks of death in a community that believes itself well and does not want to be told otherwise.'[1]

I remembered that when I read the news that the world has lost 52 per cent of its vertebrate wildlife over the past forty years.[2] It's a figure from which I'm still reeling. To love the natural world is to suffer a series of griefs, each compounding the last. It is to be overtaken by disbelief that we could treat the planet in this fashion. And, in the darkest moments, it is to succumb to helplessness, to the conviction that we will keep eroding our world of wonders until almost nothing of it remains. There is hope – real hope – as I will explain later, but at times like this it seems remote.

These wounds are inflicted not only on the world's wild-life but also on ourselves. Civilisation is but a flimsy dust sheet that we have thrown over a psyche rich in emotion and instinct, shaped by the living planet. The hominins from whom we evolved inhabited a fascinating, terrifying world, in which survival depended on constant observation and interpretation. They contended not only with lions and leopards, but with sabretooths and false sabretooths, giant hyaenas and bear dogs (monstrous creatures with a huge bite radius).

As the work of Professor Blaire van Valkenburgh at UCLA suggests, predators in the pre-human past lived at much greater densities than they do today.[3] The wear and breakage of their teeth show that competition was so intense that they were forced to consume the entire carcasses of the animals they killed, bones and all, rather than just the prime cuts, as top carnivores tend to do today. In other words, the animals with which we evolved were not just bigger than today's predators; they were also hungrier.

Navigating this world required astonishing skills. Our ancestors, in the boom-and-bust savannahs, had to travel great distances to find food, through a landscape shimmer-ing with surprise and hazard. Their survival depended upon reacting to the barest signals: the flicker of a tail in the grass, the scent of honey, a change in humidity, tracks in the dust. We still possess these capacities. We carry with us a ghost psyche, adapted to a world we no longer inhabit, which contains – though it remains locked down for much of the time – a boundless capacity for fear and wonder, curiosity and enchantment. We are pre-tuned to the natural world, wired to respond to nature.

In computer games and fantasy novels, we still grapple with the monsters of the mind. In the film of *Lord of the Rings: The Two Towers*, the Orcs rode on giant hyaenas. In the first *Hunger Games* film, bear dogs were released into the forest to prey on the contestants. I don't believe these re-creations were accidental: the directors appear to have known enough of our evolutionary history to revive the ancestral terror these animals provoke. The heroic tales that have survived – tales of Ulysses, Sinbad, Sigurd, Beowulf, Cú Chulainn, St George, Arjuna, Lạc Long Quân and Glooskap – are those that resonate with the genetic memories lodged in our minds. I suspect that their essential form has remained unchanged for hundreds of thousands of years; that the encounters with monsters recorded in writing were a consolidation of stories we have been telling since we acquired the capacity to use the past tense.

You can see how such tales might have originated in a remarkable sequence in the BBC's *Human Planet* series. Three men in southern Kenya, described by the programme as Dorobo people (though this is not a designation many ethnographers accept) stalk to within about fifty metres of a lion kill. Fifteen lions, blood dripping from their jaws, are eating the carcass of a wildebeest. The men suddenly stand and walk towards the pride. Rattled by their confidence, the lions flee. They watch from the bushes, puzzled and indecisive, as the three men walk up to the carcass, hack off one of the hind legs, then saunter away. That night, the adventurers roast the meat in their cave. 'We really robbed those lions', one of them boasts. 'How many do you think there were?' another asks. 'Fifteen, but there might have been more.'

This, surely, is how sagas begin. Those men, led by a veteran of such ruses, are heroes of the old stamp. They outwitted a party of monsters, using guile and audacity, much as Ulysses did. A few hours later, they tell the first version of a story that might echo down the generations, every time with new flourishes and embellishments. Now imagine that, thousands of years hence, lions are long extinct, and the descendants of the Dorobo have only the haziest notion of what they were. They have become monsters even bigger and more dangerous than they were in life, and the feat has become even more outrageous and unlikely. The saga remains true to its core, but the details have changed. We are those people, still telling the old stories, of encounters with the beasts that shaped us.

The world lives within us; we live within the world. By damaging the living planet we have diminished our existence.

We have been able to do this partly as a result of our ability to compartmentalise. This is another remarkable capacity we have developed, which perhaps reflects the demands of survival in the ever more complex human world we have created. By carving up the world in our minds we have learnt to shut ourselves out of it.

One of the tasks that parents set themselves is to train their children in linearity. Very young children don't do linearity. Their inner life is discursive, contingent, impulsive. They don't want to walk in a straight line down the pavement, but to wander off in the direction of whatever attracts their attention. They don't begin a task with a view to its conclusion. They throw themselves into it, engage for as long as it's exciting, then suddenly divert to something else.

This is how all animals except adult humans behave. Optimal foraging, the term biologists use to describe the way animals lock onto the best food supply, involves pursuing a task only for as long as it remains rewarding. Our own hunting and gathering would have followed a similar pattern, though it was complicated by our ability to plan and coordinate and to speculate about imagined outcomes. Broadly speaking, ours was a rambling and responsive existence, in which, by comparison with the way we live today, we had little capacity or inclination to impose our will on the world, to lay out a course of action and to follow it without deviation or distraction.

Only with the development of farming did we have to discipline ourselves to think linearly: following a plan from one point to another across weeks or months. Before long we were ploughing in straight lines, making hedges and ditches and tracks in straight lines, building houses and then towns in straight lines. Now almost every aspect of our lives is lived within grids, either concrete or abstract. Linearity, control and management dominate our lives. We fetishise progress: a continuous movement in the same direction. We impose our lines on the messy, contradictory and meandering realities of the human world, because otherwise we would be completely lost in it. We make compartments simple enough, amid the labyrinths we have created, to navigate and understand.

Thus we box ourselves out of the natural world. We become resistant to the experiences that nature has to offer; its spontaneity and serendipity, its unscripted delights, its capacity to shake us out of the frustrations and humiliations which are an inevitable product of the controlled and ordered world we have sought to create. We bully the living world into the grids we impose on ourselves. Even the areas we claim to have set aside for nature are often subjected to rigid management plans, in which the type and the height of the vegetation is precisely ordained and, through grazing or cutting or burning, nature is kept in a state of arrested development to favour an arbitrary assemblage of life over other possible outcomes. Nothing is allowed to change, to enter or leave. We preserve these places as if they were pickles in a jar.

The language we use to describe them is also rigid and compartmentalised. In the UK we protect 'sites of special scientific interest', as if the wildlife they contain is of interest only to scientists. The few parts of the seabed which are not ripped up by industrial trawling are described as 'reference areas', as if their only value is as a baseline with which to compare destruction elsewhere. And is there a more alienating term than 'reserve'? When we talk about reserve in people, we mean that they seem cold and remote. It reminds me of the old Native American joke: 'We used to like the white man, but now we have our reservations.' Even 'the environment' is an austere and technical term, which creates no pictures in the mind.

It's not that we have banished our vestigial psychological equipment from our minds, or lost our instinct for engagement with wildlife. The tremendous popularity of nature programmes testifies to its persistence. I remember sitting in a café listening to a group of bus drivers talking, with great excitement and knowledge, about the spiders they had seen on television the night before, and thinking that, for all our technological sophistication, for all the clever means by which we shield ourselves from our emotions, we remain the people we have always been.

But we have suppressed these traits, and see the world through our fingers, shutting out anything that might spoil the view. We eat meat without even remembering that it has come from an animal, let alone picturing the conditions of its rearing and slaughter. We make no connection in our compartmentalised minds between the beef on our plates and the destruction of rainforests to grow the soya that fed the cattle; between the miles we drive and the oil wells drilled in rare and precious places, and the spills that then pollute them.

In our minds we have sanitised the world. W. H. Auden's poem 'Et in Arcadia Ego' describes how

> Her jungle growths
> Are abated,
> Her exorbitant monsters abashed,
>
> Her soil mumbled,

while

> the autobahn
> Thwarts the landscape
> In godless Roman arrogance.

But the old gods, the old fears, the old knowledge, have not departed. We simply choose not to see.

> The farmer's children
> Tiptoe past the shed
> Where the gelding knife is kept.[4]

Civilisation is boring. It has many virtues, but it leaves large parts of our minds unstimulated. It uses just a fraction of our mental and physical capacities. To know what comes next has been perhaps the dominant aim of materially complex societies. Yet, having achieved it, or almost achieved it, we have been rewarded with a new collection of unmet needs. Many of us, I believe, need something that our planned and ordered lives don't offer.

I found that something once in Cardigan Bay, on the west coast of Wales. I had stupidly launched my kayak into a three-metre swell to fish about three kilometres from the shore. As I returned to land, I saw that the tide had risen, and ugly, jumbled breakers were smashing on the seawall. From where I sat, two hundred metres from the shore, I could see that the waves were stained brown by the shingle they flung up. I could hear them cracking and soughing against the wall. It was terrifying.

Behind me I heard a monstrous hiss: a freak wave was about to break over my head. I ducked and braced the paddle against the water. But nothing happened. Then a hooked grey fin, scarred and pitted, rose and skimmed just under the shaft of my paddle. I knew what it was, but the shock of it enhanced my rising fear. I glanced around, almost believing that I was under attack.

Then, from the stern, I heard a different sound: a crash and a rush of water. A gigantic bull dolphin soared into the air and almost over my head. As he flew past, he fixed his eye on mine. I stared at the sea into which he had disappeared, willing him to emerge again, filled with a wild exaltation, and a yearning of the kind that used to afflict me when I woke from that perennial pre-adolescent dream of floating down the stairs, my feet a few centimetres above the carpet. I real-ised at that moment that I had been suffering from a drought of sensation which I had come to accept as a condition of middle age, like the loss of the upper reaches of hearing.

I found that missing element again in the Białowieża Forest in eastern Poland. I was walking down a sandy path between oak and lime trees that rose for perhaps thirty metres without branching. Around them the forest floor frothed with ramsons, celandines, spring peas and May lilies. I had seen boar with their piglets, red squirrels, hazel grouse, a huge bird that might have been an eagle owl, a black wood-pecker. I rounded a curve in the path and found myself face to face with an animal that looked more like a Christian depiction of the Devil than any other creature I have seen.

I was close enough to see the mucus in her tear ducts. She had small, hooked black horns, heavy brows and eyes so dark that I could not distinguish the irises from the pupils. She wore a neat brown beard and an oddly human fringe between her horns. Her back rose to a crest then tapered away to a narrow rump, from which a black tail, slim as a whip, now twitched. She flared her nostrils and raised her chin. I fancied I could smell her sweet, beery breath. We watched each other for several minutes. I stayed so still that I could feel the blood pounding in my neck. Eventually the bison tossed her head, danced a couple of steps, then turned, trotted back down the path and cantered away through the trees.

Experiences like these are the benchmarks of my life, moments in which dormant emotions are rekindled, in which my world is re-enchanted. But such unexpected encounters are far too rare. Most of the lands in which I walk and the seas in which I swim or paddle my kayak are devoid of almost all large wildlife. I see deer, the occasional fox or badger, seals, but little else. It does not have to be like this. We can recharge the world with wonder, reverse much of the terrible harm we have done to it.

Over the past centuries, farming has expanded onto ever less suitable land. Even places of extremely low fertility have been cultivated or grazed, and the result has been a great disproportion between damage and productivity: the production of a tiny amount of food destroys the vegetation, the wild animals, the soil and the watersheds of entire mountain ranges. In the face of global trade, farming in such areas is becoming ever less viable: it cannot compete with production in fertile parts of the world. This has caused a loss of cultural diversity, which is another source of sadness.

But at the same time it means that the devastated land could be restored. In Europe, according to one forecast, 300,000 square kilometres – an area the size of Poland – will be vacated by farmers by 2030.[5] In the United States, two-thirds of those parts of the land which were once forested, then cleared, have become forested again,[6] as farming and logging have retreated, especially from the eastern half of the country. Rewilding, the mass restoration of ecosystems, which involves pulling down the redundant fences, blocking the drainage ditches, planting trees where necessary, re-establishing missing wildlife and then leaving the land to find its own way, could reverse much of the damage done to these areas. Already, animals like lynx, wolves, bears and moose, on both continents, are moving back into their former ranges.

There are also possibilities of restoring large parts of the sea. Public disgust at a fishing industry that has trashed almost every square metre of seabed on the continental shelves is now generating worldwide demands for marine parks. These are places in which commercial extraction is forbidden and the wildlife of the seas can recover. Even fishing companies can be persuaded to support them, when they discover that the fish migrating out of these places greatly boost their overall catches, a phenomenon known as the spillover effect. Such underwater parks are quickly recolonised by sessile life forms. Fish and crustacea proliferate, breeding freely and growing to great sizes once more. Dolphins, sharks and whales move in.

In these places we can leave our linearity and confinement behind, surrender to the unplanned and emergent world of nature, be surprised once more by joy, as unexpected encounters with great beasts (almost all of which, despite our fears, are harmless to us) become possible again. We can rediscover those buried emotions that otherwise remain unexercised. Why should we not have such places on our doorsteps, to escape into when we feel the need?

Rewilding offers something else, even rarer than lynx and wolves and dolphins and whales. Hope. It offers the possibility that our silent spring could be followed by a raucous summer. In seeking to persuade people to honour and protect the living planet, an ounce of hope is worth a tonne of despair. We could, perhaps, begin to heal some of the great wounds we have inflicted on the world and on ourselves.

9 December 2014

17
End of an Era

It is, perhaps, the greatest failure of collective leadership since the First World War. The Earth's living systems are collapsing, and the leaders of some of the most powerful nations – the US, the UK, Germany, Russia – could not even be bothered to turn up and discuss it. Those who did attend the Earth Summit in Rio de Janeiro in 2012 solemnly agreed to keep stoking the destructive fires: sixteen times in their text they pledged to pursue 'sustained growth', the primary cause of the biosphere's losses.[1]

The efforts of governments are concentrated not on defending the living Earth from destruction, but on defending the machine that is destroying it. Whenever consumer capitalism becomes snarled up by its own contradictions, governments scramble to mend the machine, to ensure – though it consumes the conditions that sustain our lives – that it runs faster than ever before.

The thought that it might be the wrong machine, pursuing the wrong task, cannot even be voiced in mainstream politics. The machine greatly enriches the economic elite, while insulating the political elite from the mass movements it might otherwise confront. We have our bread; now we are wandering, in spellbound reverie, among the circuses.

The world's most inventive minds are deployed not to improve the lot of humankind but to devise ever more effective means of stimulation, to counteract the diminishing satisfactions of consumption. The mutual dependencies of consumer capitalism ensure that we all unwittingly conspire in the trashing of what may be the only living planet. The failure at Rio de Janeiro belongs to us all.

It marks, more or less, the end of the multilateral effort to protect the biosphere. The only successful global instrument – the Montreal Protocol on substances that deplete the ozone layer – was agreed and implemented years before the first Earth Summit, in 1992.[2] It was one of the last fruits of a different political era, in which intervention in the market for the sake of the greater good was not considered anathema, even by the Thatcher and Reagan governments. Everything of value discussed since then has led to weak, unenforceable agreements, or to no agreements at all.

This is not to suggest that the global system and its increasingly pointless annual meetings will disappear or even change. The governments that allowed the Earth Summit, and all such meetings, to fail evince no sense of responsibility for this outcome, and appear untroubled by the thought that if a system hasn't worked for twenty years there's something wrong with the system. They walk away, aware that there are no political penalties; that the media is as absorbed in consumerist trivia as the rest of us; that, when future generations have to struggle with the mess they have left behind, their contribution will have been forgotten.

Nor is it to suggest that multilateralism should be abandoned. Agreements on biodiversity, the oceans and the trade in endangered species may achieve some marginal mitigation of the full-spectrum assault on the biosphere that the consumption machine has unleashed. But that's about it.

The action – if action there is – will mostly be elsewhere. The governments that do retain an interest in planet Earth will have to work alone, or in agreement with like-minded nations. There will be no means of restraining free riders, no means of persuading voters that their actions will be matched by those of other countries.

That we have missed the chance of preventing two degrees of global warming now seems obvious, as does the fact that most of the other planetary boundaries will be crossed. So what do we do now?

Some people will respond by giving up, or at least withdrawing from political action. Why, they will ask, should we bother, if the inevitable destination is the loss of so much of what we hold dear: the forests, the brooks, the wetlands, the coral reefs, the sea ice, the glaciers, the birdsong and the night chorus, the soft and steady climate which has treated us kindly for so long? It seems to me that there are at least three reasons.

The first is to draw out the losses over as long a period as possible, in order to allow our children and grandchildren to experience something of the wonder and delight in the natural world and of the peaceful, unharried lives with which we have been blessed. Is that not a worthy aim, even if there were no other?

The second is to preserve what we can in the hope that conditions might change. I do not believe that the planet-eating machine, maintained by an army of mechanics, oiled by constant injections of public money, will collapse before the living systems on which it feeds. But I might be wrong. Would it not be a terrible waste to allow the tiger, the rhinoceros, the bluefin tuna, the queen's executioner beetle, the scabious cuckoo bee, the hotlips fungus and the fountain anemone to disappear without a fight if this period of intense exploitation turns out to be a brief one?[3]

The third is that, while we may possess no influence over decisions made elsewhere, there is plenty that can be done within our own borders. Rewilding – the mass restoration of ecosystems – offers the best hope we have of creating refuges for the natural world, which is why I've decided to spend much of the next few years promoting it here and abroad.

Giving up on global agreements, or, more accurately, on the prospect that they will substantially alter our relationship with the natural world, is almost a relief. It means walking away from decades of anger and frustration. It means turning away from a place in which we have no agency to one in which we have, at least, a chance of being heard. But it also invokes a great sadness, as it means giving up on so much else.

Was it too much to have asked of the world's governments, which performed such miracles in developing stealth bombers and drone warfare, global markets and trillion-dollar bail-outs, that they might spend a tenth of the energy and resources they devoted to these projects on defending our living planet? It seems, sadly, that it was.

25 June 2012

18

The Population Myth

It's no coincidence that most of those who are obsessed with population growth are post-reproductive wealthy white men: it's about the only environmental issue for which they can't be blamed. The brilliant earth systems scientist James Lovelock, for example, claimed last month that, 'Those who fail to see that population growth and climate change are two sides of the same coin are either ignorant or hiding from the truth. These two huge environmental problems are insepar-able and to discuss one while ignoring the other is irrational.'[1] But it's Lovelock who is being ignorant and irrational.

A paper published in the journal *Environment and Urbanization* shows that the places where population has been growing fastest are those in which carbon dioxide has been growing most slowly, and vice versa. Between 1980 and 2005, for example, sub-Saharan Africa produced 18.5 per cent of the world's population growth and just 2.4 per cent of the growth in CO_2. North America turned out 4 per cent of the extra people, but 14 per cent of the extra emissions.

Sixty-three per cent of the world's population growth happened in places with very low emissions.[2]

Even this does not capture it. The paper points out that around one-sixth of the world's population is so poor that it produces no significant emissions at all. This is also the group whose growth rate is likely to be highest. Households in India earning less than 3,000 rupees a month use a fifth of the electricity per head and one-seventh of the transport fuel of households earning 30,000 rupees or more. Street sleepers use almost nothing. Those who live by processing waste (a large part of the urban underclass) often save more greenhouse gases than they produce.

Many of the emissions for which poorer countries are blamed should in fairness belong to us. Gas flaring by companies exporting oil from Nigeria, for example, has produced more greenhouse gases than all other sources in sub-Saharan Africa put together.[3] Even deforestation in poor countries is driven mostly by commercial operations delivering timber, meat and animal feed to rich consumers. The rural poor do far less harm.[4]

The paper's author, David Satterthwaite of the International Institute for Environment and Development, points out that the old formula taught to all students of development – that total impact equals population times affluence times technology (I = PAT) – is wrong. Total impact should be measured as I = CAT: consumers times affluence times technology. Many of the world's people use so little that they wouldn't figure in this equation. They are the ones who have most children.

While there's a weak correlation between global warming and population growth, there's a strong correlation between global warming and wealth. I've been taking a look at a few superyachts, as I'll need somewhere to entertain politicians in the style to which they're accustomed. First I went through the plans for Royal Falcon Fleet's RFF135, but when I discovered that it burns only 750 litres of fuel per hour I realised that it wasn't going to impress Lord Mandelson. I might raise half an eyebrow in Brighton with the Overmarine Mangusta 105, which sucks up 850 litres of fuel per hour. But the raft that's really caught my eye is made by Wally Yachts in Monaco. The WallyPower 118 (which gives total wallies a sensation of power) consumes 3,400 litres of fuel per hour when travelling at 60 knots. That's nearly one litre per second. Another way of putting it is thirty-one litres per kilometre.

Of course to make a real splash I'll have to shell out on teak and mahogany fittings, carry a few jet-skis and a mini-submarine, ferry my guests to the marina by private plane and helicopter, offer them bluefin tuna sushi and beluga caviar and drive the beast so fast that I mash up half the marine life of the Mediterranean. As the owner of one of these yachts I'll do more damage to the biosphere in ten minutes than most Africans inflict in a lifetime.

Someone I know who hangs out with the very rich tells me that in the banker belt of the Lower Thames Valley there are people who heat their outdoor swimming pools to bath temperature, all round the year. They like to lie in the pool on winter nights, looking up at the stars. The fuel costs them £3,000 a month. One hundred thousand people living like these bankers would knacker our life support systems faster than 10 billion people living like the African peasantry. But at least the super-wealthy have the good manners not to breed very much, so the rich old men who bang on about human reproduction leave them alone.

In May 2009, *The Sunday Times* carried an article headlined 'Billionaire Club in Bid to Curb Overpopulation'. It revealed that 'some of America's leading billionaires have met secretly' to decide which good cause they should support. 'A consensus emerged that they would back a strategy in which population growth would be tackled as a potentially disastrous environmental, social and industrial threat.'[5] The ultra-rich, in other words, have decided that it's the very poor who are trashing the planet. You grope for a metaphor, but it's impossible to satirise.

James Lovelock, like Sir David Attenborough and Jonathan Porritt, is a patron of the Optimum Population Trust (OPT). It is one of dozens of campaigns and charities whose sole purpose is to discourage people from breeding in the name of saving the biosphere. But I haven't been able to find any campaign whose sole purpose is to address the impacts of the very rich.

The obsessives could argue that the people breeding rapidly today might one day become richer. But as the super-wealthy grab an ever greater share and resources begin to run dry, this, for most of the very poor, is a diminishing prospect. There are strong social reasons for helping people to manage their reproduction, but weak environmental reasons, except among wealthier populations.

The Optimum Population Trust glosses over the fact that the world is going through demographic transition: population growth rates are slowing down almost everywhere and the number of people is likely, according to a paper in *Nature*, to peak this century,[6] probably at around 10 billion.[7] Most of the growth will take place among those who consume almost nothing.

But no one anticipates a consumption transition. People breed less as they become richer, but they don't consume less; they consume more. As the habits of the super-rich show, there are no limits to human extravagance. Consumption can be expected to rise with economic growth until the biosphere hits the buffers. Anyone who understands this and still considers that population, not consumption, is the big issue is, in Lovelock's words, 'hiding from the truth'. It is the worst kind of paternalism, blaming the poor for the excesses of the rich.

So where are the movements protesting about the stinking rich destroying our living systems? Where is the direct action against superyachts and private jets? Where's Class War when you need it?

It's time we had the guts to name the problem. It's not sex; it's money. It's not the poor; it's the rich.

29 September 2009

19

The Dawning

The first hour of the day, before the sun is over the horizon: this is the time to see wildlife. In the spring and summer, when no one else is walking, when there is no traffic and the air is dense, so that the sounds of the natural world reverberate, when both nocturnal and diurnal beasts are roaming, you will see animals that melt away like snow as the sun rises.

Whenever I stay in an unfamiliar part of the countryside, I try to wake before dawn and walk until the heat begins to rise. Many of my richest experiences with wildlife have occurred at such times. In this magical hour, I too seem to come to life. I hear more, smell more, I am more alert. I feel that at other times my perceptions are muted, my senses dulled by the white noise of the day.

Recently I camped with my family at a barn-raising party on the western foot of the Quantock Hills, in Somerset. I crept out of the tent at five a.m., when the faintest skein of red cloud netted the sky. Below me, mist filled the valley floor. I slipped through the sagging fence at the top of the field and found myself in a steep, broad coomb, covered in bracken.

I climbed for a while, as quietly as I could, until a frightful wail shattered my thoughts. I crouched and listened. I could see nothing on the dark hillside. It came again, from about 150 feet to my right, half-shriek, half-bleat, a wild, wrenching, desolate cry, a cry that the Earth might make in mourning for itself.

My mind spooled, discounting possibilities until only one remained: a fawn calling for its mother. I waited, and soon I heard her answering bark, coarse and coughing, like a dog with bronchitis. Then, to my left, I heard others bark, and soon I realised that I was standing between two halves of a herd of red deer, ranged across the hillside above me. Upwind, they were unaware of the intrusion.

Now I saw them, on a false summit a little way above me, silhouetted against the dawn sky, their great ears twitching and turning as they gazed into the valley below. The barking and grunting intensified as the two wings of the herd converged, before they crossed the ridge and vanished into the darkness of the hills.

I walked for a while along the spine of the range. As the light rose, the mist rolled up the coombs, then broke into ragged clouds on the summits. I came across another herd, grey and faint in the fog, one stag, several hinds and a line of fawns, little heads just emerging from the heather.

The high ground, as in almost all English upland conservation sites, was sheepwrecked: swarming with the white plague, reduced to low heather and gorse and bracken with scarcely a tree in sight, supporting as a result just a sparse selection of the species that might have lived there. There are some magnificent woods a little further to the east, which number among the few native forests permitted to grow above 600 feet in Britain; sessile oaks writhed and wind-bitten into fantastic shapes. But elsewhere in the Quantocks the landscape pornographers (people who insist on seeing the uplands naked) who dominate British conservation still stamp their fetish onto the hills.

As the sun turned from red to yellow to white, I followed a path down into the enclosed pastures of the lower slopes. Here I found field mushrooms poking through the dew, their gills as pink as raw flesh. I picked some and wrapped them in my shirt. Wild mushrooms collected at dawn and eaten for breakfast are sweet, nutty, faintly tinged with aniseed. They bear no resemblance to those on sale in the shops.

Walking without a map, I reached the valley floor too soon, and found myself on the main road. In some places there were no verges, and I had to press myself into the hedge as cars passed. But on such early walks, almost regard-less of where you are, there are rewards. Just as I was about to turn off the road, onto the track that would take me back to the barn, I found a squirrel hit by a car that must have just passed me, dead but still twitching. It was a male, one of this year's brood but fully grown. Blood seeped from a wound to the head.

I picked it up by its hind feet, and though I had played no part in its death, I was immediately gripped by a sensation so discrete, so distinct from all else we feel, that I believe it requires its own label: Hunter's Pride. It's the raw, feral thrill I have experienced only on the occasions when I have picked up a fresh dead animal I intend to eat. It feels to me like the opening of a hidden door, a rent in the mind through which you can glimpse a ghost psyche: vestigial emotional faculties that once helped us to survive.

One of the oldest literary motifs, a staple of metaphysical narratives for thousands of years, is the portal: the gateway through which the hero passes into another world. I have come to believe that portals are mythic representations of these perceptual openings, fissures that allow us to see, though briefly and darkly, the ancient soul of humankind. To me, this ancient soul is the psychological equipment, abandoned but not absent, with which we once navigated a world where we were both hunters and hunted. To judge by my own fleeting experiences, the land beyond the portal is an enchanting, electrifying place, in which senses and sensations are tightened and stretched, tuned as at no other time to both the inner and the outer life.

All this, in response to a dead squirrel! Well, I'm sorry, it's how I felt. Unless you have felt it too, it doubtless sounds as if I'm raving. But I am trying to describe something that I believe to be fundamental; an essential yet neglected component of our being.

I showed the squirrel to the small tribe of children that had formed in the campsite, girls and boys between the ages of three and nine, and asked them if they'd like to watch me prepare it. As I expected, they clustered round, enthralled. How wrong we are to assume that children will be repelled and horrified by dead animals! On the contrary, they want to see as much as they can. What tends to repel and horrify them is the suffering of live animals. In this respect, they often seem to me to have a keener ethical sense than adults do.

I borrowed an axe and sharpened it on a stone, told the children what I was about to do, in case any of them had qualms, then chopped off the head, tail and feet. Immediately, a lively argument erupted over who was to claim these trophies. As I opened the abdominal cavity with my penknife, they pored over the guts, fascinated by the anatomy. They asked me to cut open the heart, to see what it looked like inside. I showed them the tiny atria and ventricles, in which the blood had now clotted. Then I skinned the squirrel and stretched and salted the skin on a piece of plank, whereupon another dispute arose about who would take it home.

Squirrel meat, while the flavour is excellent, is tough, and on previous occasions I have stewed it. But that wasn't possible at the barn, where there was only a barbecue and a camping stove. So I spatchcocked it and marinated it in lemon juice for a couple of hours, before we cooked it slowly on the barbecue. It was exquisite: tender and delicately flavoured.

I've eaten plenty of roadkill. I'll take anything fresh except cats and dogs (my main concern is for the feelings of the owners, rather than the palatability of the meat, though it would require an effort to overcome the cultural barriers), but I was never before foolish enough to mention this eccentric habit on social media. I noted on Twitter how good the meat was, and was greeted by protests.

Alongside the various 'yucks' and concerns about disease and fleas, none of which seem valid to me if the meat is properly cooked, were comments questioning the ethics of what I had done:

'Disappointed, what a strange thing to do, you should have just buried it.'

'… we should treat animals as equal until they are. Eating it demonstrates that it is worthless'.

'I thought I could look up to you, you monster …'

'The big question is what makes a squirrel different from a human. Very few people would consider it OK to eat a dead person.'

'... all that good stuff you've done and then you skin a squirrel and eat it, huge fall from grace'.

I asked one of these respondents why she felt the way she did, and she was good enough to give me some answers. She told me I should 'have respect for the life and feel sorrow it has been killed. Not think skin it and eat it'. I asked her whether she would find it more or less upsetting if I had eaten some chicken or pork. She answered, 'I'm not a veggy! Please just don't scrape things off the road and skin them. Your time better spent highlighting eco/politics.'

On one level, I think I can understand these comments. We have become so far removed from the realities of meat production that anything which reminds us of where it comes from and how it is processed (let alone reared) is disturbing and dissonant. So it should be, given the realities of factory farming and slaughterhouses. But it seems to me that some people have confused what is customary with what is ethical.

Familiarity can render any kind of horror invisible, and the common modes of livestock production are no exception. It is the unfamiliar that attracts opprobrium, even if it inflicts no harm.

The great majority of farmed meat, in my view, is unethically produced. The treatment of farm animals, particularly intensively produced pigs and chickens, is a suppurating open secret, sustained by tacit consent in a nation that purports to love animals and lavishes affection on dogs and cats. Pigs are just as intelligent and capable of suffering as the pets we treat almost as if they were children.

While free-range production tends to be kinder to the animals, its environmental impacts can be much worse. Free-range chicken and pig farms pollute groundwater and rivers. Outdoor pig farming has often caused soil slumping and erosion, resulting in muddy floods downstream, some of which have repeatedly inundated people's homes.[1] A friend describes the worst examples as 'opencast pig mining'. Sheep ranching across most of our uplands inflicts environmental damage out of all proportion to the tiny amounts of meat it produces, as the sheep seek out any seedlings that rear their heads, ensuring that trees are scoured from the hills.

And most of the farmed animals in this country are fed on either soya or maize, whose impacts on the living world are terrible.[2] A new paper in the journal *Science of the Total Environment* reports that, 'Livestock production is the single largest driver of habitat loss.'[3]

Perhaps you can dismiss these problems from your mind. But the overuse of antibiotics by livestock farms that can lead to resistant strains of pathogens, and the competition for scarce arable land between the production of animal feed and grain for human consumption, must surely trouble anyone with a concern for other people.

Even organic, low-input, high-welfare production could be described as ethical only if we ate less meat. Then, if manure production were in balance with crop production, it would make sense. But we are swimming in animal manure in this country (sometimes, given the state of our rivers and coastal waters, literally[4]). We need less of it, not more. In the context of overconsumption across the spectrum, and the vast land-take this requires, any form of meat production exacerbates the problems.

I don't regard the eating of meat as wrong in itself; it is contingent on circumstance. I don't have a problem, for example, with eating wild rabbits, pigeons or deer. All live here in great abundance, as they benefit from the way we manage the land. Deer are, by any reckoning, overpopulated, due to the absence of predators.

I see rabbit, pigeon and deer meat as by-products. The animals are killed primarily for pest control, and will continue to be killed, like the squirrel on the road, whether or not we eat the meat. Suppressing their populations does not damage ecological processes; in the case of deer it tends to enhance them. If some of the millions of grey squirrels killed every year in this country were sold for meat, it would be no bad thing. The same does not apply to pheasants laid down by shooting estates or grouse slaughtered by driven shoots. In both cases, their management, designed to boost their numbers, causes grave environmental problems,[5] and any purchases that help to make these industries more viable contribute to the damage.

Perhaps if we engaged more with the natural world, and developed a better understanding of our evolutionary history and our psychological place within it, we might spend more time thinking about what we eat. In doing so, I believe, we would enrich our lives, as well as the life of the more-than-human world. To seek enlightenment about ourselves and the world around us: this is what makes a life worth living.

27 August 2015

Part 4
Feeding Frenzy

20

Sheepwrecked

The section of the A83 that runs between Loch Long and Loch Fyne in western Scotland is known as the Rest and Be Thankful. It would be better described as the Get the Hell out of Here. For this, as far as I can tell, is the British trunk road most afflicted by landslips.

The soil on the brae above the road is highly unstable. There have been six major slips since 2007, which have shut the road for a total of thirty-four days.[1] The cost of these closures is estimated at about £290,000 a year.[2] It's a minor miracle that no one has yet been killed. The Scottish government has already spent millions on clearing the road and building culverts and barriers. It's about to launch a new engineering project, at a cost of £10 million, which, it hopes, will reduce the frequency of these disasters.[3]

Sensible, logical? Yes – until you hear this. One of the factors destabilising the soil is the presence of sheep on the hillside. A report the government commissioned notes that the sheep make landslips more likely because they compact and erode the soil and prevent trees and shrubs (whose roots might otherwise have fixed the slope) from growing.[4] The number of sheep on the hillside exceeds the danger point identified by scientists, beyond which erosion becomes severe.[5]

Yet throughout the years of consultants' reports and engineering solutions, repeated landslips and continuing danger to the public, the sheep have remained on the hillside. Every one of those animals must have cost the taxpayer thousands of pounds. But they are worth next to nothing: the government describes the value of the grazing as 'negligible'.[6]

It's an extreme example, but it's indicative of a wider issue: we pay billions to service a national obsession with sheep, in return for which the woolly maggots kindly trash the countryside. The white plague has done more extensive environmental damage than all the building that has ever taken place here, but to identify it as an agent of destruction is little short of blasphemy. Britain is being shagged by sheep, but hardly anyone dares say so.

I blame Theocritus. His development in the third century BC of the pastoral tradition – the literary convention that associates shepherding with virtue and purity – helps to inspire our wilful blindness towards its destructive impacts. His theme was embraced by Virgil and the New Testament, in which Christ is portrayed both as the Good Shepherd and as Agnus Dei, the Lamb of God, 'which taketh away the sin of the world'. The Elizabethans revived the tradition, and the beautiful nonsense Marlowe, Spenser and others published about the uncorrupted pastoral life resonates with us still. Their eclogues and idylls, bucolics and mimes persist today on Sunday night television, through which we wistfully immerse ourselves in the lives of hunky shepherds and adorable lambs, sheepdog trials and market days.

This tradition, coupled with an urban cultural cringe towards those who make their living from the land, means that challenging the claims and demands of hill farmers is, politically, almost impossible. Instead we throw money at them. I've used Wales as my case study. Here, according to figures from 2010, the average subsidy for sheep farms on the hills is £53,000. Average net farm income is £33,000. The contribution the farmer makes to his income by keeping animals, in other words, is minus £20,000.

But that's just the beginning. Hill farmers are used to justify the entire subsidy system. Farmers' unions and governments throughout Europe push them forward and tell moving stories about their plight to justify the €50 billion the EU spends every year. The barley barons and oilseed oligarchs hiding behind them must scarcely believe their luck.

Farmers argue that keeping sheep in the hills makes an essential contribution to Britain's food supply. But does it? Just over three-quarters of the area of Wales is devoted to live-stock farming,[7] largely to produce meat.[8] But according to the UK's National Ecosystem Assessment, Wales imports by value seven times as much meat as it exports.[9] This remarkable fact suggests a shocking failure of productivity.

That's not quite the end of the issue. Deep vegetation on the hills absorbs rain when it falls and releases it gradually, delivering a steady supply of water to the lowlands. When grazing prevents trees and shrubs from growing and when the small, sharp hooves of sheep compact the soil, rain flashes off the hills, causing floods downstream. When the floods abate, water levels fall rapidly. Upland grazing, in other words, contributes to a cycle of flood and drought. This restricts the productivity of more fertile lands downstream, both drowning them and depriving them of irrigation water. Given the remarkably low output in the upland areas of Britain, it is within the range of possibility that hill farming creates a net loss of food.

Sheep have reduced most of our uplands to bowling greens with contours. Only the merest remnants of life persist. Spend two hours sitting in a bushy suburban garden and you are likely to see more birds and of a greater range of species than in walking five miles across almost any part of the British uplands. The land has been sheepwrecked.

I accept that hill farmers are only trying to survive, and that theirs is a tough, thankless and precarious occupation. I'm not calling for the entire tradition of hill farming to be abandoned (not that there's much left of it in this age of quad bikes, consolidation and absentee ranchers). I am calling for a good deal more scepticism about the claims of those who champion it. And for a sweeping reassessment of a subsidy system which has been sold to us with a series of falsehoods. Do we really believe that keeping the hills bare, wiping out wildlife, helping to flood homes and farms and exacerbating landslips is a good use of public money?

30 May 2013

21

Ripping Apart the Fabric of the Nation

'British soils are reaching crisis point.' Don't take my word for it – this is a quote from a loyal friend of the farming industry, *Farmers' Weekly*.

You would expect farmers to try to protect their soils, which are the foundations of their livelihood, and many do. There are some excellent farmers in Britain, careful, well informed and always thinking of the future. But across large areas of land, short-termism now triumphs over common sense. Farmers are often in debt to the banks, and seek to clear that debt as quickly as they can. Many are growing crops that are simply incompatible with protecting the soil. Some don't seem to know very much about soil erosion and why it happens. Others – especially contract farmers working on other people's land – don't seem to care. Sensible land use is giving way to smash-and-grab exploitation.

I always flinch at the name given to soil in the US: dirt. Here there's a similar conflation: something dirty is said to have been soiled. But soil is a remarkable substance, a delicately structured cushion between rock and air, formed from thousands of years of physical and biological processes. It supports an ecosystem that turns unusable materials into plant food; it stores carbon, filters water and protects us from floods. Oh, and there's the small consideration that without it we would starve. It is, as it takes so long to re-form once it is lost, effectively non-renewable.

Yet this great gift of nature is being squandered at a horrifying rate. One study suggests that soil in Devon is being lost at the rate of five tonnes per hectare per year. There are several reasons for this, mostly to do with bad practice, but the problem has been exacerbated by an increase in the cultivation of maize.

Like the growing of potatoes, maize cultivation with conventional methods in this country is a perfect formula for ripping the soil off the land, as the ground is ploughed deeply, then left almost bare for several months. A study in south-west England suggests that the soil structure has broken down in 75 per cent of the maize fields there.[1] Maize cultivation has expanded from 1,400 hectares to 160,000 since 1970.[2] It is not grown to feed people, but to feed livestock and to supply anaerobic digestion plants producing biogas. If the National Farmers' Union gets its way, maize growing will expand by another 100,000 hectares in the next six years, solely to make biogas.[3]

Subsidies which were meant to encourage farmers to turn their slurry and crop wastes into biogas – a sensible and commendable idea – are instead being used to grow virgin feedstocks on the best arable land. Across the European Union, thanks to this perverse incentive, virgin crops (mostly maize) now account for 55 per cent of all the feedstock being poured into biogas plants. Our soils are being torn apart for no good reason.

Soil erosion and an associated problem, soil compaction

– mostly caused by using heavy machinery in the wrong conditions – is a major contributor to floods. Rain percolates into soils whose structure is intact, but flashes off fields where the structure has broken down, taking the soil – and the pesticides and fertiliser – with it. This means that the rivers fill up more quickly with both water and silt (which is what we call soil once it has entered a waterway). Siltation blocks channels and smothers the places where wildlife lives, including the gravel beds where fish spawn.

In some parts of Britain, soil erosion is now so severe that it causes floods without the help of exceptional rainfall, as saturated fields simply slump down the slopes into the houses below.[4] In some places, soil compaction has increased the rate of instant run-off from 2 per cent of all the rain that falls on the land to 60 per cent.

All this is a result of a complete failure of effective regulation. The only rules that seek to protect soils in this country are the conditions applied to farm subsidies, which are called cross-compliance. Just as social security claimants have to abide by certain rules in order to qualify for public money, so, in theory, farmers are meant to meet certain conditions in return for their much larger pay-outs. But while the rules applied to social security have been tightened to the point at which they have become degrading and oppressive, the rules attached to farm subsidies have been loosened by Defra, the Department for Environment, Food and Rural Affairs, until they are almost useless.

What they now amount to in practice is filling out the Soil Protection Review, a booklet or online form in which you state how well you are looking after your soil. Rural Payments Agency inspectors, whose job is to ensure that farmers aren't taking public money while also taking the piss, visit 1 per cent of farms a year, which means, on average, that a farm can expect a visit once every century. They seldom check whether there is any connection between what the farmer has written on the form and what is happening on the farm.

And even if there is a problem, they can't do anything about it. As the Rivers Trust notes, 'The Soil Protection Review is an unenforceable mechanism because provided a farmer has completed his SPR, identified a risk level for each field and allocated the appropriate number of optional measures, he cannot be deemed non-compliant even if he is causing a significant soil erosion problem on his farm.'[5]

You doubt it can be as bad as this? Then take a look at this exchange between two farmers on the *Farming Forum*:

QUESTION: Is the Soil Protection Review the biggest load of red tape codswallop that Defra have ever written? Farmers do have common sense, so this should be scrapped.

RESPONSE: 'The Soil Management Review is an entirely paperwork based affair that Defra invented to satisfy the EU that they were 'doing something' about soil management, without actually doing anything. In fact its [*sic*] an example of the UK civil service learning from our European cousins about how to play the EU system without hamstringing the people on the ground . . . Defra only want to see that it's been filled in, that's it. They will fine you if you don't so they can say to their EU masters 'Look we're enforcing the rules like you told us too.' But beyond that they pretty much let the farmers get on with it. They know we fill the thing in at the end of the year with any old rubbish – they don't care, as long as the farm doesn't look like a warzone. Its [*sic*] the ultimate in 'We pretend to abide by the

rules, and you pretend to enforce the rules, and everyone's happy'
concepts. Take 10 mins to fill your form in once a year and be very
glad Defra have decided this is the way to go.[6]

Yet even this is now deemed too onerous. Soon after it took
office, the coalition government set up a Farming Regulation
Task Force, chaired by a former director-general of the
National Farmers' Union. I've come across plenty of self-
serving reports by old boys' networks, but seldom anything
as bad as this. It insisted that 'food and farming businesses
must be freed from unnecessary bureaucracy', by which it
appeared to mean almost any regulation at all. 'Government
must trust industry . . . we suggest that Government should
invite industry to play a leading role in drafting guidance.'[7]

On protecting the soil, it had this to say: 'We recommend:
that the Soil Protection Review becomes voluntary . . . not
completing the Review correctly (or at all) should not result
in a breach.'[8]

In other words, give us the subsidies, but please remove
the last remaining conditions attached to them. We want
your money, no strings attached. Imagine how the government would respond to a report by ordinary benefit claimants, making the same demand. But these are landowners, so
an entirely different set of political rules apply.

At this year's conference of the National Farmers' Union,
the farming minister, George Eustice, announced that, 'I
want to bear down on the burden of regulation today. We've
just published the conclusion to the Red Tape Challenge on
Agriculture. In total we will scrap 156 regulations and
simplify 134 more. And we're going to slash guidance.'[9]

There will, he promised, be even fewer farm inspections

(fewer than one per century, in other words). If, by some miracle, a farmer is found to be in breach of rules so feeble that they're almost impossible to break, Eustice promised that they would lose as few of their subsidies as he could manage: 'We are pushing hard at an EU level for sanctions and penalties to be more proportionate.'

That is the sum total of the protection given to our soils in the UK: no meaningful protection at all.

You may detest the European Union and all its works, but I think even the most indurated sceptic would struggle to explain what was wrong with the measures it proposed for defending soils. Since 2006 it has been seeking to extend to soil the same basic protections which now apply to air and water. To this end it drafted something called the Soil Framework Directive.

The draft directive asked the member states to take precautions to minimise soil erosion and compaction, to maintain the organic matter soil contains, to prevent landslides and to prevent soil from being contaminated with toxic substances.[10] Terrified yet?

At the end of last month, unreported by any British newspaper or broadcaster, something unprecedented happened: a European legislative proposal was withdrawn. The Soil Framework Directive has been scrapped.

The National Farmers' Union took credit for the decision:

> From the early stages of the negotiations on the draft Soils Directive, and since the halt on its progress at the end of 2007, the NFU has actively called for these proposals to be thrown out. Our long held and firm belief has been that there is no need for additional legislation in this area – soils in the UK, and across the EU, are already protected by a range of laws and other measures.[11]

Farmers' Weekly, which must have forgotten that 'British soils are reaching crisis point', celebrated with the headline 'Red tape victory as soils rules axed'.

For eight years the NFU and its counterparts in other European nations lobbied against the directive. They were supported by a small number of member states, led by the United Kingdom. Both the Labour and coalition governments collaborated with the union on this project. Under these administrations, Defra has been captured by the industry it is supposed to regulate, until it now stands for Doing Everything Farmers' Representatives Ask.

The people who got this directive ditched claim to love their country. But they've ensured that it will continue to run down the rivers and into the sea. You want to get Britain out of Europe? Well how about ensuring that our soils stop ending up on the coastlines of France and Holland and Germany?

Where is the 'range of laws and other measures' which, the NFU claims, already protect our soils? There are words on paper, but nothing that amounts to anything resembling actual protection.

So goodbye fertility. Goodbye to the land's capacity to absorb and filter water, hold carbon and support crops. Goodbye to clean and healthy rivers. If the NFU and the British government had set out to damage the interests of this country they could scarcely have done a better job. Their work is a monument to short-termism and stupidity. Remember, next time you hear them say that Britain should produce as much of our food as it can, how they have helped to destroy our capacity to do so.

5 June 2014

22

Drowning in Money

We all know what's gone wrong, or we think we do: not enough spending on flood defences. It's true that the government's cuts have exposed thousands of homes to greater risk, and that the cuts will become more dangerous as climate change kicks in.[1] But too little public spending is a small part of problem. It is dwarfed by another factor, which has been overlooked in discussions in the media and statements by the government: too much public spending.

Vast amounts of public money – running into the billions – are spent every year on policies that make devastating floods inevitable.

Flood defence, or so we are told almost everywhere, is about how much concrete you can pour. It's about not building houses in stupid places on the floodplain, and about using clever new engineering techniques to defend those already there. None of that is untrue, but it's a small part of the story. To listen to the dismal debates in January 2014, you could be forgiven for believing that rivers arise in the plains; that there is no such thing as upstream; that mountains, hills, catchments and watersheds are irrelevant to the question of whether or not homes and infrastructure get drowned.

The story begins with a group of visionary farmers at Pontbren, in the headwaters of Britain's longest river, the Severn. In the 1990s they realised that the usual hill farming strategy – loading the land with more and bigger sheep, grubbing up the trees and hedges, digging more drains – wasn't working. It made no economic sense, the animals had nowhere to shelter, the farmers were breaking their backs to wreck their own land.

So they devised something beautiful. They began planting shelter belts of trees along the contours. They stopped draining the wettest ground and built ponds to catch the water instead. They cut and chipped some of the wood they grew to make bedding for their animals, which meant that they no longer spent a fortune buying straw. Then they used the composted bedding, in a perfect closed loop, to cultivate more trees.[2]

One day a government consultant was walking over their fields during a rainstorm. He noticed something that fascinated him: the water flashing off the land suddenly disappeared when it reached the belts of trees the farmers had planted. This prompted a major research programme, which produced the following astonishing results: water sinks into the soil under the trees at sixty-seven times the rate at which it sinks into the soil under the grass.[3] The roots of the trees provide channels down which the water flows, deep into the ground. The soil there becomes a sponge, a reservoir which sucks up water and then releases it slowly. In the pastures, by contrast, the small, sharp hooves of the sheep puddle the ground, making it almost impermeable: a hard pan off which the rain gushes.

One of the research papers estimates that, even though only 5 per cent of the Pontbren land has been reforested, if all the farmers in the catchment did the same thing, flooding peaks downstream would be reduced by some 29 per cent.[4] Full reforestation would reduce the peaks by around 50 per cent.[5] For the residents of Shrewsbury, Gloucester and the other towns ravaged by endless Severn floods, that means, more or less, problem solved.

Did I say the results were astonishing? Well, not to anyone who has studied hydrology elsewhere. For decades the British government has been funding scientists working in the tropics, and using their findings to advise other countries to protect the forests or to replant trees in the hills, to prevent communities downstream from being swept away. But we forgot to bring the lesson home.

So will the rest of the Severn catchment, and the catchments of the other unruly waterways of Britain, follow the Pontbren model? The authorities say they would love to do it.[6] In theory. Natural Resources Wales told me that these techniques 'are hard wired in to the actions we want land managers to undertake'.[7] What it forgot to say is that tree-planting grants in Wales have now been stopped. Some of the offices responsible for administering them are in the process of closing down.[8] If other farmers want to copy the Pontbren model, not only must they pay for the trees themselves; but they must sacrifice the money they would otherwise have been paid for farming that land.

For – and here we start to approach the nub of the problem – there is an unbreakable rule laid down by the Common

Agricultural Policy. If you want to receive your single farm payment – by far the biggest component of farm subsidies – that land has to be free from what it calls 'unwanted vegetation'.[9] Land that is allowed to reforest naturally is not eligible. The subsidy rules have enforced the mass clearance of vegetation from the hills.

Just as the tree planting grants have stopped, the land clearing grants have risen. In his speech to the Oxford Farming Conference, made during the height of the floods, the Environment Secretary Owen Paterson boasted that hill farmers 'on the least-productive land' will now receive 'the same direct payment rate on their upland farmland as their lowland counterparts'.[10] In other words, even in places where farming makes no sense because the land is so poor, farmers will now be paid more money to keep animals there. But to receive this money, they must first remove the trees and scrub that absorb the water falling on the hills.

And that's just the start of it. One result of the latest round of subsidy negotiations – concluded in June last year – is that governments can now raise the special mountain payments, whose purpose is to encourage farming at the top of the watersheds, from €250 per hectare to €450.[11] This money should be renamed the flooding subsidy: it pays for the wreckage of homes, the evacuation of entire settlements, the drowning of people who don't get away in time, all over Europe. Pig-headed idiocy doesn't begin to describe it.

The problem is not confined to livestock in the mountains. In the foothills and lowlands, the misuse of heavy machinery, overstocking with animals and other forms of bad management can – by compacting the soil – increase the rates of instant run-off from 2 per cent of all the rain that falls on the land to 60 per cent.[12]

Sometimes, ploughing a hillside in the wrong way at the wrong time of year can cause a flood – of both mud and water – even without exceptional rainfall. This practice has blighted homes around the South Downs (that arguably should never have been ploughed at all). One house was flooded thirty-one times in the winter of 2000–1 by muddy floods caused by ploughing.[13] Another, in Suffolk, above which the fields had been churned up by pigs, was hit fifty times.[14] But a paper on floods of this kind found that, 'There are no (or only very few) control measures taken yet in the UK.'[15]

Under the worst Environment Secretary this country has ever suffered, there seems little chance that much of this will change. In November 2013, in response to calls to reforest the hills, Owen Paterson told Parliament, 'I am absolutely clear that we have a real role to play in helping hill farmers to keep the hills looking as they do.'[16] In other words: bare. When asked by a parliamentary committee to discuss how the resilience of river catchments could be improved, the only thing he could think of was building more reservoirs.[17]

But while he is cavalier and ignorant when it comes to managing land to reduce the likelihood of flooding, he goes out of his way to sow chaos when it comes to managing rivers.

Many years ago, river managers believed that the best way to prevent floods was to straighten, canalise and dredge rivers along much of their length, to enhance their capacity for carrying water. They soon discovered that this was not just wrong but counterproductive. A river can, at any moment, carry very little of the water that falls on its catchment: the great majority must be stored in the soils and on the floodplains.

By building ever higher banks around the rivers, by reducing their length through taking out the bends and by scooping out the snags and obstructions along the way, engineers unintentionally did two things. They increased the rate of flow, meaning that flood waters poured down the rivers and into the nearest towns much faster. And, by separating the rivers from the rural land through which they passed, they greatly decreased the area of functional floodplains.[18]

The result, as authorities all over the world now recognise, was catastrophic. In many countries, chastened engineers are now putting snags back into the rivers, reconnecting them to uninhabited land that they can safely flood and allowing them to braid and twist and form oxbow lakes. These features catch the sediment and the tree trunks and rocks which otherwise pile up on urban bridges, and take much of the energy and speed out of the river. Rivers, as I was told by the people who had just rewilded one in the Lake District – greatly reducing the likelihood that it would cause floods downstream – 'need something to chew on'.[19]

There are one or two other such projects in the UK: Paterson's department is funding four rewilding schemes, to which it has allocated a grand total of, er, £1 million.[20] Otherwise, the Secretary of State is doing everything he can to prevent these lessons from being applied. Last year he was reported to have told a conference that 'the purpose of waterways is to get rid of water'.[21] In another speech he lambasted the previous government for a 'blind adherence to Rousseauism' in refusing to dredge.[22] Not only will there be more public dredging, he insists, but there will also be private dredging: landowners can now do it themselves.[23]

After he announced this policy, the Environment Agency, which is his department's statutory adviser, warned that dredging could 'speed up flow and potentially increase the risk of flooding downstream'.[24] Elsewhere, his officials have pointed out that, 'Protecting large areas of agricultural land in the floodplain tends to increase flood risk for downstream communities.'[25] The Pitt Review, commissioned by the previous government after the horrible 2007 floods, concluded that, 'Dredging can make the river banks prone to erosion, and hence stimulate a further build-up of silt, exacerbating rather than improving problems with water capacity.'[26] Paterson has been told repeatedly that it makes more sense to pay farmers to store water in their fields, rather than shoving it off their land and into the towns.

But he has ignored all this advice and started seven pilot projects in which farmers will be permitted to drag all that messy wildlife habitat out of their rivers, to hurry the water down to the nearest urban pinch point.[27] Perhaps we shouldn't be surprised to discover that Paterson has demanded massive cuts at the Environment Agency, including many of the staff responsible for preventing floods.[28]

Since 2007, there has been a review, a parliamentary enquiry, two bills, new flood management programmes, but next to nothing has changed.[29] Floods, because of the way we manage our land and rivers, remain inevitable. We pay a fortune in farm subsidies and river-mangling projects to have our towns flooded and homes and lives wrecked. We pay again in the form of the flood defences necessitated by these crazy policies, and through the extra insurance payments – perhaps we should call them the Paterson tax – levied on all homes. But we also pay through the loss of everything else that watersheds give us: beauty, tranquillity, wildlife and, oh yes, the small matter of water in the taps.

In *The Compleat Angler*, published in 1653, Izaak Walton wrote this: 'I think the best Trout-anglers be in Derbyshire; for the waters there are clear to an extremity.'[30] No longer. Last summer I spent a weekend walking along the River Dove and its tributaries, where Walton used to fish. All along the river, including the stretch on which the fishing hut built for him by Charles Cotton still stands, the water was a murky blueish brown. The beds of clean gravel he celebrated were smothered in silt: on some bends the accretions of mud were several feet deep.

You had only to raise your eyes to see the problem: the badly ploughed hills of the mid-catchment and, above them, the drained and burnt moors of the Peak District National Park, comprehensively trashed by grouse shooting estates. A recent report by Animal Aid found that grouse estates in England, though they serve only the super-rich, receive some £37 million of public money every year in the form of subsidies.[31] Much of this money is used to cut and burn them, which is likely to be a major cause of flooding.[32] Though there had been plenty of rain throughout the winter and early spring, the river was already low and sluggish.

A combination of several disastrous forms of upland management has been helping Walton's beloved river to flood, with the result that both government and local people have had to invest heavily in the Lower Dove flood defence scheme.[33] But this wreckage has also caused it to dry up when the rain doesn't fall.

That's the flipside of a philosophy which believes that land exists only to support landowners, and waterways exist only 'to get rid of water'. Instead of a steady flow sustained around the year by trees in the hills, by sensitive farming methods, by rivers which are allowed to find their own course and their own level, to filter and hold back their waters through bends and braiding and obstructions, we get a cycle of flood and drought. We get filthy water and empty aquifers and huge insurance premiums and ruined carpets. And all of it at public expense.

13 January 2014

23

Small Is Bountiful

Robert Mugabe is right. At the 2008 global Food Summit in Rome, he was the only leader to speak of 'the importance . . . of land in agricultural production and food security'.[1] Countries should follow Zimbabwe's lead, he said, in democratising ownership.

Of course the old bastard has done just the opposite. He has evicted his opponents and given land to his supporters. He has failed to support the new settlements with credit or expertise, with the result that farming in Zimbabwe has collapsed. The country was in desperate need of land reform when Mugabe became president. It remains in desperate need of land reform today.

But he is right in theory. Though the rich world's governments won't hear it, the issue of whether or not the world will be fed is partly a function of ownership. This reflects an unexpected discovery. It was first made in 1962 by the Nobel economist Amartya Sen, and has since been confirmed by dozens of further studies.[2] There is an inverse relationship between the size of farms and the amount of crops they produce per hectare. The smaller they are, the greater the yield.

In some cases, the difference is enormous. A recent study of farming in Turkey, for example, found that farms of less than one hectare are twenty times as productive as farms of over ten hectares.[3] Sen's observation has been tested in India, Pakistan, Nepal, Malaysia, Thailand, Java, the Philippines, Brazil, Colombia and Paraguay. It appears to hold almost everywhere.

The finding would be surprising in any industry, as we have come to associate efficiency with scale. In farming, it seems particularly odd, because small producers are less likely to own machinery, less likely to have capital or access to credit, and less likely to know about the latest techniques.

There's a good deal of controversy about why this relationship exists. Some researchers argued that it was the result of a statistical artefact: fertile soils support higher populations than barren lands, so farm size could be a result of productivity, rather than the other way around. But further studies have shown that the inverse relationship holds across an area of fertile land. Moreover, it works even in countries like Brazil, where the biggest farmers have grabbed the best land.[4]

The most plausible explanation is that small farmers use more labour per hectare than big farmers.[5] Their workforce largely consists of members of their own families, which means that labour costs are lower than on large farms (they don't have to spend money recruiting or supervising workers), while the quality of the work is higher. With more labour, farmers can cultivate their land more intensively:

they spend more time terracing and building irrigation systems; they sow again immediately after the harvest; they might grow several different crops in the same field.

In the early days of the Green Revolution, this relationship seemed to go into reverse: the bigger farms, with access to credit, were able to invest in new varieties and boost their yields. But as the new varieties have spread to smaller farmers, the inverse relationship has reasserted itself.[6] If governments are serious about feeding the world, they should be breaking up large landholdings, redistributing them to the poor and concentrating their research and their funding on supporting small farms.

There are plenty of other reasons for defending small farmers in poor countries. The economic miracles in South Korea, Taiwan and Japan arose from their land reform programmes. Peasant farmers used the cash they made to build small businesses. The same thing seems to have happened in China, though it was delayed for forty years by collectivisation and the Great Leap Backwards: the economic benefits of the redistribution that began in 1949 were not felt until the early 1980s.[7] Growth based on small farms tends to be more equitable than growth built around capital-intensive industries.[8] Though their land is used intensively, the total ecological impact of smallholdings is lower. When small farms are bought up by big ones, the displaced workers move into new land to try to scratch out a living. I once followed evicted peasants from the Brazilian state of Maranhão 2,000 miles across the Amazon to the land of the Yanomami Indians, then watched them rip it apart.

But the prejudice against small farmers is unshakeable. It gives rise to the oddest insult in the English language: when you call someone a peasant, you are accusing them of being self-reliant and productive. Peasants are detested by capitalists and communists alike. Both have sought to seize their land, and have a powerful vested interest in demeaning and demonising them. In its profile of Turkey, the country whose small farmers are twenty times more productive than its large ones, the UN's Food and Agriculture Organisation states that, as a result of small landholdings, 'farm output . . . remains low.'[9] The OECD states that 'stopping land fragmentation' in Turkey 'and consolidating the highly fragmented land is indispensable for raising agricultural productivity.'[10] Neither body provides any supporting evidence. A rootless, half-starved labouring class suits capital very well.

Like Mugabe, the donor countries and the big international bodies loudly demand that small farmers be supported, while quietly shafting them. Rome's 2008 Food Summit agreed 'to help farmers, particularly small-scale producers, increase production and integrate with local, regional, and international markets'. But when, earlier this year, the International Assessment of Agricultural Knowledge proposed a means of doing just this, the US, Australia and Canada refused to endorse it as it offended big business,[11] while the United Kingdom remains the only country that won't reveal whether or not it supports the study.[12]

Big business is killing small farming. By extending intellectual property rights over every aspect of production, by developing plants which either won't breed true or which don't reproduce at all, it ensures that only those with access to capital can cultivate.[13] As it captures both the wholesale and retail markets, it seeks to reduce its transaction costs by engaging only with major sellers. If you think that supermarkets are giving farmers in the UK a hard time, you should see what they are doing to growers in the poor world. As developing countries sweep away street markets and hawkers' stalls and replace them with superstores and glossy malls, the most productive farmers lose their customers and are forced to sell up. The rich nations support this process by demanding access for their companies. Their agricultural subsidies still help their own large farmers to compete unfairly with the small producers of the poor world.

This leads to an interesting conclusion. For many years, well-meaning liberals have supported the Fairtrade movement because of the benefits it delivers directly to the people it buys from. But the structure of the global food market is changing so rapidly that fair trade is now becoming one of the few means by which small farmers in poor nations might survive. A shift from small to large farms will cause a major decline in global production, just as food supplies become tight. Fair trade might now be necessary not only as a means of redistributing income, but also to feed the world.

10 June 2008

Part 5
Energy Vampires

24

Leave It in the Ground

As far as I can tell, this was the first article calling for fossil fuels to be kept in the ground. It began the discussion that eventually helped lead to the development of a global movement.

Ladies and Gentlemen, I have the answer! Incredible as it might seem, I have stumbled across the single technology that will save us from runaway climate change! From the goodness of my heart I offer it to you for free. No patents, no small print, no hidden clauses. Already this technology, a radical new kind of carbon capture and storage, is causing a stir among scientists. It is cheap, it is efficient and it can be deployed straight away. It is called . . . leaving fossil fuels in the ground.

On a filthy day in December 2007, as governments gathered in Bali to prevaricate about climate change, a group of us tried to put this policy into effect. We swarmed into the opencast coal mine being dug at Ffos-y-fran in South Wales and occupied the excavators, shutting down the works for the day. We were motivated by a fact which the wise heads in Bali have somehow missed: if fossil fuels are extracted, they will be used.

Most of the governments of the rich world now exhort their citizens to use less carbon. They encourage us to use energy-efficient light bulbs, insulate our lofts, turn our TVs off at the mains. In other words, they have a demand-side policy for tackling climate change. But as far as I can determine not one of them has a supply-side policy. None seeks to reduce the supply of fossil fuel. So the demand-side policy will fail. Every barrel of oil and tonne of coal that comes to the surface will be burnt.

Or perhaps I should say that they do have a supply-side policy: to extract as much as they can. Since 2000 the British government has given coal firms £220 million to help them open new mines or to keep existing mines working.[1] According to the energy White Paper, the government intends to 'maximise economic recovery . . . from remaining coal reserves.'[2]

The pit at Ffos-y-fran received planning permission after two ministers in the Westminster government jumped up and down on Rhodri Morgan, the First Minister in Wales. Stephen Timms at the department of trade and industry listed the benefits of the scheme and demanded that the application 'is resolved with the minimum of further delay'.[3] His successor, Mike O'Brien, warned of dire consequences if the pit was not granted permission.[4] The coal extracted from Ffos-y-fran alone will produce 29.5 million tonnes of carbon dioxide: equivalent, according to the latest figures from the Intergovernmental Panel on Climate Change, to the sustainable emissions of 55 million people for one year.[5]

In 2007, British planning authorities considered twelve new applications for opencast coal mines. They approved all but two of them. Later Hazel Blears, the Secretary of State in charge of planning, overruled Northumberland County Council in order to grant permission for an opencast mine at Shotton, on the grounds that the scheme (which will produce 9.3 million tonnes of CO_2[6]) is 'environmentally acceptable'.[7]

The British government also has a policy of 'maximising the UK's existing oil and gas reserves'.[8] To promote new production, it has granted companies a 90 per cent discount on the licence fees they pay for prospecting the continental shelf. It hopes the prospecting firms will open a new frontier in the seas to the west of the Shetland Isles.[9] The government also has two schemes for 'forcing unworked blocks back into play'. If oil companies don't use their licences to the full, it revokes them and hands them to someone else. In other words it is prepared to be ruthlessly interventionist when promoting climate change, but not when preventing it: no minister talks of 'forcing' companies to reduce their emissions. Ministers hope the industry will extract up to 28 billion barrels of oil and gas.

Following that, the government announced a new tax break for the companies working in the North Sea. The Treasury minister Angela Eagle explained that its purpose is 'to make sure we are not leaving any oil in the ground that could be recovered.'[10] The government's climate change policy works like this: extract every last drop of fossil fuel then pray to God that no one uses it.

The same wishful thinking is applied worldwide. The International Energy Agency's new outlook report warns that 'urgent action is needed' to cut carbon emissions. The action it recommends is investing $22 trillion in new energy infrastructure, most of which will be spent on extracting, transporting and burning fossil fuels.[11]

Aha, you say, but what about carbon capture and storage? When governments use this term, they mean catching and burying the carbon dioxide produced by burning fossil fuels. It is feasible, but there are three problems. The first is that fossil fuels are being extracted and burnt today, and scarcely any carbon capture schemes yet exist. The second is that the technology works only for power stations and large industrial processes: there is no plausible means of catching and storing emissions from cars, planes and heating systems. The third, as Alistair Darling, then in charge of energy, admitted in the House of Commons in May 2007, is that the technologies required for commercial carbon capture 'might never become available'.[12] (The government is prepared to admit this when making the case – as Darling was – for nuclear power, but not when making the case for coal.)

Almost every week I receive an email from someone asking what the heck I am talking about. Don't I realise that peak oil will solve this problem for us? Fossil fuels will run out, we'll go back to living in caves and no one will need to worry about climate change again. These correspondents make the mistake of conflating conventional oil supplies with all fossil fuels. Yes, at some point the production of petroleum will peak, and then go into decline. I don't know when this will happen, and I urge environmentalists to remember that while we have been proved right about most things, we have been consistently wrong about the dates for mineral exhaustion. But before oil peaks, demand is likely to outstrip supply and the price will soar. The result is that the oil firms will have an even greater incentive to extract the stuff.

Already, encouraged by prices, the pollutocrats are pouring billions into unconventional oil. In December 2007, BP announced a massive investment in Canadian tar sands. Oil produced from tar sands creates even more carbon emissions than the extraction of petroleum. There's enough tar and kerogen in North America to cook the planet several times over.

If that runs out, they switch to coal, of which there is hundreds of years' supply. Sasol, the South African company founded during the apartheid period (when supplies of oil were blocked) to turn coal into liquid transport fuel, is conducting feasibility studies for new plants in India, China and the US.[13] Neither geology nor market forces will save us from climate change.

When you review the plans for fossil fuel extraction, the horrible truth dawns that every carbon-cutting programme on earth is a con. Without supply-side policies, runaway climate change is inevitable, however hard we try to cut demand. International talks, like those in Bali, are meaningless unless they produce a programme for leaving fossil fuels in the ground.

11 December 2007

25

Applauding Themselves to Death

If you visit the website of the UN body that oversees the world's climate negotiations, you will find dozens of pictures, taken across twenty years, of people clapping.[1] These photos should be of interest to anthropologists and psychologists, for they show hundreds of intelligent, educated, well-paid and elegantly dressed people wasting their lives.

The celebratory nature of the images testifies to the world of make-believe these people inhabit. They are surrounded by objectives, principles, commitments, instruments and protocols, which create a reassuring phantasm of progress while the ship on which they travel slowly founders. Leafing through these photos, I imagine I can hear what the delegates are saying through their expensive dentistry: 'Darling you've rearranged the deckchairs beautifully. It's a breakthrough! We'll have to invent a mechanism for holding them in place, as the deck has developed a bit of a tilt, but we'll do that at the next conference.'

This process is futile because they have addressed the problem only from one end, and it happens to be the wrong end. They have sought to prevent climate breakdown by limiting the amount of greenhouse gases that is released; in other words, by constraining the consumption of fossil fuels. But, throughout the twenty-three years since the world's governments decided to begin this process, the delegates have uttered not one coherent word about constraining production.

Compare this to any other treaty-making process. Imagine, for example, that the Biological Weapons Convention made no attempt to restrain the production or possession of weaponised smallpox and anthrax, but only to prohibit their use. How effective do you reckon it would be? (You don't have to guess: look at the US gun laws, which prohibit the lethal use of guns but not their sale and carriage. You can see the results in the news every week.) Imagine trying to protect elephants and rhinos by only banning the purchase of their tusks and horns, without limiting killing, export or sale. Imagine trying to bring slavery to an end not by stopping the transatlantic trade, but by seeking only to discourage people from buying slaves once they had arrived in the Americas. If you want to discourage a harmful trade, you must address it at both ends: production and consumption. Of the two, production is the most important.

The extraction of fossil fuels is a hard fact. The rules that governments have developed to prevent their use are weak, inconsistent and negotiable. In other words, when coal, oil and gas are produced, they will be used. Continued production will overwhelm attempts to restrict consumption. Even if efforts to restrict consumption temporarily succeed, they are likely to be self-defeating. A reduction in demand when supply is unconstrained lowers the price, favouring carbon-intensive industry.

You can search through the UN's website for any recognition of this issue, but you would be wasting your time. In its gushing catalogue of self-congratulation, at Kyoto, Doha, Bali, Copenhagen, Cancun, Durban, Lima and all stops en route, the phrase 'fossil fuel' does not occur once.[2] Nor do the words 'coal' or 'oil'. But gas: oh yes, there are plenty of mentions of gas. Not natural gas, of course, but of greenhouse gases, the sole topic of official interest.

The closest any of the twenty international conferences convened so far has come to acknowledging the problem is in the resolution adopted in Lima in December 2014. It pledged 'cooperation' in 'the phasing down of high-carbon investments and fossil fuel subsidies', but proposed no budget or timetable, instrument or mechanism, required to make it happen.[3] It's progress of a sort, I suppose, and perhaps, after just twenty-three years, we should be grateful.

There is nothing random about the pattern of silence that surrounds our lives. Silences occur where powerful interests are at risk of exposure. They protect these interests from democratic scrutiny. I'm not suggesting that the negotiators decided not to talk about fossil fuels, or signed a common accord to waste their lives. Far from it: they have gone to great lengths to invest their efforts with the appearance of meaning and purpose. Creating a silence requires only an instinct for avoiding conflict. It is a conditioned and unconscious reflex, part of the package of social skills that secures our survival. Don't name the Devil for fear that you'll summon him.

Breaking such silences requires a conscious and painful effort. I remember as if it were yesterday how I felt when I first raised this issue in the media.[4] I had been working with a group of young activists in Wales, campaigning against opencast coalmines.[5] Talking it over with them, it seemed so obvious, so overwhelming, that I couldn't understand why it wasn't on everyone's lips. Before writing about it, I circled the topic like a dog investigating a suspicious carcass. Why, I wondered, is no one touching this? Is it toxic?

You cannot solve a problem without naming it. The absence of official recognition of the role of fossil fuel production in causing climate change – blitheringly obvious as it is – permits governments to pursue directly contradictory policies. While almost all governments claim to support the aim of preventing more than two degrees centigrade of global warming, they also seek to 'maximise economic recovery' of their fossil fuel reserves. (Then they cross their fingers, walk three times widdershins around the office and pray that no one burns it.) But few governments go as far as the UK has gone.

In the Infrastructure Act that received royal assent in February 2015, maximising the economic recovery of petroleum from the UK's continental shelf became a statutory duty.[6] Future governments are now legally bound to squeeze every possible drop out of the ground.

The idea came from a government review conducted by Sir Ian Wood, the billionaire owner of an inherited company – the Wood Group – that provides services to the oil and gas industry. While Sir Ian says his recommendations 'received overwhelming industry support', his team interviewed no one outside either the oil business or government. It contains no sign that I can detect of any feedback from environment groups or scientists.

His review demanded government powers to enhance both the exploration of new reserves and the exploitation of existing ones. This, it insisted, 'will help take us closer to the 24 billion [barrel] prize potentially still to come.' The government promised to implement his recommendations in full and without delay.[7] In fact it went some way beyond them. It is prepared to be ruthlessly interventionist when promoting climate change, but not when restraining it.

During the December 2014 climate talks in Lima, the UK's Energy Secretary, Ed Davey, did something unwise. He broke the silence. He warned that if climate change policies meant that fossil fuel reserves could no longer be exploited, pension funds could be investing in 'the sub-prime assets of the future'.[8] Echoing the Bank of England and financial analysts such as the Carbon Tracker Initiative, Mr Davey suggested that if governments were serious about preventing climate breakdown, fossil fuel could become a stranded asset.

This provoked a furious response from the industry. The head of Oil and Gas UK wrote to express his confusion, pointing out that Mr Davey's statements came 'at a time when you, your Department and the Treasury are putting great effort into [making] the UK North Sea *more* attractive to investors in oil and gas, not less. I'm intrigued to understand how such opposing viewpoints can be reconciled.'[9] He's not the only one. Ed Davey quickly explained that his comments were not to be taken seriously, as 'I did not offer any suggestions on what investors should choose to do.'[10]

Barack Obama has the same problem. During a television interview, he confessed that, 'We're not going to be able to burn it all.'[11] So why, he was asked, has his government been encouraging ever more exploration and extraction of fossil fuels? His administration has opened up marine oil exploration from Florida to Delaware – in waters that were formally off-limits.[12] It has increased the number of leases sold for drilling on federal lands and, most incongruously, rushed through the process to enable Shell to prospect in the highly vulnerable Arctic waters of the Chukchi Sea.[13]

Similar contradictions beset most governments with environmental pretentions. Norway, for example, intends to be 'carbon-neutral' by 2030. Perhaps it hopes to export its entire oil and gas output, while relying on wind farms at home.[14] A motion put to the Norwegian parliament last year to halt new drilling because it is incompatible with Norway's climate change policies was defeated by ninety-five votes to three.[15]

Obama explained that, 'I don't always lead with the climate change issue because if you right now are worried about whether you've got a job or if you can pay the bills, the first thing you want to hear is how do I meet the immediate problem?'[16]

Money is certainly a problem, but not necessarily for the reasons Obama suggested. The bigger issue is the bankrolling of politics by big oil and big coal, and the tremendous lobbying power they purchase.[17] These companies have, in the past, financed wars to protect their position; they will not surrender the bulk of their reserves without a monumental fight.[18] This fight would test the very limits of state power; I wonder whether our nominal democracies would survive it.

Fossil fuel companies have become glutted on silence: their power has grown as a result of numberless failures to challenge and expose them. It's no wonder that the manicured negotiators at the UN conferences, so careful never to break a nail, have spent so long avoiding the issue.

I believe there are ways of resolving this problem, ways that might recruit other powerful interests against these corporations. For example, a global auction in pollution permits would mean that governments had to regulate just a few thousand oil refineries, coal washeries, gas pipelines and cement and fertiliser factories, rather than the activities of 7 billion people.[19] It would create a fund from the sale of permits that's likely to run into trillions: money that could be used for anything from renewable energy to health care. By reducing fluctuations in the supply of energy, this auction would deliver more predictable prices, which would be welcomed by many businesses. Most importantly, unlike the current framework for negotiations, it could work, producing a real possibility of averting climate breakdown.

Left to themselves, the negotiators will continue to avoid this issue until they have wasted everyone else's lives as well as their own. They keep telling us that the conference in Paris in December 2015 is the make-or-break meeting (presumably they intend to unveil a radical new deckchair design). We should take them at their word, and demand that they start confronting the real problem.

With the help of George Marshall at the Climate Outreach and Information Network, I've drafted a paragraph of the kind that the Paris agreement should contain. It's far from perfect, and I would love to see other people refining it. But, I hope, it's a start:

Scientific assessments of the carbon contained in existing fossil fuel reserves suggest that full exploitation of these reserves is incompatible with the agreed target of no more than 2°C of global warming. The unrestricted extraction of these reserves undermines attempts to limit greenhouse gas emissions. We will start negotiating a global budget for the extraction of fossil fuels from existing reserves, as well as a date for a moratorium on the exploration and development of new reserves. In line with the quantification of the fossil carbon that can be extracted without a high chance of exceeding 2°C of global warming, we will develop a timetable for annual reductions towards that budget. We will develop mechanisms for allocating production within this budget and for enforcement and monitoring.

If something of that kind were to emerge from Paris, it will not have been a total waste of time, and the delegates would be able to congratulate themselves on a real achievement rather than yet another false one. Then, for once, they would deserve their own applause.

10 March 2015

26

The Grime behind the Crime

It seemed, at first, preposterous. The hypothesis was so exotic that I laughed. The rise and fall of violent crime during the second half of the twentieth century and first years of the twenty-first were caused, it proposed, not by changes in policing or imprisonment, single-parenthood, recession, crack cocaine or the legalisation of abortion, but mainly by . . . lead.

I don't mean bullets. The crime waves that afflicted many parts of the world and then, against all predictions, collapsed, were ascribed, in an article published by *Mother Jones* in January 2013, to the rise and fall in the use of lead-based paint and leaded petrol.[1]

It's ridiculous – until you see the evidence. Studies between cities, states and nations show that the rise and fall in crime follows, with a roughly twenty-year lag, the rise and fall in the exposure of infants to trace quantities of lead.[2] But all that gives us is correlation: an association that could be coincidental. The *Mother Jones* article, based on several scientific papers, claimed causation.

I began by reading the papers. Do they say what the article claims? They do. Then I looked up the citations: the discussion of those papers in the scientific literature. The three whose citations I checked have been mentioned, between them, 301 times.[3] I went through all these papers (except the handful in foreign languages), as well as dozens of others. To my astonishment, I could find just one study attacking the thesis, and this was sponsored by the Ethyl Corporation, which happens to have been a major manufacturer of the petrol additive tetraethyl lead.[4] I found many more supporting it. Crazy as this seems, it really does look as if lead poisoning could be the major cause of the rise and fall of violent crime.

The curve is much the same in all the countries these papers have studied. Lead was withdrawn first from paint and then from petrol at different times in different places (beginning in the 1970s in the US in the case of petrol, and the 1990s in many parts of Europe), yet, despite these different times and different circumstances, the pattern is the same: violent crime peaks around twenty years after lead pollution peaks.[5] The crime rates in big and small cities in the US, once wildly different, have now converged, also some twenty years after the phase-out.[6]

Nothing else seems to explain these trends. The researchers have taken great pains to correct for the obvious complicating variables: social, economic and legal factors. One paper found, after fifteen variables had been taken into account, a fourfold increase in homicides in US counties with the highest lead pollution.[7] Another discovered that lead levels appeared to explain 90 per cent of the difference in rates of aggravated assault between various American cities.[8]

A study in Cincinnati finds that young people prosecuted for delinquency are four times more likely than the general population to have high levels of lead in their bones.[9] A meta-analysis (a study of studies) of nineteen papers found no evidence that other factors could explain the correlation between exposure to lead and conduct problems among young people.[10]

Is it really so surprising that a highly potent nerve toxin causes behavioural change? The devastating and permanent impacts of even very low levels of lead on IQ have been known for many decades. Behavioural effects were first documented in 1943: infants who had tragically chewed the leaded paint off the railings of their cots were found, years after they had recovered from acute poisoning, to be highly disposed to aggression and violence.[11]

Lead poisoning in infancy, even at very low levels, impairs the development of those parts of the brain (the anterior cingulate cortex and prefrontal cortex) that regulate behaviour and mood.[12] The effect is stronger in boys than in girls. Lead poisoning is associated with attention deficit disorder, impulsiveness, aggression and, according to one paper, psychopathy.[13] Lead is so toxic that it is unsafe at any level.[14]

Because they were more likely to live in inner cities, in unrenovated housing whose lead paint was peeling and beside busy roads, African Americans have been subjected to higher average levels of lead poisoning than white Americans. One study, published in 1986, found that 18 per cent of white children but 52 per cent of black children in the US had over twenty microgrammes per decilitre of lead in their blood;[15] another that, between 1976 and 1980, black infants were eight times more likely to be carrying the horrendous load of forty microgrammes per decilitre.[16] This, two papers propose, could explain much of the difference in crime rates between black and white Americans,[17] and the supposed difference in IQ trumpeted by the book *The Bell Curve*.[18]

There is only one remaining manufacturer of tetraethyl lead on earth. It's based in Ellesmere Port in Britain, and it's called Innospec. The product has long been banned from general sale in the UK, but the company admits on its website that it's still selling this poison to other countries.[19] Innospec refuses to talk to me, but other reports claim that tetraethyl lead is being exported to Afghanistan, Algeria, Burma, Iraq, North Korea, Sierra Leone and Yemen, countries afflicted either by chaos or by governments who don't give a damn about their people.[20]

In 2010, the company admitted that, under the name Associated Octel, it had paid millions of dollars in bribes to officials in Iraq and Indonesia to be allowed to continue, at immense profit, selling tetratethyl lead.[21] Through an agreement with the British and American courts, Innospec was let off so lightly that Lord Justice Thomas complained that 'no such arrangement should be made again'.[22] God knows how many lives this firm has ruined.

The UK government tells me that because tetraethyl lead is not on the European list of controlled exports, there is nothing to prevent Innospec from selling it to whomever it wants.[23] There's a term for this: environmental racism.

If it is true that lead pollution, whose wider impacts have been recognised for decades, has driven the rise and fall of violence, then there lies, behind the crimes that have destroyed so many lives and filled so many prisons, a much greater crime.

7 January 2013

27

Going Critical

You will not be surprised to hear that the nuclear catastrophe at Fukushima has changed my view of nuclear power. You will be surprised to hear how it has changed it. As a result of the disaster, I am no longer nuclear-neutral. I now support the technology.

A crappy old plant with inadequate safety features was hit by a monster earthquake and a vast tsunami. The electricity supply failed, knocking out the cooling system. The reactors began to explode and melt down. The disaster exposed a familiar legacy of poor design and corner-cutting.[1] Yet, as far as we know, no one has yet received a lethal dose of radiation.

Some Greens have wildly exaggerated the dangers of radioactive pollution. For a clearer view, look at the graphic published by xkcd.com.[2] It shows that the average total dose from the Three-Mile Island disaster for someone living within ten miles of the plant was one 625th of the maximum yearly amount permitted for US radiation workers. This, in turn, is half of the lowest one-year dose clearly linked to an increased cancer risk, which, in its turn, is one-eightieth of an invariably fatal exposure. I'm not proposing complacency here. I am proposing perspective.

If other forms of energy production caused no damage, these impacts would weigh more heavily. But energy is like medicine: if there are no side-effects, the chances are that it doesn't work.

Like most Greens, I favour a major expansion of renewables. I can also sympathise with the complaints of their opponents. It's not just the onshore windfarms that bother people, but also the new grid connections (pylons and power lines). As the proportion of renewable electricity on the grid rises, more pumped storage will be needed to keep the lights on. That means reservoirs on mountains: they aren't popular either.

The impacts and costs of renewables rise with the proportion of power they supply, as the need for both storage and redundancy increases. It may well be the case (I have yet to see a comparative study) that up to a certain grid penetration – 50 or 70 per cent, perhaps? – renewables have smaller carbon impacts than nukes, while beyond that point, nukes have smaller impacts than renewables.

Like others, I have called for renewable power to be used both to replace the electricity produced by fossil fuel and to expand the total supply, displacing the oil used for transport and the gas used for heating fuel. Are we also to demand that it replace current nuclear capacity? The more work we expect renewables to do, the greater the impacts on the landscape will be, and the tougher the task of public persuasion.

But expanding the grid to connect people and industry to rich, distant sources of ambient energy is also rejected by many environmentalists, who want us to power down and produce our energy locally. Some have even called for the abandonment of the grid. Their bucolic vision sounds lovely, until you read the small print.

At high latitudes like ours, most small-scale ambient power production is a dead loss. Generating solar power in the UK involves a spectacular waste of scarce resources.[3] It's hopelessly inefficient and poorly matched to the pattern of demand. Wind power in populated areas is largely worthless. This is partly because we have built our settlements in sheltered places; partly because turbulence caused by the buildings interferes with the airflow and chews up the mechanism. Micro-hydropower might work for a farmhouse in Wales; it's not much use in Birmingham.

And how do we drive our textile mills, brick kilns, blast furnaces and electric railways – not to mention advanced industrial processes? Rooftop solar panels? The moment you consider the demands of the whole economy is the moment at which you fall out of love with local energy production. A national (or, better still, international) grid is the essential prerequisite for a largely renewable energy supply.

Some Greens go even further: why waste renewable resources by turning them into electricity? Why not use them to provide energy directly? To answer this question, look at what happened in Britain before the Industrial Revolution.

The damming and weiring of British rivers for watermills was small-scale, renewable, picturesque and devastating. By blocking the rivers and silting up the spawning beds, they helped bring to an end the gigantic runs of migratory fish that were once among our great natural spectacles and which fed much of Britain: wiping out sturgeon, lampreys and shad as well as most sea trout and salmon.[4]

Traction was intimately linked with starvation. The more land was set aside for feeding draft animals for industry and transport, the less was available for feeding humans. It was the seventeenth-century equivalent of today's biofuels crisis. The same applied to heating fuel. As E. A. Wrigley points out in his new book *Energy and the English Industrial Revolution*, the 11 million tonnes of coal mined in England in 1800 produced as much energy as 11 million acres of woodland (one-third of the land surface) would have generated.[5]

Before coal became widely available, wood was used not just for heating homes but also for industrial processes: if half the land surface of Britain had been covered with woodland, Wrigley shows, we could have made 1.25 million tonnes of bar iron a year (a fraction of current consumption[6]) and nothing else.[7] Even with a much lower population than today's, manufactured goods in the land-based economy were the preserve of the elite. Deep green energy production – decentralised, based on the products of the land – is far more damaging to humanity than nuclear meltdown.

But the energy source to which most economies will revert if they shut down their nuclear plants is not wood, water, wind or sun, but fossil fuel. On every measure (climate change, mining impact, local pollution, industrial injury and death, even radioactive discharges) coal is much worse than nuclear power.[8] Thanks to the expansion of shale gas production, the impacts of natural gas are catching up fast.[9]

Yes, I still loathe the liars who run the nuclear industry. Yes, I would prefer to see the entire sector shut down, if there were harmless alternatives. But there are no ideal solutions. Every energy technology carries a cost; so does the absence of energy technologies. Atomic energy has just been subjected to one of the harshest of possible tests, and the impact on people and the planet has been small. The crisis at Fukushima has converted me to the cause of nuclear power.

21 March 2011

28
Power Crazed

Most of the afflictions wrongly attributed to nuclear power can rightly be attributed to coal. I was struck by this thought when I saw the graphics published by Greenpeace, showing the premature deaths caused by coal plants in China.[1] The research it commissioned suggests that a quarter of a million deaths a year could be avoided if coal power were shut down in China.[2] Yes, a quarter of a million.

Were Greenpeace to plot the impacts of nuclear power on the same scale, the vast red splodges depicting the air pollution catastrophe suffered by several Chinese cities would be replaced by dots invisible to the naked eye.

This is not to suggest that there are no impacts, but they are tiny by comparison. The World Health Organisation's analysis of the Fukushima disaster concludes that, 'For the general population inside and outside of Japan . . . no observable increases in cancer rates above baseline rates are anticipated.'[3] Only the most contaminated parts of Fukushima prefecture are exposed to any significant threat:

a slight increase in the chances of contracting cancer. Even the majority of the emergency workers have no higher cancer risk than that of the general population.[4] And this, remember, was caused by an unprecedented disaster. The deaths in China are caused by business as usual.

The tiny risk imposed by nuclear power has both obscured and invoked the far greater risk imposed by coal. Scare stories about nuclear power are a gift to the coal industry. When these stories are taken seriously by politicians – as they have been in Japan – causing a switch from nuclear to coal, they kill people.[5]

Since the tsunami in 2011, the Internet has been awash with ever more lurid claims about Fukushima. Millions have read reports which state that children on the western seaboard of the US are dying as a result of radiation released by the damaged plant.[6] It doesn't seem to matter how often and effectively these claims are debunked: they keep on coming.[7] But children in the US really are dying as a result of pollution from coal plants, and we hear almost nothing about it.

Plenty of reports also propose that the water on the Pacific coast of North America is now dangerous to swimmers, and the fish there too radioactive to eat.[8] Again, it's not true. Except in the immediate vicinity of the plant, any extra radiation to which fish in the Pacific are exposed is minute by comparison with the concentration in their tissues of polonium-210, which occurs naturally in seawater.[9] There are, however, genuine dangers associated with another toxic contaminant found in fish: mercury. What is the primary source of mercury pollution? Ah yes, coal burning.[10]

In October 2013, for the first time, the World Health Organisation officially listed both gaseous outdoor pollution and airborne particulates as carcinogenic to humans. Exposure levels, it notes, are rising sharply in some parts of the world. In 2010 an estimated 223,000 deaths from lung cancer were caused by air pollution.[11]

But these cancers, though wildly outstripping those correctly attributed to man-made radiation, are just a small part of the pollution problem. Far greater numbers are afflicted by other diseases, including asthma, bronchitis, emphysema, heart disease, hypertension, strokes, low birth weight, pre-term delivery, pre-eclampsia and (through heavy metal exposure in the womb) impaired brain function.

Three hundred microgrammes of fine particulates per cubic metre of air is classed as severe pollution, the point at which children and elderly people should not leave their homes. As Greenpeace pointed out, in Shanghai in December 2013 and in Harbin in October of the same year, concentrations exceeded 500 microgrammes.[12] By far the greatest source of these particles is coal burning. In total, air pollution in northern China, according to a study published in *Proceedings of the National Academy of Sciences*, has cut average life expectancy by five and a half years.[13]

We have exported much of our pollution – and its associated deaths – but the residue in our own countries is still severe. A study by the Clean Air Task Force suggests that coal power in the US causes 13,200 premature deaths a year.[14] In Europe, according to the Health and Environment Alliance, the figure is 18,200.[15] A study it cites suggests that around 200,000 children born in Europe each year have been exposed to 'critical levels' of methylmercury in the womb.[16]

It estimates the health costs inflicted by coal burning at between €15 and €42 billion a year. Do you still reckon coal is cheap?

You're picturing filthy plants in Poland and Romania, aren't you? But among the most polluting power stations in Europe, Longannet in Scotland is ranked eleventh. Drax, in England, is ranked seventh.[17] The House of Lords has just failed to pass an amendment which would have forced a gradual shutdown of our coal-burning power plants: they remain exempted from the emissions standards other power stations have to meet.[18]

While nuclear power is faltering, coal is booming. Almost 1,200 new plants are being developed worldwide: many will use coal exported from the United States and Australia.[19] The exports are now a massive source of income for these supposedly greening economies.[20] By 2030, China is expected to import almost five times as much coal as it does today.[21] The International Energy Agency estimates that the global use of coal will increase by 65 per cent by 2035.[22] Even before you consider climate change, this is a disaster.

You don't have to be an enthusiast for atomic energy to see that it scarcely features as a health risk beside its rival. I wonder whether the nuclear panic might be a way of not seeing. Displacement is something we all do: fixing on something small to avoid engaging with something big. Coal, on which industrialism was built, which over the past 200 years has come to seem central to our identity, is an industry much bigger and nastier and more embedded than the one we have chosen to fear. I don't believe our choice is accidental.

16 December 2013

Part 6
Riches and Ruins

29

The Impossibility of Growth

Let us imagine that in 3030 BC the total possessions of the people of Egypt filled one cubic metre. Let us propose that these possessions grew by 4.5 per cent a year. How big would that stash have been by the Battle of Actium in 30 BC? This is the calculation performed by the investment banker Jeremy Grantham.[1]

Go on, take a guess. Ten times the size of the pyramids? All the sand in the Sahara? The Atlantic ocean? The volume of the planet? A little more? It's 2.5 billion billion solar systems.[2] It does not take you long, pondering this outcome, to reach the paradoxical position that salvation lies in collapse.

To succeed is to destroy ourselves. To fail is to destroy ourselves. That is the bind we have created. Ignore, if you must, climate change, biodiversity collapse, the depletion of water, soil, minerals, oil; even if all these issues were miraculously to vanish, the mathematics of compound growth make continuity impossible.

Economic growth is an artefact of the use of fossil fuels. Before large amounts of coal were extracted, every upswing in industrial production would be met with a downswing in agricultural production, as the charcoal or horsepower required by industry reduced the land available for growing food. Every prior industrial revolution collapsed, as growth could not be sustained.[3] But coal broke this cycle and enabled – for a few hundred years – the phenomenon we now call sustained growth.

It was neither capitalism nor communism that made possible the progress and the pathologies (total war, the unprecedented concentration of global wealth, planetary destruction) of the modern age. It was coal, followed by oil and gas. The meta-trend, the mother narrative, is carbon-fuelled expansion. Our ideologies are mere subplots. Now, as the most accessible reserves have been exhausted, we must ransack the hidden corners of the planet to sustain our impossible proposition.

A few days after scientists announced that the collapse of the West Antarctic ice sheet is now inevitable,[4] the Ecuadorean government decided that oil drilling would go ahead in the heart of the Yasuni national park.[5] It had made an offer to other governments: if they gave it half the value of the oil in that part of the park, it would leave the stuff in the ground. You could see this as blackmail or you could see it as fair trade. Ecuador is poor, its oil deposits are rich: why, the government argued, should it leave them untouched without compensation when everyone else is drilling down to the inner circle of hell? It asked for $3.6 billion and received $13 million. The result is that Petroamazonas, a company with a colourful record of destruction and spills,[6] will now enter one of the most biodiverse places on the planet, in which a hectare of rainforest is said to contain more species than exist in the entire continent of North America.[7]

The UK oil company Soco is now hoping to penetrate Africa's oldest national park, Virunga, in the Democratic Republic of Congo, one of the last strongholds of the mountain gorilla and the okapi, of chimpanzees and forest elephants.[8] In Britain, where a possible 4.4 billion barrels of shale oil has just been identified in the south-east, the government fantasises about turning the leafy suburbs into a new Niger delta.[9] To this end it's changing the trespass laws to enable drilling without consent and offering lavish bribes to local people.[10] These new reserves solve nothing. They do not end our hunger for resources; they exacerbate it.

The trajectory of compound growth shows that the scouring of the planet has only just begun. As the volume of the global economy expands, everywhere that contains something concentrated, unusual, precious will be sought out and exploited, its resources extracted and dispersed, the world's diverse and differentiated marvels reduced to the same grey stubble.

Some people try to solve the impossible equation with the myth of dematerialisation: the claim that as processes become more efficient and gadgets are miniaturised, we use, in aggregate, fewer materials. There is no sign that this is happening. Iron ore production has risen 180 per cent in ten years.[11] The trade body Forest Industries tell us that, 'Global paper consumption is at a record high level and it will continue to grow.'[12] If, in the digital age, we won't reduce even our consumption of paper, what hope is there for other commodities?

Look at the lives of the super-rich, who set the pace for global consumption. Are their yachts getting smaller? Their houses? Their artworks? Their purchase of rare woods, rare fish, rare stone? Those with the means buy ever bigger houses to store the growing stash of stuff they will not live long enough to use. By unremarked accretions, ever more of the surface of the planet is used to extract, manufacture and store things we don't need. Perhaps it's unsurprising that fantasies about the colonisation of space – which tell us we can export our problems instead of solving them – have resurfaced.[13]

As the philosopher Michael Rowan points out, the inevitabilities of compound growth mean that if last year's predicted global growth rate for 2014 (3.1 per cent) is sustained, even if we were miraculously to reduce the consumption of raw materials by 90 per cent we delay the inevitable by just seventy-five years.[14] Efficiency solves nothing while growth continues.

The inescapable failure of a society built upon growth and its destruction of the Earth's living systems are the overwhelming facts of our existence. As a result they are mentioned almost nowhere. They are the twenty-first century's great taboo, the subjects guaranteed to alienate your friends and neighbours. We live as if trapped inside a Sunday supplement: obsessed with fame, fashion, recipes and home improvements. Anything but the topic that demands our attention.

Statements of the bleeding obvious, the outcomes of basic arithmetic, are treated as exotic and unpardonable distractions, while the impossible proposition by which we live is regarded as so sane and normal and unremarkable that it isn't worthy of mention. That's how you measure the depth of this problem: by our inability even to discuss it.

27 May 2014

30
Curb Your Malthusiasm

Kindness is cruelty; cruelty is kindness: this is the core belief of compassionate conservatism. If the state makes excessive provision for the poor, it traps them in a culture of dependency, destroying their self-respect, locking them into unemployment. Cuts and coercion are a moral duty, to be pursued with the holy fervour of Inquisitors overseeing an auto-da-fé.

This belief persists despite reams of countervailing evidence, showing that severity does nothing to cure the structural causes of unemployment.[1] In Britain it is used to justify a £12 billion reduction of a social security system already so harsh that it drives some recipients to suicide. The belief arises from a deep and dearly held fallacy that has persisted for over 200 years.

Poverty was once widely understood as a social condition: it described the fate of those who did not possess property. England's Old Poor Law, introduced in 1597 and 1601, had its own cruelties, some of which were extreme. But as the US academics Fred Block and Margaret Somers explain in their fascinating book *The Power of Market Fundamentalism*, those who implemented it seemed to recognise that occasional unemployment was an intrinsic feature of working life.[2]

But in 1786, as economic crises threw rising numbers onto the mercy of their parishes, the clergyman Joseph Townsend sought to recast poverty as a moral or even biological condition. 'The poor know little of the motives which stimulate the higher ranks to action – pride, honour, and ambition', he argued in his *Dissertation on the Poor Laws*.[3] 'In general it is only hunger which can spur and goad them onto labour; yet our laws have said, they shall never hunger.'

Thomas Malthus expands on this theme in his *Essay on the Principle of Population*, published in 1798.[4] Poor relief, he maintained, causes poverty. It destroys the work ethic, reducing productivity. It also creates an incentive to reproduce, as payments rise with every family member. The higher the population, the hungrier the poor become: kindness results in cruelty.

Poverty, he argued, should be tackled through shame ('dependent poverty ought to be held disgraceful') and the withdrawal of assistance from all able-bodied workers. Nature should be allowed to take its course: if people were left to starve to death, the balance between population and food supply would be restored. Malthus ignored the means by which people limit their reproduction or increase their food supply, characterising the poor, in effect, as unthinking beasts.

His argument was highly controversial, but support grew rapidly among the propertied classes. In 1832, the franchise was extended to include more property owners: in other words, those who paid the poor rate. The poor, of course, were not entitled to vote. In the same year, the government launched a Royal Commission into the Operation of the Poor Laws.[5]

Like Malthus, the commissioners blamed the problems of the rural poor not on structural factors but on immorality, improvidence and low productivity, all caused by the system of poor relief, which had 'educated a new generation in idleness, ignorance and dishonesty'.[6] It called for the abolition of 'outdoor relief' for able-bodied people. Help should be offered only in circumstances so shameful, degrading and punitive that anyone would seek to avoid them: namely the workhouse. The government responded with the 1834 Poor Law Amendment Act, which instituted, for the sake of the poor, a regime of the utmost cruelty.[7] Destitute families were broken up and, in effect, imprisoned.

The commission was a fraud. It began with fixed conclusions and sought evidence to support them. Its interviews were conducted with like-minded members of the propertied classes, who were helped towards the right replies with leading questions. Anecdote took the place of data.

In reality, poverty in the countryside had risen as a result of structural forces over which the poor had no control. After the Napoleonic wars, the price of wheat slumped, triggering the collapse of rural banks and a severe credit crunch. Swayed by the arguments of David Ricardo, the government re-established the gold standard, which locked in austerity and aggravated hardship, much as George Osborne's legal enforcement of a permanent budget surplus will do.[8] Threshing machines reduced the need for labour in the autumn and winter, when employment was most precarious. Cottage industries were undercut by urban factories, while enclosure prevented the poor from producing their own food.

Far from undermining employment, poor relief sustained rural workers during the winter months, ensuring that they remained available for hire when they were needed by farms in the spring and summer. By contrast to the loss of agricultural productivity that Malthus predicted and the commission reported, between 1790 and 1834 wheat production more than doubled.[9]

As Block and Somers point out, the rise in unemployment and extreme poverty in the 1820s and 1830s represented the first great failure of Ricardian, laissez-faire economics. But Malthus's doctrines allowed this failure to be imputed to something quite different: the turpitude of the poor. Macroeconomic policy mistakes were blamed on the victims. Does that sound familiar?

This helps to explain the persistence of the fallacy. Those who promoted laissez-faire economics required an explanation when the magic of the markets failed to deliver their promised utopia. Malthus gave them the answer they needed.

And still does. People are poor and unemployed, George Osborne and Iain Duncan Smith claimed in *The Sunday Times*, because of 'the damaging culture of welfare dependency'.[10] Earlier, Duncan Smith, in a burst of Malthusiasm, sought to restrict child benefit to two children per family, to discourage the poor from reproducing.[11] A new analysis by the Wellcome Trust suggests that the government, which is about to place 350 psychologists in job centres, now treats unemployment as a mental health disorder.[12]

The media's campaign of vilification associates social security with disgrace, and proposes even more humiliation, exhortation, intrusion, bullying and sanctions. New household income figures are likely to show a sharp rise in child poverty, after sustained reductions under the Labour government.[13] Doubtless the poor will be blamed for improvidence and feckless procreation, and urged to overcome their moral failings through aspiration.

For 230 years, this convenient myth has resisted all falsification. Expect that to persist.

23 January 2015

31

Kleptoremuneration

There is an inverse relationship between utility and reward. The most lucrative, prestigious jobs tend to cause the greatest harm. The most useful workers tend to be paid the least and treated the worst.

I was reminded of this while listening to a care worker describing her job. Carole's company gives her a rota of, er, three half-hour visits per hour. It takes no account of the time required to travel between jobs, and doesn't pay her for it either, which means she makes less than the minimum wage. During the few minutes she spends with a client, she might have to get them out of bed, help them on the toilet, wash them, dress them, make breakfast and give them their medicines. If she ever gets a break, she told the radio programme *You and Yours*, she spends it with her clients. For some, she is the only person they see all day.

Is there more difficult or worthwhile employment? Yet she is paid in criticism and insults as well as pennies. She is shouted at by family members for being late and not spending enough time with each client, then upbraided by the company because of the complaints it receives. Her profession is assailed in the media, as the problems created by the corporate model are blamed on the workers. 'I love going to people; I love helping them, but the constant criticism is depressing,' she says. 'It's like always being in the wrong.'

Her experience is unexceptional. A report by the Resolution Foundation reveals that two-thirds of frontline care workers receive less than the living wage.[1] Ten per cent, like Carole, are illegally paid less than the minimum wage. This abuse is not confined to the UK: in the US, 27 per cent of care workers who make home visits are paid less than the legal minimum wage.[2]

Let's imagine the lives of those who own or run the company. We have to imagine it, as, for good reasons, neither the care worker's real name nor the company she works for were revealed. The more costs and corners they cut, the more profitable their business will be. In other words, the less they care, the better they will do. The perfect chief executive, from the point of view of the shareholders, is a fully fledged sociopath.

Such people will soon become very rich. They will be praised by the government as wealth creators.[3] If they donate enough money to party funds, they have a high chance of becoming peers of the realm.[4] Gushing profiles in the press will commend their entrepreneurial chutzpah and flair.

They'll acquire a wide investment portfolio, perhaps including a few properties, so that – even if they cease to do anything resembling work – they can continue living off the labour of people like Carole, as she struggles to pay extortionate rents. Their descendants, perhaps for many generations, will need never take a job of the kind she does.

Care workers function as a human loom, shuttling from one home to another, stitching the social fabric back together, while many of their employers, shareholders and government ministers slash blindly at the cloth, downsizing, outsourcing and deregulating in the cause of profit.

It doesn't matter how many times the myth of meritocracy is debunked. It keeps re-emerging, as you could see in the 2015 election campaign. How else, after all, can the government justify stupendous inequality?

One of the most painful lessons a young adult learns is that the wrong traits are rewarded. We celebrate originality and courage, but those who rise to the top are often conformists and sycophants. We are taught that cheats never prosper, yet the country is run by spivs.

If you possess the one indispensable skill – battering and blustering your way to the top – incompetence in other areas is no impediment. The former chief executive of Hewlett-Packard, Carly Fiorina, features prominently on lists of the USA's worst bosses: quite an achievement when you consider the competition.[5] She fired 30,000 workers in the name of efficiency, yet oversaw a halving of the company's stock price. Morale and communication became so bad that she was booed at company meetings. She was forced out, with a $42 million severance package. Where is she now? About to launch her campaign as presidential candidate for the Republican party, where, apparently, she's considered a serious contender. It's the Mitt Romney story all over again.

At university, I watched in horror as the grand plans of my ambitious friends dissolved. It took them about a minute, on walking into the corporate recruitment fair, to see that the careers they had pictured – working for Oxfam, becoming a photographer, defending the living world – paid about one-fiftieth of what they might earn in the City. They all swore that they would leave to follow their dreams after two or three years of making money. Need I remark that none did? They soon adjusted their morality to their circumstances. One, a firebrand who wanted to nationalise the banks and overthrow capitalism, plunged first into banking, then into politics. Claire Perry now sits on the front bench of the Conservative Party.

Flinch once, at the beginning of your career, and they will have you for life. The world is wrecked by clever young people making apparently sensible choices.

The inverse relationship doesn't always hold. There are plenty of useless, badly paid jobs, and a few useful, well-paid jobs. But surgeons and film directors are greatly outnumbered by corporate lawyers, lobbyists, advertisers, management consultants, financiers and parasitic bosses consuming the utility their workers provide. As the pay gap widens – chief executives in the UK took sixty times as much as the average worker in the 1990s and take 180 times as much today – the uselessness ratio is going through the roof.[6] I propose a name for this phenomenon: kleptoremuneration.

There is no end to this theft except robust government intervention: a redistribution of wages through maximum ratios and enhanced taxation. But this won't happen until we challenge the infrastructure of justification, built so carefully by politicians and the press. Our lives are damaged not by the undeserving poor but by the undeserving rich.

31 March 2015

32

The Self-Attribution Fallacy

If wealth were the inevitable result of hard work and enterprise, every woman in Africa would be a millionaire. The claims that the ultra-rich 1 per cent make for themselves – that they are possessed of unique intelligence or creativity or drive – are examples of the self-attribution fallacy. This means crediting yourself with outcomes for which you weren't responsible. Many of those who are rich today got there because they were able to capture certain jobs. This capture owes less to talent and intelligence than to a combination of the ruthless exploitation of others and accidents of birth, as such jobs are taken disproportionately by people born in certain places and into certain classes.

The findings of the psychologist Daniel Kahneman, winner of a Nobel economics prize, are devastating to the beliefs that financial high-fliers entertain about themselves. He discovered that their apparent success is a cognitive illusion. For example, he studied the results achieved by twenty-five wealth advisers, across eight years. He found that the consistency of their performance was zero. 'The results resembled what you would expect from a dice-rolling contest, not a game of skill.' Those who received the biggest bonuses had simply got lucky.

Such results have been widely replicated. They show that traders and fund managers across Wall Street receive their massive remuneration for doing no better than would a chimpanzee flipping a coin. When Kahneman tried to point this out they blanked him. 'The illusion of skill . . . is deeply ingrained in their culture.'[1]

So much for the financial sector and its super-educated analysts. As for other kinds of business, you tell me. Is your boss possessed of judgement, vision and management skills superior to those of anyone else in the firm, or did he or she get there through bluff, bullshit and bullying?

In a study published by the journal *Psychology, Crime and Law*, Belinda Board and Katarina Fritzon tested thirty-nine senior managers and chief executives from leading British businesses.[2] They compared the results to the same tests on patients at Broadmoor special hospital, where people who have been convicted of serious crimes are incarcerated. On certain indicators of psychopathy, the bosses' scores either matched or exceeded those of the patients. In fact on these criteria they beat even the subset of patients who had been diagnosed with psychopathic personality disorders.

The psychopathic traits on which the bosses scored so highly, Board and Fritzon point out, closely resemble the characteristics that companies look for. Those who have these traits often possess great skill in flattering and manipu-lating powerful people. Egocentricity, a strong sense of entitlement, a readiness to exploit others and a lack of empathy and conscience are also unlikely to damage their prospects in many corporations.

In their book *Snakes in Suits*, Paul Babiak and Robert Hare point out that as the old corporate bureaucracies have been replaced by flexible, ever-changing structures, and as team players are deemed less valuable than competitive risk-takers, psychopathic traits are more likely to be selected and rewarded.[3] Reading their work, it seems to me that if you have psychopathic tendencies and are born to a poor family you're likely to go to prison. If you have psychopathic tendencies and are born to a rich family you're likely to go to business school.

This is not to suggest that all executives are psychopaths. It is to suggest that the economy has been rewarding the wrong skills. As the bosses have shaken off the trade unions and captured both regulators and tax authorities, the distinction between the productive and rentier upper classes has broken down. CEOs now behave like dukes, extracting from their financial estates sums out of all proportion to the work they do or the value they generate, sums that sometimes exhaust the businesses they parasitise. They are no more deserving of the share of wealth they've captured than oil sheikhs.

The rest of us are invited, by governments and by fawning interviews in the press, to subscribe to their myth of election: the belief that they are the chosen ones, possessed of superhuman talents. The very rich are often described as wealth creators. But they have preyed upon the Earth's natural wealth and their workers' labour and creativity, impoverishing both people and planet. Now they have almost bankrupted us. The wealth creators of neoliberal mythology are some of the most effective wealth destroyers the world has ever seen.

What has happened over the past thirty years is the capture of the world's common treasury by a handful of people, assisted by neoliberal policies which were first imposed on rich nations by Thatcher and Reagan. I am now going to bombard you with figures. I'm sorry about that, but these numbers need to be tattooed on our minds. Between 1947 and 1979, productivity in the US rose by 119 per cent, while the income of the bottom fifth of the population rose by 122 per cent. But between 1979 and 2009, productivity rose by 80 per cent, while the income of the bottom fifth fell by 4 per cent.[4] In roughly the same period, the income of the top 1 per cent rose by 270 per cent.[5]

In the UK, the money earned by the poorest tenth fell by 12 per cent between 1999 and 2009, while the money made by the richest tenth rose by 37 per cent.[6] The Gini coefficient, which measures income inequality, climbed in this country from twenty-six in 1979 to forty in 2009.[7]

In his book *The Haves and the Have-Nots*, Branko Milanovic tries to discover who was the richest person who has ever lived.[8] Beginning with the loaded Roman triumvir Marcus Crassus, he measures wealth according to the quantity of his compatriots' labour a rich man could buy. It appears that the richest man to have lived in the past 2,000 years is alive today. Carlos Slim could buy the labour of 440,000 average Mexicans. This makes him fourteen times as rich as Crassus, nine times as rich as Carnegie and four times as rich as Rockefeller.

Until recently, we were mesmerised by the bosses' self-attribution. Their acolytes, in academia, the media, think tanks and government, created an extensive infrastructure of junk economics and flattery to justify their seizure of other people's wealth. So immersed in this nonsense did we become that we seldom challenged its veracity.

This is now changing. I have just witnessed a remarkable thing: a debate on the steps of St Paul's Cathedral between Stuart Fraser, chairman of the Corporation of the City of London, another official from the Corporation, the turbulent priest Father William Taylor, John Christensen of the Tax Justice Network and the people of Occupy London.[9] It had something of the flavour of the Putney debates of 1647. For the first time in decades – and all credit to the Corporation officials for turning up – financial power was obliged to answer directly to the people.

It felt like history being made. The undeserving rich are now in the frame, and the rest of us want our money back.

7 November 2011

33

The Lairds of Learning

Who are the most ruthless capitalists in the Western world? Whose monopolistic practices make Wal-Mart look like a corner shop and Rupert Murdoch look like a socialist? You won't guess the answer in a month of Sundays. While there are plenty of candidates, my vote goes not to the banks, the oil companies or the health insurers, but – wait for it – to academic publishers. Theirs might sound like a fusty and insignificant sector. It is anything but. Of all corporate scams, the racket they run is most urgently in need of referral to the competition authorities.

Everyone claims to agree that people should be encouraged to understand science and other academic research. Without current knowledge, we cannot make coherent democratic decisions. But the publishers have slapped a padlock and a Keep Out sign on the gates.

You might resent Murdoch's paywall policy, in which he charges £1 for twenty-four hours of access to the *The Times* and *The Sunday Times*. But at least in that period you can read and download as many articles as you like. Reading a single article published by one of Elsevier's journals will cost you $31.50. Springer charges €34.95, Wiley-Blackwell, $42.[1] Read ten and you pay ten times. And the journals retain perpetual copyright. You want to read a letter printed in 1981? That'll be $31.50.[2]

Of course, you could go into the library (if it still exists). But they too have been hit by cosmic fees. The average cost of an annual subscription to a chemistry journal is $3,792.[3] Some journals cost $10,000 a year or more to stock. The most expensive I've seen, Elsevier's *Biochimica et Biophysica Acta*, is $20,930.[4] Though academic libraries have been frantically cutting subscriptions to make ends meet, journals now consume 65 per cent of their budgets, which means they have had to reduce the number of books they buy.[5] Journal fees account for a significant component of universities' costs, which are being passed to their students.

Murdoch pays his journalists and editors, and his companies generate much of the content they use. But the academic publishers get their articles, their peer reviewing (vetting by other researchers) and even much of their editing for free. The material they publish was commissioned and funded not by them but by us, through government research grants and academic stipends. But to see it, we must pay again, and through the nose.

The returns are astronomical: in the past financial year, for example, Elsevier's operating profit margin was 36 per cent (£724 million on revenues of £2 billion).[6] They result from a stranglehold on the market. Elsevier, Springer and Wiley, who have bought up many of their competitors, now publish 42 per cent of journal articles.[7]

More importantly, universities are locked into buying their products. Academic papers are published in only one place, and they have to be read by researchers trying to keep up with their subject. Demand is inelastic and competition non-existent, because different journals can't publish the same material. In many cases the publishers oblige the libraries to buy a large package of journals, whether or not they want them all. Perhaps it's not surprising that one of the biggest crooks ever to have preyed upon the people of this country – Robert Maxwell – made much of his money through academic publishing.

The publishers claim that they have to charge these fees as a result of the costs of production and distribution, and that they add value (in Springer's words) because they 'develop journal brands and maintain and improve the digital infrastructure which has revolutionized scientific communication in the past 15 years'. But an analysis by Deutsche Bank reaches different conclusions. 'We believe the publisher adds relatively little value to the publishing process . . . if the process really were as complex, costly and value-added as the publishers protest that it is, 40 per cent margins wouldn't be available.'[8] Far from assisting the dissemination of research, the big publishers impede it, as their long turnaround times can delay the release of findings by a year or more.[9]

What we see here is pure rentier capitalism: monopolising a public resource then charging exorbitant fees to use it. Another term for it is economic parasitism. To obtain the knowledge for which we have already paid, we must surrender our feu to the lairds of learning.

It's bad enough for academics; it's worse for the laity. I refer readers to peer-reviewed papers, on the principle that claims should be followed to their sources. The readers tell me that they can't afford to judge for themselves whether or not I have represented the research fairly. Independent researchers who try to inform themselves about important scientific issues have to fork out thousands.[10] This is a tax on education, a stifling of the public mind. It appears to contravene the Universal Declaration of Human Rights, which says that, 'Everyone has the right freely to . . . share in scientific advancement and its benefits.'[11]

Open-access publishing, despite its promise, and some excellent resources such as the Public Library of Science and the physics database arxiv.org, have failed to displace the monopolists. In 1998 the *Economist*, surveying the opportunities offered by electronic publishing, predicted that 'the days of 40% profit margins may soon be as dead as Robert Maxwell'.[12] But in 2010 Elsevier's operating profit margins were the same (36 per cent) as they were in 1998.[13]

The reason is that the big publishers have rounded up the journals with the highest academic impact factors, in which publication is essential for researchers trying to secure grants and advance their careers.[14] You can start reading open-access journals, but you can't stop reading the closed ones.

Government bodies, with a few exceptions, have failed to confront them. The National Institutes of Health in the US oblige anyone taking their grants to put their papers in an open-access archive. But Research Councils UK, whose statement on public access is a masterpiece of meaningless waffle, relies on 'the assumption that publishers will maintain the spirit of their current policies'.[15] You bet they will.

In the short term, governments should refer the academic publishers to their competition watchdogs, and insist that all papers arising from publicly funded research are placed in a free public database.[16] In the longer term, they should work with researchers to cut out the middleman altogether, creating, along the lines proposed by Bjorn Brembs, a single global archive of academic literature and data.[17] Peer review would be overseen by an independent body. It could be funded by the library budgets which are currently being diverted into the hands of privateers.

The knowledge monopoly is as unwarranted and anachronistic as the Corn Laws. Let's throw off these parasitic overlords and liberate the research which belongs to us.

29 August 2011

34

The Man Who Wants to Northern Rock the Planet

Brass neck doesn't begin to describe it. Matt Ridley used to make his living partly by writing state-bashing columns in the *Daily Telegraph*. The government, he complained, is 'a self-seeking flea on the backs of the more productive people of this world . . . governments do not run countries, they parasitise them'.[1] Taxes, bail-outs, regulations, subsidies, intervention of any kind, he argued, are an unwarranted restraint on market freedom.

Then he became chairman of Northern Rock, where he was able to put his free market principles into practice. Under his chairmanship, the bank pursued what the Treasury Select Committee later described as a 'high-risk, reckless business strategy'.[2] It was able to do so because the government agency which oversees the banks, the Financial Services Authority, 'systematically failed in its regulatory duty'.[3]

On 16 August 2007, Dr Ridley rang an agent of the detested state to explore the possibility of a bail-out. The self-seeking fleas agreed to his request, and in September the government opened a support facility for the floundering bank. The taxpayer eventually bailed out Northern Rock to the tune of £27 billion.

When news of the crisis leaked, it caused the first run on a bank in this country since 1878. The parasitic state had to intervene a second time: the run was halted only when the government guaranteed the depositors' money. Eventually the government was obliged to nationalise the bank. Investors, knowing that their money would now be safe as it was protected by the state, began to return.

While the crisis was made possible by a 'substantial failure of regulation', MPs identified the directors of Northern Rock as 'the principal authors of the difficulties that the company has faced'. They singled Ridley out for having failed 'to provide against the risks that [Northern Rock] was taking and to act as an effective restraining force on the strategy of the executive members'.[4]

This, you might think, must have been a salutary experience. You would be wrong. Last week Dr Ridley published a new book called *The Rational Optimist*.[5] He uses it as a platform to attack governments which, among other crimes, 'bail out big corporations'.[6] He lambasts intervention and state regulation, insisting that markets deliver the greatest possible benefits to society when left to their own devices. Has there ever been a clearer case of the triumph of faith over experience?

Free market fundamentalists, apparently unaware of Ridley's own experiment in market liberation, are currently filling cyberspace and the mainstream media with gasps of enthusiasm about his thesis. Ridley provides what he claims is a scientific justification for unregulated business. He maintains that rising consumption will keep enriching us for 'centuries and millennia' to come, but only if governments don't impede innovation.[7] He dismisses or denies the environmental consequences, laments our risk-aversion, and claims that the market system makes self-interest 'thoroughly virtuous.'[8] All will be well in the best of all possible worlds, as long as the 'parasitic bureaucracy' keeps its nose out of our lives.[9]

His book is elegantly written and cast in the language of evolution, but it's the same old cornutopian nonsense we've heard one hundred times before (cornutopians are people who envisage a utopia of limitless abundance).[10] In this case, however, it has already been spectacularly disproved by the author's experience.

The Rational Optimist is riddled with excruciating errors and distortions. Ridley claims, for example, that 'every country that tried protectionism' after the Second World War suffered as a result. He cites South Korea and Taiwan as 'countries that went the other way', and experienced miraculous growth.[11] In reality, the governments of both nations subsidised key industries, actively promoted exports and used tariffs and laws to shut out competing imports. In both countries the state owned all the major commercial banks, allowing it to make decisions about investment.[12]

Ridley maintains that 'Enron funded climate alarmism'.[13] The reference he gives demonstrates nothing of the sort, nor can I find evidence for this claim elsewhere.[14] He says that 'no significant error has come to light' in Bjorn Lomborg's book *The Sceptical Environmentalist*.[15] In fact it contains so many significant errors that an entire book – *The Lomborg Deception* by Howard Friel – was required to document them.[16]

Ridley asserts that average temperature changes over 'the last three decades' have been 'relatively slow'.[17] In reality the rise over this period has been the most rapid since instrumental records began.[18] He maintains that 'eleven of thirteen populations' of polar bears are 'growing or steady'.[19] There are in fact nineteen populations of polar bears. Of those whose fluctuations have been measured, one is increasing, three are stable and eight are declining.[20]

Ridley uses blatant cherry-picking to create the impression that ecosystems are recovering: water snake numbers in Lake Erie, fish populations in the Thames, bird's eggs in Sweden.[21] But as the Millennium Ecosystem Assessment shows, of sixty-five global indicators of human impacts on biodiversity, only one – the extent of temperate forests – is improving. Eighteen are stable, but in all the other cases the impacts are increasing.[22]

Northern Rock grew rapidly by externalising its costs, pursuing money-making schemes that would eventually be paid for by other people. Ridley encourages us to treat the planet in the same way. He either ignores or glosses over the costs of ever-expanding trade and perpetual growth. His timing, as BP fails to contain the oil spill in the Gulf of Mexico, is unfortunate. Like the collapse of Northern Rock, the Deepwater Horizon disaster was made possible by weak regulation. Ridley would weaken it even further, leaving public protection to the invisible hand of the market.

He might not have been chastened by experience, but it would be wrong to claim that he has learnt nothing. On the contrary, he has developed a fine line in blame-shifting and post-rational justification. He mentions Northern Rock only once in his book, where he blames the crisis on 'government housing and monetary policy'.[23] It was the state wot made him do it. He asserts that while he wants to reduce the regulation of markets in goods and services, he has 'always supported' the careful regulation of financial markets.[24] He provides no evidence for this and I cannot find it in anything he wrote before the crisis.

Other than that, he claims, he can say nothing, due to the terms of his former employment at the bank. I suspect this constraint is overstated: it's unlikely that it forbids him from accepting his share of the blame.

It is only from the safety of the regulated economy, in which governments pick up the pieces when business screws up, that people like Dr Ridley can pursue their magical thinking. Had the state he despises not bailed out his bank and rescued its depositors' money, his head would probably be on a pike by now. Instead we see it on our television screens, instructing us to apply his irrational optimism more widely. And no one has yet been rude enough to use the word 'discredited'.

1 June 2010

35

The Gift of Death

There's nothing they need, nothing they don't own already, nothing they even want. So you buy them a solar-powered waving queen; a belly button brush; a silver-plated ice cream tub holder; a 'hilarious' inflatable zimmer frame; a confection of plastic and electronics called Terry the Swearing Turtle; or – and somehow I find this significant – a Scratch Off World wall map.

They seem amusing on the first day of Christmas, daft on the second, embarrassing on the third. By the twelfth they're in landfill. For thirty seconds of dubious entertainment, or a hedonic stimulus that lasts no longer than a nicotine hit, we commission the use of materials whose impacts will ramify for generations.

Researching her film *The Story of Stuff*, Annie Leonard discovered that of the materials flowing through the consumer economy, only 1 per cent remain in use six months after sale.[1] Even the goods we might have expected to hold onto are soon condemned to destruction through either planned obsolescence (breaking quickly) or perceived obsolescence (becoming unfashionable).

But many of the products we buy, especially for Christmas, cannot become obsolescent. The term implies a loss of utility, but they had no utility in the first place. An electronic drum-machine T-shirt; a Darth Vader talking piggy bank; an ear-shaped iPhone case; an individual beer can chiller; an electronic wine breather; a sonic screwdriver remote control; bacon toothpaste; a dancing dog: no one is expected to use them, or even look at them, after Christmas Day. They are designed to elicit thanks, perhaps a snigger or two, and then be thrown away.

The fatuity of the products is matched by the profundity of the impacts. Rare materials, complex electronics, the energy needed for manufacture and transport are extracted and refined and combined into compounds of utter pointlessness. When you take account of the fossil fuels whose use we commission in other countries, manufacturing and consumption are responsible for more than half of our carbon dioxide production.[2] We are screwing the planet to make solar-powered bath thermometers and desktop crazy golfers.

People in eastern Congo are massacred to facilitate smartphone upgrades of ever-diminishing marginal utility.[3] Forests are felled to make 'personalised heart-shaped wooden cheese board sets'. Rivers are poisoned to manufacture talking fish. This is pathological consumption: a world-consuming epidemic of collective madness, rendered so normal by advertising and the media that we scarcely notice what has happened to us.

In 2007, the journalist Adam Welz records that thirteen rhinos were killed by poachers in South Africa. In 2012, 668 were shot.[4] No one is entirely sure why. But one answer is that very rich people in Vietnam are now sprinkling ground rhino horn on their food or snorting it like cocaine to display their wealth. It's grotesque, but it scarcely differs from what almost everyone in industrialised nations is doing: trashing the living world through pointless consumption.

This boom has not happened by accident. Our lives have been corralled and shaped in order to encourage it. World trade rules force countries to participate in the festival of junk. Governments cut taxes, deregulate business, manipulate interest rates to stimulate spending. But seldom do the engineers of these policies stop and ask 'spending on what?' When every conceivable want and need has been met (among those who have disposable money), growth depends on selling the utterly useless. The solemnity of the state, its might and majesty, are harnessed to the task of delivering Terry the Swearing Turtle to our doors.

Grown men and women devote their lives to manufacturing and marketing this rubbish, and dissing the idea of living without it. 'I always knit my gifts', says a woman in a television ad for an electronics outlet. 'Well you shouldn't', replies the narrator.[5] An advertisement for Google's latest tablet shows a father and son camping in the woods. Their enjoyment depends on the Nexus 7's special features. The best things in life are free, but we've found a way of selling them to you.

The growth of inequality that has accompanied the consumer boom ensures that the rising economic tide no longer lifts all boats. In the US in 2010 a remarkable 93 per cent of the growth in incomes accrued to the top 1 per cent of the population.[6] The old excuse, that we must trash the planet to help the poor, simply does not wash. For a few decades of extra enrichment for those who already possess more money than they know how to spend, the prospects of everyone else who will live on this Earth are diminished.

So effectively have governments, the media and advertisers associated consumption with prosperity and happiness that to say these things is to expose yourself to opprobrium and ridicule. Witness one of the BBC's *Moral Maze* programmes from December 2012, in which most of the panel lined up to decry the idea of consuming less, and to associate it, somehow, with authoritarianism.[7] When the world goes mad, those who resist are denounced as lunatics.

Bake them a cake, write them a poem, give them a kiss, tell them a joke, but for god's sake stop trashing the planet to tell someone you care. All it shows is that you don't.

10 December 2012

Part 7

Dance with the One Who Brung You

36

How the Billionaires Broke the System

There are two ways of cutting a deficit: raising taxes or reducing spending. Raising taxes means taking money from the rich. Cutting spending means taking money from the poor. Not in all cases of course: some taxation is regressive; some state spending takes money from ordinary citizens and gives it to banks, arms companies, oil barons and farmers. But in most cases the state transfers wealth from rich to poor, while tax cuts shift it from poor to rich.

So the rich, in a nominal democracy, have a struggle on their hands. Somehow they must persuade the other 99 per cent to vote against their own interests: to shrink the state, supporting spending cuts rather than tax rises. In the US they appear to be succeeding.

Partly as a result of the Bush tax cuts of 2001, 2003 and 2005 (shamefully extended by Barack Obama), taxation of the wealthy, in Obama's words, 'is at its lowest level in half a century'.[1] The consequence of such regressive policies is a level of inequality unknown in other developed nations. As the Nobel laureate Joseph Stiglitz points out, in the past ten years the income of the top 1 per cent has risen by 18 per cent, while that of blue-collar male workers has fallen by 12 per cent.[2]

The deal that was being thrashed out in Congress as this article went to press in July 2011 sought only to cut state spending. As the former Republican senator Alan Simpson said, 'The little guy is going to be cremated.'[3] That, in turn, will mean further economic decline, which means a bigger deficit.[4] It's insane. But how did it happen?

The immediate reason is that Republican members of Congress supported by the Tea Party movement wouldn't budge. But this explains nothing. The Tea Party movement mostly consists of people who have been harmed by tax cuts for the rich and spending cuts for the poor and middle. Why would they mobilise against their own welfare? You can understand what is happening in Washington only if you remember what everyone seems to have forgotten: how this movement began.

The *Observer* claimed that, 'The Tea Party rose out of anger over the scale of federal spending, and in particular in bailing out the banks.'[5] This is what its members claim. It's nonsense.

The movement started with Rick Santelli's call on CNBC for a tea party of city traders to dump securities in Lake Michigan, in protest at Obama's plan to 'subsidise the losers'.[6] In other words, it was a demand for a financiers' mobilisation against the bail-out of their victims: people losing their homes. This is the opposite of the *Observer*'s story. On the same day, a group called Americans for Prosperity (AFP) set up a Tea Party Facebook page and started organising Tea Party events.[7] The movement, whose programme is still lavishly supported by AFP, took off from there.

So who or what is Americans for Prosperity? It was founded and is funded by Charles and David Koch.[8] They run what they call 'the biggest company you've never heard of',[9] and between them they are worth $43 billion.[10]

Koch Industries is a massive oil, gas, minerals, timber and chemicals company. Over the past fifteen years the brothers have poured at least $85 million into lobby groups arguing for lower taxes for the rich and weaker regulations for industry.[11] The groups and politicians funded by the Kochs also lobby to destroy collective bargaining, to stop laws reducing carbon emissions, to stymie health care reform and to hobble attempts to control the banks. During the 2010 election cycle, Americans for Prosperity spent $45 million supporting its favoured candidates.[12]

But the Kochs' greatest political triumph is the creation of the Tea Party movement. Taki Oldham's film *Astro Turf Wars* shows Tea Party organisers from all over the Union reporting back to David Koch at their 2009 Defending the Dream Summit, explaining the events and protests they've started with AFP help. 'Five years ago,' he tells them, 'my brother Charles and I provided the funds to start Americans for Prosperity. It's beyond my wildest dreams how AFP has grown into this enormous organisation.'

AFP mobilised the anger of people who found their conditions of life declining, and channelled it into a campaign to make them worse. Tea Party campaigners appear to be unaware of the origins of their own movement. Like the guard in Geoffrey Household's novel *Rogue Male* who has been conned into working for the enemy, they take to the streets to demand less tax for billionaires and worse health, education and social insurance for themselves.

Are they stupid? No. They have been systematically misled by another instrument of corporate power: the media. The Tea Party movement has been relentlessly promoted by Fox News, which belongs to a more familiar billionaire. Like the Kochs, Rupert Murdoch aims to misrepresent the democratic choices we face, in order to persuade us to vote against our own interests and in favour of his.

What's taking place in Congress right now is a kind of political coup. A handful of billionaires has shoved a spanner into the legislative process. Through the candidates they've bought and the movement that supports them, they are now breaking and reshaping the system to serve their interests. We knew this once, but now we've forgotten. What hope do we have of resisting a force we won't even see?

1 August 2011

37

Plutocracy's Boot Boys

To subvert means to turn from below. We need a new word, which means to turn from above. The primary threat to the democratic state and its functions comes not from mob rule or leftwing insurrection, but from the very rich and the corporations they run.

These forces have refined their assault on democratic governance. There is no need – as Sir James Goldsmith, John Aspinall, Lord Lucan and others did in the 1970s – to discuss the possibility of launching a military coup against the British government: the plutocrats have other means of turning it.[1]

Over the past few years I have been trying better to understand how the demands of big business and the very rich are projected into policy-making, and I have come to see the neoliberal think tanks as central to this process. These are the groups which claim to champion the free market, but whose proposals often look like a prescription for corporate power.

David Frum, formerly a fellow of one of these think tanks – the American Enterprise Institute – argues that they 'increasingly function as public-relations agencies'.[2] But in this case we don't know who the clients are. As the corporate lobbyist Jeff Judson enthuses, they are 'virtually immune to retribution . . . the identity of donors to think tanks is protected from involuntary disclosure'.[3] A consultant who worked for the billionaire Koch brothers claims that they see the funding of think tanks 'as a way to get things done without getting dirty themselves'.[4]

This much I knew, but over the past few days I've learnt a lot more. In *Think Tank: The Story of the Adam Smith Institute*, the institute's founder, Madsen Pirie, provides an unintentional but invaluable guide to how power in this country really works.[5] Soon after it was founded in 1977, the institute approached 'all the top companies'. About twenty of them responded by sending cheques.[6] Its most enthusiastic supporter was the coup-plotter Sir James Goldsmith, one of the most unscrupulous asset strippers of that time. Before making one of his donations, Pirie writes, 'He listened carefully as we outlined the project, his eyes twinkling at the audacity and scale of it. Then he had his secretary hand us a cheque for £12,000 as we left.'[7]

From the beginning, senior journalists on the *Daily Telegraph*, *The Times* and the *Daily Mail* volunteered their services. Every Saturday, in a wine bar called the Cork and Bottle, Margaret Thatcher's researchers and leader writers and columnists from *The Times* and *Telegraph* met staff from the Adam Smith Institute and the Institute of Economic Affairs. Over lunch, they 'planned strategy for the week ahead'.[8] These meetings would 'co-ordinate our activities to make us more effective collectively'. The journalists would then turn the institute's proposals into leader columns while the researchers buttonholed shadow ministers.

Soon, Pirie says, the *Daily Mail* began running a supportive article on the leader page every time the Adam Smith Institute published something.[9] The paper's editor, David English, oversaw these articles himself, and helped the institute to refine its arguments.[10]

As Pirie's history progresses, all references to funding cease. Apart from tickets donated by British Airways, no sponsors are named beyond the early 1980s.[11] While the institute claims to campaign on behalf of 'the open society', it is secretive and unaccountable.[12] Today it flatly refuses to say who funds it.[13]

Pirie describes how his group devised and refined many of the headline policies implemented by Margaret Thatcher and John Major. He claims (and produces plenty of evidence) either full or partial credit for the privatisation of the railways and other industries, the contracting out of public services to private companies, the poll tax, the sale of council houses, the internal markets in education and health, the establishment of private prisons, GP fund-holding and commissioning and, later, George Osborne's tax policies.

Pirie also wrote the manifesto of the neoliberal wing of Mrs Thatcher's government, *No Turning Back*.[14] Officially, the authors of this document – which was published by the party – were MPs such as Michael Forsyth, Peter Lilley and Michael Portillo. 'Nowhere was there any mention of, or connection to, myself or the Adam Smith Institute. They paid me my £1,000 and we were all happy.'[15] Pirie's report became the central charter of the doctrine we now call Thatcherism, whose praetorian guard called itself the No Turning Back group.

Today's parliamentary equivalent is the Free Enterprise Group. Five of its members have just published a similar manifesto, *Britannia Unchained*.[16] Echoing the narrative developed by the neoliberal think tanks, they blame welfare payments and the mindset of the poor for the UK's appalling record on social mobility, and suggest the need for much greater cuts and hint that the answer is the comprehensive demolition of the welfare system. It is subtler than *No Turning Back*. There are fewer of the direct demands and terrifying plans: these movements have learnt something in the past thirty years.

It is hard to think how their manifesto could have been better tailored to corporate interests. As if to reinforce the point, the front cover carries a quote from Sir Terry Leahy, until recently the chief executive of Tesco: 'The path is clear. We have to be brave enough to take it.'

Once more the press has taken up the call. In the approach to publication, the *Daily Telegraph* commissioned a series of articles called *Britain Unleashed*, promoting the same dreary agenda of less tax for the rich, less help for the poor and less regulation for business.[17] Another article in the same paper, published in September 2012 by its head of personal finance Ian Cowie, proposes that there be no representation without taxation. People who don't pay enough income tax shouldn't be allowed to vote.[18]

I see these people as rightwing vanguardists, mobilising first to break and then to capture a political system that is meant to belong to all of us. Like Marxist insurrectionaries, they often talk about smashing things, about 'creative destruction', about the breaking of chains and the slipping of leashes.[19] But in this case they appear to be trying to free the rich from the constraints of democracy. And at the moment they are winning.

1 October 2012

38

How Did We Get Into This Mess?

For the first time, the United Kingdom's consumer debt now exceeds our gross national product: a new report shows that we owe £1.35 trillion.[1] Inspectors in the United States have discovered that 77,000 road bridges are in the same perilous state as the one which collapsed into the Mississippi in August 2007.[2] Two years after Hurricane Katrina struck in 2005, 120,000 people from New Orleans were still living in trailer homes and temporary lodgings.[3] As runaway climate change approaches, governments refuse to take the necessary action. Booming inequality threatens to create the most divided societies the world has seen since before the First World War. A financial crisis caused by unregulated lending could turf hundreds of thousands out of their homes and trigger a cascade of economic troubles.

These problems appear unrelated, but they all have something in common. They arise in large part from a meeting that took place sixty years ago in a Swiss spa resort. It laid the foundations for a philosophy of government that is responsible for many, perhaps most, of our contemporary crises.

When the Mont Pelerin Society first met, in 1947, its political project did not have a name. But it knew where it was going. The society's founder, Friedrich von Hayek, remarked that the battle for ideas would take at least a generation to win, but he knew that his intellectual army would attract powerful backers. Its philosophy, which later came to be known as neoliberalism, accorded with the interests of the ultra-rich, so the ultra-rich would promote it.

Neoliberalism claims that we are best served by maximum market freedom and minimum intervention by the state. The role of government should be confined to creating and defending markets, protecting private property and defending the realm. All other functions are better discharged by private enterprise, which will be prompted by the profit motive to supply essential services. By this means, enterprise is liberated, rational decisions are made and citizens are freed from the dehumanising hand of the state.

This, at any rate, is the theory. But as David Harvey proposes in his book *A Brief History of Neoliberalism*, wherever the neoliberal programme has been implemented, it has caused a massive shift of wealth not just to the top one per cent, but to the top tenth of the top one per cent.[4] In the United States, for example, the upper 0.1 per cent has already regained the position it held at the beginning of the 1920s.[5] The conditions that neoliberalism demands in order to free human beings from the slavery of the state – minimal taxes, the dismantling of public services and social security, deregulation, the breaking of the unions – just happen to be the conditions required to make the elite even richer, while leaving everyone else to sink or swim.

So the question is this. Given that the crises I have listed are predictable effects of the dismantling of public services and the deregulation of business and financial markets, given that it damages the interests of nearly everyone, how has neoliberalism come to dominate public life?

Richard Nixon was once forced to concede that 'we are all Keynesians now': even the Republicans supported the interventionist doctrines of John Maynard Keynes. But we are all neoliberals now. Mrs Thatcher kept telling us that 'there is no alternative', and by implementing her programmes, Clinton, Blair, Brown and the other leaders of what were once progressive parties appear to prove her right.

The first great advantage the neoliberals possessed was an unceasing fountain of money. American oligarchs and their foundations – Coors, Olin, Scaife, Pew and others – have poured hundreds of millions into setting up think tanks, founding business schools and transforming university economics departments into bastions of almost totalitarian neoliberal thinking. The Heritage Foundation, the Hoover Institute, the American Enterprise Institute and many others in the US, as well as the Institute of Economic Affairs, the Centre for Policy Studies and the Adam Smith Institute in the UK were all established to promote this project. Their purpose was to develop the ideas and the language which would mask the real intent of the programme – the restoration of the power of the elite – and package it as a proposal for the betterment of humankind.

Their project was assisted by ideas which arose in a very different quarter. The revolutionary movements of 1968 also sought greater individual liberties, and many of the soixante-huitards saw the state as their oppressor. As Harvey shows, the neoliberals co-opted their language and ideas. Some of the anarchists I know still voice notions almost identical to those of the neoliberals: the intent is different, but the consequences very similar.

Hayek's disciples were also able to make use of economic crises. One of their first experiments took place in New York City, which was hit by budgetary disaster in 1975. Its bankers demanded that the city follow their prescriptions: massive cuts in public services, the smashing of the unions, public subsidies for business.[6] In the United Kingdom, stagflation, strikes and budgetary breakdown allowed Margaret Thatcher, whose ideas were framed by her neoliberal adviser Keith Joseph, to come to the rescue. Her programme worked, but created a new set of crises.

If these opportunities were insufficient, the neoliberals and their backers would use bribery or force. In the US, the Democrats were neutered by new laws on campaign finance. To compete successfully with the Republicans, they would have to give big business what it wanted. The first neoliberal programme of all was implemented in Chile following Pinochet's coup, with the backing of the US government and economists taught by Milton Friedman, one of the founding members of the Mont Pelerin Society. Drumming up support for the project was a simple matter: if you disagreed, you got shot. The International Monetary Fund and the World Bank used their power over developing nations to demand the same policies.

But the most powerful promoter of this programme was the media. Most media outlets are owned by multi-millionaires who use it to project the ideas that support their interests. Those which threaten their plans are either ignored or ridiculed. It is through the newspapers and television channels that the socially destructive ideas of a small group of extremists have come to look like common sense. The corporations' tame thinkers sell the project by reframing our political language.[7] Nowadays I hear even my progressive friends using terms like wealth creators, tax relief, big government, consumer democracy, red tape, compensation culture, job seekers and benefit cheats. These terms, all deliberately invented or promoted by neoliberals, have become so commonplace that they now seem almost neutral.

Neoliberalism, if unchecked, will catalyse crisis after crisis, all of which can be solved only by the means it forbids: greater intervention on the part of the state. In confronting it, we must recognise that we will never be able to mobilise the resources its exponents have been given. But as the disasters they have caused develop, the public will need ever less persuading that it has been misled.

28 August 2007

39

Going Naked

Journalists are good at dishing it out, less good at taking it. We demand from others standards we would never dream of applying to ourselves. Tabloid newsrooms fuelled by cocaine excoriate celebrity drug-takers. Hacks who have made a lifetime's study of abusing expense accounts lambast MPs for fiddling theirs. Columnists demand accountability, but demonstrate none themselves. Should we be surprised that the public places us somewhere on the narrow spectrum between derivatives traders and sewer rats?

No one will be shocked to discover hypocrisy among hacks, but there's also a more substantial issue here. A good deal of reporting looks almost indistinguishable from corporate press releases. Often that's because it does consist of corporate press releases, mindlessly recycled by overstretched staff: a process known as churnalism.[1] Or it could be because the reporters work for people who see themselves, as Max Hastings said of his employer Conrad Black, as 'members of the rich men's trade union', whose mission is to defend the proprietorial class to which they belong.[2]

But there are sometimes other influences at play, which are even less visible to the public. From time to time a payola scandal surfaces, in which journalists are shown to have received money from people whose interests they write or talk about.

For example, two columnists in the US, Doug Bandow and Peter Ferrara, were exposed for taking undisclosed payments from the disgraced corporate lobbyist Jack Abramoff.[3] On top of the payments he received from the newspapers he worked for, Bandow was given $2,000 for every column he wrote which favoured Abramoff's clients. Armstrong Williams, a television presenter, secretly signed a $240,000 contract with George W. Bush's Department of Education to promote Bush's education bill and ensure that the education secretary was offered slots on his programme.[4] In the UK, a leaked email revealed that Professor Roger Scruton, a columnist for the *Financial Times* and a contributor to other newspapers, was being paid £4,500 a month by Japan Tobacco International to write on 'major topics of current concern' to the industry.[5]

These revelations were accidental. For all we know, such deals could be commonplace. While journalists are not subject to the accountability they demand of others, their powerful position – helping to shape public opinion – is wide open to abuse.

The question of who pays for public advocacy has become an obsession of mine. I've seen how groups purporting to be spontaneous gatherings of grass-roots activists, fighting the regulation of tobacco or demanding that governments should take no action on climate change, have in fact been created and paid for by corporations: a practice known as astroturfing.[6] I've asked the bodies which call themselves free market think tanks, yet spend much of their time promoting corporate talking-points, to tell me who funds them. All but one have refused to answer.[7]

But if I'm to subject other people to this scrutiny, I should also be prepared to expose myself to it. So I have done something which might be foolhardy, but which I feel is necessary: I've opened a registry of my interests on my website, in which I will detail all the payments, gifts and hospitality (except from family and friends) I receive, as well as the investments I've made.[8] I hope it will encourage other journalists to do the same. In fact I urge you, their readers, to demand it of them.

Like many British people, I feel embarrassed talking about money, and publishing the amounts I receive from the *Guardian* and other employers makes me feel naked. I fear I will be attacked by some people for earning so much and mocked by others for earning so little. Even so, the more I think about it, the more I wonder why it didn't occur to me to do this before.

A voluntary register is a small step towards transparency. What I would really like to see is a mandatory list of journalists' financial interests, similar to the House of Commons registry.[9] I believe that everyone who steps into public life should be obliged to show who is paying them, and how much. Publishing this register could be one of the duties of whatever replaces the discredited Press Complaints Commission.

Journalists would still wield influence without responsibility. That's written into the job description. But at least we would then have some idea of whether it's the organ-grinder talking or his monkey.

29 September 2011

Part 8

Out of Sight, Out of Mind

40

The Holocaust We Will Not See

Avatar, James Cameron's blockbusting 3-D film, is both profoundly silly and profound. It's profound because, like most films about aliens, it is a metaphor for contact between different human cultures. But in this case the metaphor is conscious and precise: this is the story of European engagement with the native peoples of the Americas. It's profoundly silly because engineering a happy ending demands a plot so stupid and predictable that it rips the heart out of the film. The fate of the Native Americans is much closer to the story told in another new film, *The Road*, in which a remnant population flees in terror as it is hunted to extinction.

But this is a story no one wants to hear, because of the challenge it presents to the way we choose to see ourselves. Europe was massively enriched by the genocides in the Americas; the American nations were founded on them. This is a history we cannot accept.

In his book *American Holocaust*, the American scholar David Stannard documents the greatest acts of genocide the world has ever experienced.[1] In 1492, some 100 million native peoples lived in the Americas. By the end of the nineteenth century almost all of them had been exterminated. Many died as a result of disease. But the mass extinction was also engineered.

When the Spanish arrived in the Americas, they described a world which could scarcely have been more different from their own. Europe was ravaged by war, oppression, slavery, fanaticism, disease and starvation. The populations they encountered were healthy, well nourished and mostly (with exceptions like the Aztecs and Incas) peaceable, democratic and egalitarian. Throughout the Americas the earliest explorers, including Columbus, remarked on the natives' extraordinary hospitality. The conquistadores marvelled at the amazing roads, canals, buildings and art they found, which in some cases outstripped anything they had seen at home. None of this stopped them from destroying everything and everyone they encountered.

The butchery began with Columbus. He slaughtered the native people of Hispaniola (now Haiti and the Dominican Republic) by unimaginably brutal means. His soldiers tore babies from their mothers and dashed their heads against rocks. They fed their dogs on living children. On one occasion they hung thirteen Indians in honour of Christ and the twelve disciples, on a gibbet just low enough for their toes to touch the ground, then disembowelled them and burnt them alive. Columbus ordered all the native people to deliver a certain amount of gold every three months; anyone who failed had his hands cut off. By 1535 the native population of Hispaniola had fallen from 8 million to zero: partly as a result of disease, partly as a result of murder, overwork and starvation.

The conquistadores spread this civilising mission across Central and South America. When they failed to reveal where their mythical treasures were hidden, the indigenous people were flogged, hanged, drowned, dismembered, ripped apart by dogs, buried alive or burnt. The soldiers cut off women's breasts, sent people back to their villages with their severed hands and noses hung round their necks and hunted Indians with their dogs for sport. But most were killed by enslavement and disease. The Spanish discovered that it was cheaper to work Indians to death and replace them than to keep them alive: the life expectancy in their mines and plantations was three to four months. Within a century of their arrival, around 95 per cent of the population of South and Central America had been destroyed.

In California during the eighteenth century the Spanish systematised this extermination. A Franciscan missionary called Junipero Serra set up a series of 'missions', which were in reality concentration camps using slave labour. The native people were herded in under force of arms and made to work in the fields on one-fifth of the calories fed to African American slaves in the nineteenth century. They died from overwork, starvation and disease at astonishing rates, and were continually replaced, wiping out the indigenous populations. Junipero Serra, the Eichmann of California, was beatified by the Vatican in 1988. He now requires one more miracle to be pronounced a saint.[2]

While the Spanish were mostly driven by the lust for gold, the British who colonised North America wanted land. In New England they surrounded the villages of the Native Americans and murdered them as they slept. As genocide spread westwards, it was endorsed at the highest levels.

George Washington ordered the total destruction of the homes and land of the Iroquois. Thomas Jefferson declared that his nation's wars with the Indians should be pursued until each tribe 'is exterminated or is driven beyond the Mississippi'. During the Sand Creek Massacre of 1864, troops in Colorado slaughtered unarmed people gathered under a flag of peace, killing children and babies, mutilating all the corpses and keeping their victims' genitals to use as tobacco pouches or to wear on their hats. Theodore Roosevelt called this event 'as rightful and beneficial a deed as ever took place on the frontier'.

The butchery hasn't yet ended: the *Guardian* reports that Brazilian ranchers in the western Amazon, having slaughtered all the rest, tried to kill the last surviving member of a forest tribe.[3] Yet the greatest acts of genocide in history scarcely ruffle our collective conscience. Perhaps this is what would have happened had the Nazis won the Second World War: the Holocaust would have been denied, excused or minimised in the same way, even as it continued. The people of the nations responsible – Spain, Britain, the United States and others – will tolerate no comparisons, but the final solutions pursued in the Americas were far more successful. Those who commissioned or endorsed them remain national or religious heroes. Those who seek to prompt our memories are ignored or condemned.

This is why the right hates *Avatar*. In the neocon *Weekly Standard*, John Podhoretz complains that the film resembles a 'revisionist western' in which 'the Indians became the good guys and the Americans the bad guys'.[4] He says it asks the audience 'to root for the defeat of American soldiers at the hands of an insurgency'. Insurgency is an interesting word for an attempt to resist invasion: insurgent, like savage, is what you call someone who has something you want. *L'Osservatore Romano*, the official newspaper of the Vatican, condemned the film as 'just . . . an anti-imperialistic, anti-militaristic parable'.[5]

But at least the right knows what it is attacking. In the *New York Times* the liberal critic Adam Cohen praises *Avatar* for championing the need to see clearly.[6] It reveals, he says, 'a well-known principle of totalitarianism and genocide – that it is easiest to oppress those we cannot see'. But in a marvellous unconscious irony, he bypasses the crashingly obvious metaphor and talks instead about the light it casts on Nazi and Soviet atrocities. We have all become skilled in the art of not seeing.

I agree with its rightwing critics that *Avatar* is crass, mawkish and clichéd. But it speaks of a truth more important – and more dangerous – than those contained in a thousand arthouse movies.

11 January 2010

41

The Empire Strikes Back

Over the gates of Auschwitz were the words 'Work Makes You Free'. Over the gates of the Solovetsky camp in Lenin's gulag: 'Through Labour – Freedom!' Over the gates of the Ngenya detention camp, run by the British in Kenya: 'Labour and Freedom'.[1] Dehumanisation appears to follow an almost inexorable course.

In October 2014, three elderly Kenyans established the right to sue the British government for the torture they suffered – castration, beating and rape – in the Kikuyu detention camps it ran in the 1950s.[2]

Many tens of thousands were detained and tortured in the camps. I won't spare you the details: we have been sparing ourselves the details for far too long. Large numbers of men were castrated with pliers.[3] Others were anally raped, sometimes with the use of knives, broken bottles, rifle barrels and scorpions.[4] Women had similar instruments forced into their vaginas. The guards and officials sliced off ears and fingers, gouged out eyes, mutilated women's breasts with pliers, poured paraffin over people and set them alight.[5] Untold thousands died.

The government's secret archive, revealed in April 2012, shows that the Attorney General, the colonial governor and the colonial secretary knew what was happening.[6] The governor ensured that the perpetrators had legal immunity: including the British officers reported to him for roasting prisoners to death.[7] In public the colonial secretary lied and kept lying.[8]

Little distinguishes the British imperial project from any other. In all cases the purpose of empire was loot, land and labour. When people resisted (as some of the Kikuyu did during the Mau Mau rebellion), the response everywhere was the same: extreme and indiscriminate brutality, hidden from public view by distance and official lies.

Successive governments have sought to deny the Kikuyu justice: destroying most of the paperwork, lying about the existence of the rest, seeking to have the case dismissed on technicalities.[9] Their handling of this issue, and the widespread British disavowal of what happened in Kenya, reflect the way in which this country has been brutalised by its colonial history. Empire did almost as much harm to the imperial nations as it did to their subject peoples.

In his book *'Exterminate All the Brutes'*, Sven Lindqvist shows how the ideology that led to Hitler's war and the Holocaust was developed by the colonial powers.[10] Imperialism required an exculpatory myth. It was supplied, primarily, by British theorists.

In 1799, Charles White began the process of identifying Europeans as inherently superior to other peoples.[11] By 1850, the disgraced anatomist Robert Knox had developed the theme into fully fledged racism.[12] His book *The Races of Man* asserted that dark-skinned people were destined first to be enslaved and then annihilated by the 'lighter races'. Dark meant almost everyone: 'what a field of extermination lies before the Saxon, Celtic, and Sarmatian races!'[13]

Remarkable as it may sound, this view soon came to dominate British thought. In common with most of the political class, W. Winwood Reade, Alfred Russel Wallace, Herbert Spencer, Frederick Farrar, Francis Galton, Benjamin Kidd, even Charles Darwin saw the extermination of dark-skinned people as an inevitable law of nature.[14] Some of them argued that Europeans had a duty to speed it up: both to save the integrity of the species and to put the inferior 'races' out of their misery.

These themes were picked up by German theorists. In 1893, Alexander Tille, drawing on British writers, claimed that 'it is the right of the stronger race to annihilate the lower'.[15] In 1901, Friedrich Ratzel argued in *Der Lebensraum* that Germany had a right and duty to displace 'primitive peoples', as the Europeans had done in the Americas. In *Mein Kampf*, Hitler explained that the eastward expansion of the German empire would mirror the western and southern extension of British interests.[16] He systematised and industrialised what the imperial nations had been doing for the past five centuries. The scale was greater, the location different, the ideology broadly the same.

I believe that the brutalisation of empire also made the pointless slaughter of the First World War possible. A ruling class which had shut down its feelings to the extent that it could engineer a famine in India in the 1870s in which between 12 and 29 million people died was capable of almost anything.[17] Empire had tested not only the long-range weaponry that would later be deployed in northern France, but also the ideas.

Nor have we wholly abandoned them. Commenting on the Kikuyu case in the *Daily Mail*, Max Hastings charged that the plaintiffs had come to London 'to exploit our feeble-minded justice system'.[18] Hearing them 'represents an exercise in state masochism'. I suspect that if members of Hastings's club had been treated like the Kikuyu, he would be shouting from the rooftops for redress. But Kenyans remain, as colonial logic demanded, the 'other', bereft of the features and feelings that establish our common humanity.

So, in the eyes of much of the elite, do welfare recipients, 'problem families', Muslims and asylum seekers. The process of dehumanisation, so necessary to the colonial project, turns inwards. Until this nation is prepared to recognise what happened and how it was justified, Britain, like the countries it occupied, will remain blighted by imperialism.

8 October 2012

42

Unremitting Pain

Let me introduce you to the world's most powerful terrorist recruiting sergeant. It's a US federal agency called the Office of the Comptroller of the Currency. Its decision to cause a humanitarian catastrophe in one of the poorest and most troubled places on earth could resonate around the world for decades.

In February 2015, after the Office had sent it a cease and desist order, the last bank in the United States still processing money transfers to Somalia closed its service.[1] The Office – which reports to the US Treasury – reasoned that some of this money might find its way into the hands of the Somali terrorist group al-Shabaab. It's true that some of it might, just as some resources in any nation will find their way into the hands of criminals. So why don't we shut down the phone networks to hamper terrorism? Why don't we ban agriculture, in case fertiliser is used to make explosives? Why don't we stop all the clocks, to prevent armed gangs from planning their next atrocity?

Ridiculous? In fact it's not far off. Remittances from the diaspora amount to between $1.2 and 1.6 billion a year,[2] which is roughly 50 per cent of Somalia's gross national income.[3] Forty per cent of the population relies on these remittances for survival.[4] Over the past ten years, the money known to have been transferred to suspected terrorists in Somalia amounts to a few thousand dollars.[5] Cutting off remittances is likely to kill more people than terrorists will ever manage.

During the 2011 famine in Somalia, according to a report by the British government, 'British Somalis saved hundreds of thousands of lives by remitting money . . . reaching family members before aid agencies could mobilise'.[6] Government aid agencies then used the same informal banking system (the xawala) to send money to 1.5 million people, saving hundreds of thousands more. Today, roughly 3 million of the 7 million people in Somalia are short of food.[7] Shut off the funds and the results are likely to be terrible. Money transfers from abroad also pay for schooling, housing, business start-ups and all the means by which a country can lift itself out of dependency and chaos.[8] Yes, banking has its uses, as well as its abuses.

Somalia might be the second-poorest nation on earth, but its remittance system is widely seen as a model for other nations. Shifting e-money via the mobile phone network, the xawala brokers charge only 5 per cent, against a global average of 9 per cent and an African average of 12 per cent.[9] In a nation held to ransom by well-armed thugs and lacking almost all infrastructure, these remarkable people – often motivated as much by a desire to keep their country alive as to make money – supply tiny desert settlements all over the nation with scarcely any losses. The xawala system is one of Africa's great success stories. But it cannot work unless banks in the donor nations are permitted to transfer funds to Somalia. The US Treasury's paranoid rules threaten remittances from all over the world, as no bank wants to lose American business.

No one suffers more from al-Shabaab than the Somalis. Preventing these crucial transfers of funds epitomises that combination of menace and absurdity satirised in Chris Morris's film *Four Lions*. In the areas these few thousand men control, they have tried to ban samosas, on the grounds that their triangular shape invokes the Holy Trinity.[10] They whip women for wearing bras,[11] have pledged to prohibit the Internet, have imposed fundamentalist Wahhabi doctrines on a largely Sufi population, have tried to stop food aid and have waged war on vaccination programmes, causing outbreaks of polio and measles.[12] They have just murdered another MP.[13]

So you take a country suffering from terrorism, massive youth unemployment and the threat of famine and you seek to shut off half its foreign earnings. You force money transfers underground, where they are more likely to be captured by terrorists. You destroy hope, making young men more susceptible to recruitment by an organisation promising loot and status. Through an iniquitous mass punishment, you mobilise the anger and grievance on which terrorist organisations thrive. You help al-Shabaab to destroy Somalia's economic life.

Compare this pointless destruction to the US government's continued licensing of HSBC. In 2012 the bank was condemned by a Senate committee for circumventing safeguards 'designed to block transactions involving terrorists, drug lords, and rogue regimes'.[14] It processed billions of dollars for Mexican drug barons and provided services to Saudi and Bangladeshi banks linked to the financing of terrorists.[15] But there was no criminal prosecution because, the Attorney General's office argued, too many jobs were at stake.[16] The further outrageous practices that have since been revealed will doubtless be treated with the same leniency.[17]

So the US government fails to prosecute the illegal transfer of billions of dollars, in order to protect American jobs, while sentencing people in the Horn of Africa to death because of the illegal transfer of a few thousand. There is a word for these double standards: racism.

By contrast, the British government comes through this surprisingly well. While recognising that money could be transferred to terrorists in Somalia, its response is not to ban the remittance system but to try to make it more transparent. Last year, working with people throughout the money chain, it ran a pilot project to improve the system's security.[18]

But the US has simply shut the door and walked away. It offers no alternatives (why can't the Federal Reserve be used for transfers?),[19] and no useful guidance about how existing remittances could meet its exacting standards.[20] The Office remarks that, 'The Somali situation is a terrible human tragedy that cannot be solved by bank regulators.'[21] Perhaps not. But they can exacerbate it. The solution, it says, is 'humanitarian assistance'. Just two problems: the US isn't offering any more than before, and replacing an autonomous system with state aid contradicts everything the government says about African development. If the result is a mountain of corpses, the Office of the Comptroller of Currency will neither know nor care.

Somalis, like many of the world's people, are significant only when they are considered a threat. And if US policies make that threat more likely, well, that will be another department's problem. Until then, they count for nothing.

10 February 2015

43

Bomb Everyone

Let's bomb the Muslim world — all of it — to save the lives of its people. Surely this is the only consistent moral course? Why stop at blowing up Islamic State, when the Syrian government has murdered and tortured so many? This, after all, was 2013's moral imperative. What's changed?

How about blasting the Shia militias in Iraq? One of them selected forty people from the streets of Baghdad in June 2014, and murdered them for being Sunnis.[1] Another massacred sixty-eight people at a mosque in August the same year.[2] They now talk openly of 'cleansing' and 'erasure', once Islamic State has been defeated.[3] As a senior Shia politician warns, 'We are in the process of creating Shia al-Qaida radical groups equal in their radicalisation to the Sunni Qaida.'[4]

What humanitarian principle instructs you to stop there? In Gaza in 2014, 2,100 Palestinians were massacred: including people taking shelter in schools and hospitals. Surely these atrocities demand an air war against Israel? And what's the moral basis for refusing to liquidate Iran? Mohsen Amir-Aslani was hanged there last week for making 'innovations in the religion' (suggesting that the story of Jonah in the Qu'ran was symbolic rather than literal).[5] Surely that should inspire humanitarian action from above? Pakistan is crying out for friendly bombs: an elderly British man, Mohammed Asghar, who suffers from paranoid schizophrenia, is, like other blasphemers, awaiting execution there after claiming to be a holy prophet.[6] One of his prison guards has already shot him in the back.

Is there not an urgent duty to blow up Saudi Arabia? It has beheaded fifty-nine people so far this year, for offences that include adultery, sorcery and witchcraft.[7] It has long presented a greater threat to the West than ISIS now poses. In 2009, Hillary Clinton warned in a secret memo that 'Saudi Arabia remains a critical financial support base for al-Qa'ida, the Taliban . . . and other terrorist groups.'[8] In July, the former head of MI6, Sir Richard Dearlove, revealed that Prince Bandar bin Sultan, until recently the head of Saudi intelligence, told him: 'The time is not far off in the Middle East, Richard, when it will be literally "God help the Shia". More than a billion Sunnis have simply had enough of them.'[9] Saudi support for extreme Sunni militias in Syria during Bandar's tenure is widely blamed for the rapid rise of ISIS.[10] Why take out the subsidiary and spare the headquarters?

The humanitarian arguments aired in Parliament, if consistently applied, could be used to flatten the entire Middle East and West Asia.[11] By this means you could end all human suffering, liberating the people of these regions from the vale of tears in which they live.

Perhaps this is the plan: Barack Obama has now bombed seven largely Muslim countries, in each case citing a moral imperative.[12] The result, as you can see in Libya, Iraq, Pakistan, Afghanistan, Yemen, Somalia and Syria, has been the eradication of jihadi groups, of conflict, chaos, murder, oppression and torture. Evil has been driven from the face of the earth by the destroying angels of the West.

Now we have a new target, and a new reason to dispense mercy from the sky, with similar prospects of success. Yes, the agenda and practices of ISIS are disgusting. It murders and tortures, terrorises and threatens. As Obama says, it is a 'network of death'.[13] But it's one of many networks of death. Worse still, a Western crusade appears to be exactly what it wants.[14]

Already Obama's bombings have brought ISIS and Jabhat al-Nusra, a rival militia affiliated to Al Qaeda, together.[15] More than 6,000 fighters have joined ISIS since the bombardment began.[16] They dangled the heads of their victims in front of the cameras as bait for warplanes. And our governments were stupid enough to take it.

And if the bombing succeeds? If – and it's a big if – it manages to tilt the balance against ISIS, what then? Then we'll start hearing once more about Shia death squads and the moral imperative to destroy them too – and any civilians who happen to get in the way. The targets change; the policy doesn't. Never mind the question, the answer is bombs. In the name of peace and the preservation of life, our governments wage perpetual war.

While the bombs fall, our states befriend and defend other networks of death. The US government still refuses – despite Obama's promise – to release the twenty-eight redacted pages from the Joint Congressional Inquiry into 9/11, which document Saudi Arabian complicity in the attack on America.[17] In the UK, in 2004 the Serious Fraud Office began investigating allegations of massive bribes paid by the British weapons company BAE to Saudi ministers and middlemen. Just as the crucial evidence was about to be released, Tony Blair intervened to stop the investigation.[18] The biggest alleged beneficiary was Prince Bandar, mentioned above. The Serious Fraud Office was investigating a claim that, with the approval of the British government, he received £1 billion in secret payments from BAE.[19]

And still it goes on. *Private Eye*, drawing on a dossier of recordings and emails, alleges that a British company has paid £300 million in bribes to facilitate weapons sales to the Saudi National Guard.[20] When a whistleblower in the company reported these payments to the British Ministry of Defence, instead of taking action it alerted his bosses. He had to flee the country to avoid being thrown into a Saudi jail. Smirking, lying, two-faced bastards – this scarcely begins to touch it.

There are no good solutions that military intervention by the UK or the US can engineer. There are political solutions in which our governments could play a minor role: supporting the development of effective states that don't rely on murder and militias, building civic institutions that don't depend on terror, helping to create safe passage and aid for people at risk. Oh, and ceasing to protect and sponsor and arm selected networks of death. Whenever our armed forces have bombed or invaded Muslim nations, they have made life worse for those who live there. The regions in which our governments have intervened most are those which suffer most from terrorism and war. That is neither coincidental nor surprising.

Yet our politicians affect to learn nothing. Insisting that more killing will magically resolve deep-rooted conflicts, they scatter bombs like fairy dust.

30 September 2014

Part 9
Holding Us Down

44

A Global Ban on Leftwing Politics

I wrote this article in the spirit of despair. I felt that this issue was both critically important and so witheringly dull that hardly anyone would pay attention to it: this, at least, had been my experience when I discussed it two weeks before. I told myself that I was writing this column so that I could tell my children that I had at least tried. To my astonishment, the article went viral, and TTIP was suddenly on the map.

Remember that referendum about whether we should create a single market with the United States? You know, the one that asked whether corporations should have the power to strike down our laws? No, I don't either. Mind you, I spent ten minutes looking for my watch the other day, before I realised I was wearing it. Forgetting about the referendum is another sign of ageing. Because there must have been one, mustn't there? After all that agonising over whether or not we should stay in the European Union,[1] the government wouldn't cede our sovereignty to some shadowy, undemocratic body without consulting us. Would it?

The purpose of the Transatlantic Trade and Investment Partnership (TTIP) is to remove the regulatory differences between the Unites States and European nations. I mentioned it in an opinion piece on the *Guardian* website in October 2013.[2] But I left out the most important issue: the remarkable ability it would grant big business to sue the living daylights out of governments which try to defend their citizens. It would allow a secretive panel of corporate lawyers to over-rule the will of Parliament and destroy our legal protections. Yet the defenders of our sovereignty say nothing.

The mechanism is called investor–state dispute settlement. It's already being used in many parts of the world to kill regulations protecting people and the living planet.

The Australian government, after massive debates in and out of Parliament, decided that cigarettes should be sold in plain packets, marked only with shocking health warnings. The decision was validated by the Australian Supreme Court. But, using a trade agreement Australia struck with Hong Kong, the tobacco company Philip Morris has asked an offshore tribunal to award it a vast sum in compensation for the loss of what it calls its intellectual property.[3]

During its financial crisis, and in response to public anger over rocketing charges, Argentina imposed a freeze on people's energy and water bills. It was sued by the international utility companies whose vast bills had prompted the government to act. For this and other such crimes, it has been forced to pay out over a billion dollars in compensation.[4]

In El Salvador, local communities managed at great cost (three campaigners were murdered) to persuade the government to refuse permission for a vast gold mine which threatened to contaminate their water supplies. A victory for democracy? Not for long, perhaps. The Canadian company which sought to dig the mine is now suing El Salvador for $315 million – for the loss of its anticipated future profits.[5]

In Canada, the courts revoked two patents owned by the US drugs firm Eli Lilly, on the grounds that the company had not produced enough evidence that they had the beneficial effects it claimed. Eli Lilly is now suing the Canadian government for C$500 million, and demanding that Canada's patent laws be changed.[6]

These companies (and hundreds of others) are using the investor–state dispute rules embedded in trade treaties signed by the countries they are suing. The rules are enforced by panels which have none of the safeguards we expect in our own courts.[7] The hearings are held in secret. The judges are corporate lawyers, many of whom work for corporations of the kind whose cases they hear. Citizens and communities affected by their decisions have no legal standing. There is no right of appeal on the merits of the case. Yet they can overthrow the sovereignty of parliaments and the rulings of supreme courts.

You don't believe it? Here's what one of the judges on these tribunals says about his work:

> When I wake up at night and think about arbitration, it never ceases to amaze me that sovereign states have agreed to investment arbitration at all . . . Three private individuals are entrusted with the power to review, without any restriction or appeal procedure, all actions of the government, all decisions of the courts, and all laws and regulations emanating from parliament.[8]

There are no corresponding rights for citizens. We can't use these tribunals to demand better protections from corporate greed. As the Democracy Centre says, this is 'a privatised justice system for global corporations'.[9]

Even if these suits don't succeed, they can exert a powerful and chilling effect on legislation. One Canadian government official, speaking about the rules introduced by the North American Free Trade Agreement, remarked:

> I've seen the letters from the New York and DC law firms coming up to the Canadian government on virtually every new environmental regulation and proposition in the last five years. They involved dry-cleaning chemicals, pharmaceuticals, pesticides, patent law. Virtually all of the new initiatives were targeted and most of them never saw the light of day.[10]

Democracy, as a meaningful proposition, is impossible under these circumstances.

This is the system to which we will be subject if the transatlantic treaty goes ahead. The US and the European Commission, both of which have been captured by the corporations they are supposed to regulate, are pressing for investor–state dispute resolution to be included in the agreement.

The Commission justifies this policy by claiming that domestic courts don't offer corporations sufficient protection because they 'might be biased or lack independence'.[11] Which courts is it talking about? Those of the US? Its own member states? It doesn't say. In fact it fails to produce a single concrete example demonstrating the need for a new, extra-judicial system. It is precisely because our courts are generally not biased or lacking independence that the corporations want to bypass them. The European Commission seeks to replace open, accountable, sovereign courts with a closed, corrupt system riddled with conflicts of interest and arbitrary powers.

Investor–state rules could be used to smash any attempt to save the NHS from corporate control, to re-regulate the banks, to curb the greed of the energy companies, to renationalise the railways, to leave fossil fuels in the ground. These rules shut down democratic alternatives. They outlaw leftwing politics.

This is why there has been no attempt by our government to inform us about this monstrous assault on democracy, let alone consult us. This is why the Conservatives who huff and puff about sovereignty are silent. Wake up people, we're being shafted.

4 November 2013

45

Innocent until Proved Dead

Did the FBI execute Ibragim Todashev? He appears to have been shot seven times while being interviewed at his home in Orlando, Florida about his connection to one of the Boston bombing suspects. Among the shots was the assassin's hall-mark: a bullet to the back of the head.[1] What kind of an interview was it?

An irregular one. There was no lawyer present. It was not recorded.[2] By the time Todashev was shot, he had apparently been interrogated by three agents for five hours.[3] And then? Who knows? First, we were told, he lunged at them with a knife.[4] How he acquired it, five hours into a police interview, was not explained. How he posed such a threat while recovering from a knee operation also remains perplexing.

At first he drew the knife while being interviewed. Then he acquired it during a break from the interview.[5] Then it ceased to be a knife and became a sword, then a pipe, then a metal pole, then a broomstick, then a table, then a chair.[6] In one account all the agents were in the room at the time of the attack; in another, all but one had mysteriously departed, leaving the remaining officer to face his assailant alone.

If – and it remains a big if – this was an extra-judicial execution, it was one of hundreds commissioned by US agencies since Barack Obama first took office. The difference in this case is that it took place on American soil. Elsewhere, suspects are bumped off without even the right to the lawyerless interview Ibragim Todashev was given.

In his speech two days after Todashev was killed, President Obama maintained that 'our commitment to Constitutional principles has weathered every war'.[7] But he failed to explain which Constitutional principles permit him to authorise the killing of people in nations with which the United States is not at war. When his Attorney General, Eric Holder, tried to do so last year, he got himself into a terrible mess, ending with the extraordinary claim that, '"Due process" and "judicial process" are not one and the same . . . the Constitution guarantees due process, not judicial process.'[8] So what is due process if it doesn't involve the courts? Whatever the president says it is?

Er, yes. In the same speech Obama admitted for the first time that four US citizens had been killed by US drone strikes in other countries. In the next sentence he said, 'I do not believe it would be constitutional for the government to target and kill any US citizen – with a drone, or a shotgun – without due process.'[9] This suggests he believes that the legal rights of those four people had been respected before they were killed.

Given that they might not even have known that they were accused of the alleged crimes for which they were executed, that they had no opportunities to contest the charges, let alone be granted judge or jury, this suggests that the former law professor's interpretation of Constitutional rights is somewhat elastic. If Obama and his nameless advisers say someone is a terrorist, he stands convicted and can be put to death.

Left hanging in his speech is the implication that non-US citizens may be executed without even the pretence of due process. The many hundreds killed by drone strikes (who, civilian or combatant, retrospectively become terrorists by virtue of having been killed in a US anti-terrorism operation) are afforded no rights even in principle.[10]

As the process of decision-making remains secret, as the US government refuses even to acknowledge – let alone to document or investigate – the killing by its drones of people who patently had nothing to do with terrorism or any other known crime, miscarriages of justice are not just a risk emerging from the deployment of the president's kill-list. They are an inevitable outcome. Under the Obama doctrine, innocent until proved guilty has mutated to innocent until proved dead.

The president made his rejection of habeas corpus and his assumption of a godlike capacity for judgement explicit later in the speech, while discussing another matter. How, he wondered, should the US deal with detainees in Guantánamo Bay 'who we know have participated in dangerous plots or attacks, but who cannot be prosecuted – for example because the evidence against them has been compromised or is inadmissible in a court of law'? If the evidence has been compromised or is inadmissible, how can he know that they have participated? He can suspect, he can allege, but he cannot know until his suspicion has been tested in a court of law.

Global powers have an anti-social habit of bringing their work back home. The British government, for example, imported some of the methods it used against its colonial subjects to suppress domestic protests and strikes. Once an administrative class becomes accustomed to treating foreigners as if they have no rights, and once the domestic population broadly accepts their justifications, it is almost inevitable that the habit migrates from one arena into another. If hundreds of people living abroad can be executed by US agents on no more than suspicion, should we be surprised if residents of the United States began to be treated the same way?

3 June 2013

46

The Paranoia Squad

When you hear the term 'domestic extremist', whom do you picture? How about someone like Dr Peter Harbour? He's a retired physicist and university lecturer, who worked on the nuclear fusion reactor run by European governments at Culham in Oxfordshire. He's seventy next year. He has never been tried or convicted of an offence, except the odd speeding ticket. He has never failed a security check. Not the sort of person you had in mind? Then you don't work for the police.

Dr Harbour was one of the people who campaigned to save a local beauty spot – Thrupp Lake – between the Oxfordshire villages of Radley and Abingdon. They used to walk and swim and picnic there, and watch otters and kingfishers. RWE npower, which owns Didcot power station, wanted to empty the lake and fill it with pulverised fly ash.[1]

The villagers marched, demonstrated and sent in letters and petitions. Some people tried to stop the company from cutting down trees by standing in the way. Their campaign was entirely peaceful. But RWE npower discovered that it was legally empowered to shut the protests down.

Using the Protection from Harassment Act 1997, it obtained an injunction against the villagers and anyone else who might protest. This forbids them from 'coming to, remaining on, trespassing or conducting any demonstrations or protesting or other activities' on land near the lake.[2] If anyone breaks this injunction they could spend five years in prison.

The Act, Parliament was told, was meant to protect women from stalkers. But as soon as it came onto the statute books, it was used to stop peaceful protest. To obtain an injunction, a company needs to show only that someone feels 'alarmed or distressed' by the protesters, a requirement so vague that it can mean almost anything. Was this an accident of sloppy drafting? No. Timothy Lawson-Cruttenden, the solicitor who specialises in using this law against protesters, boasts that his company 'assisted in the drafting of the . . . Protection from Harassment Act 1997'.[3] In 2005, Parliament was duped again, when a new clause, undebated in either chamber, was slipped into the Serious Organised Crime and Police Act.[4] It peps up the 1997 Act, which can now be used to ban protest of any kind.

Mr Lawson-Cruttenden, who represented RWE npower, brags that the purpose of obtaining injunctions under the act is 'the criminalisation of civil disobedience'.[5] One of the advantages of this approach is that very low standards of proof are required: 'hearsay evidence . . . is admissible in civil courts'. The injunctions he obtains criminalise all further activity, even though, as he admits, 'any allegations made remain untested and unproven'.[6]

Last week, stung by bad publicity, npower backed down. The villagers had just started to celebrate when they made a shocking discovery: they now feature on an official list of domestic extremists.

The National Extremism Tactical Co-ordination Unit (NETCU) is the police team coordinating the fight against extremists. To illustrate the threats it confronts, the NETCU site carries images of people marching with banners, of peace campaigners standing outside a military base and of the Rebel Clown Army (whose members dress up as clowns to show that they have peaceful intentions). It publishes press releases about Greenpeace and the climate camp at Kingsnorth.[7] All this, the site suggests, is domestic extremism.

NETCU publishes a manual for officers policing protests. To help them identify dangerous elements, it directs them to a list of 'High Court Injunctions that relate to domestic extremism campaigns', published on NETCU's website.[8] On the first page is the injunction obtained by npower against the Radley villagers, which names Peter Harbour and others. Dr Harbour wrote to the head of NETCU, Steve Pearl, to ask for his name to be removed from the site. Mr Pearl refused. So Dr Harbour remains a domestic extremist.

It was this Paranoia Squad which briefed the *Observer* about 'eco-terrorists'. The article maintained that, 'A lone maverick eco-extremist may attempt a terrorist attack aimed at killing large numbers of Britons.'[9] The only evidence it put forward was that someone in Earth First! had stated that the world is overpopulated. This, it claimed, meant that the movement might attempt a campaign of mass annihilation. The same could be said about the United Nations, the

Optimum Population Trust and anyone else who has expressed concern about population levels.

The *Observer* withdrew the article after NETCU failed to provide any justification for its claims.[10] NETCU now tells me that the report 'wasn't an accurate reflection of our views'.[11] But the article contained a clue as to why the police might wish to spread such stories. 'The rise of eco-extremism coincides with the fall of the animal rights activist movement. Police said the animal rights movement was in disarray' and that 'its critical mass of hardcore extremists was sufficiently depleted to have halted its effectiveness'.[12] If, as the police maintain, animal rights extremism is no longer dangerous, it is hard for NETCU to justify its existence: unless it can demonstrate that domestic extremism exists elsewhere. A better headline for the article might have been 'Keep funding us, say police, or civilisation collapses'.

NETCU claims that domestic extremism 'is most often associated with single-issue protests, such as animal rights, anti-war, anti-globalisation and anti-GM crops'.[13] With the exception of animal rights protests, these campaigns in the UK have been overwhelmingly peaceful. As the writer and activist Merrick Godhaven points out, the groups whose tactics come closest to those of violent animal rights activists are anti-abortion campaigns. The UK Life League, for example, has published the names and addresses of people involved in abortion and family planning.[14] Two of its members have been convicted of sending pictures of mutilated foetuses to doctors and pharmacies.[15] Anti-abortionists in the US have murdered doctors, nurses and receptionists. Yet there is no mention of the UK Life League or anti-abortion campaigning on the NETCU site.

Just as the misleading claims of the security services were used to launch an illegal and unnecessary war against Iraq, NETCU's exaggerations will be used to justify the heavy-handed treatment of peaceful protesters. In both cases police and spies are distracted from dealing with genuine threats of terrorism and violence.

For how much longer will the government permit the police forces to drum up business like this? And at what point do we decide that this country is beginning to look like a police state?

23 November 2008

47

Union with the Devil

Gordon Brown appears to have tested them. It is as if he wanted to discover how far he could go before the affiliated trade unions – which provide most of the Labour Party's funds – decide that they have had enough. The results must reassure him: they will tolerate any level of abuse. Turkeys led by chickens, they will never stop voting for Christmas.

His government of all the talents has room for no professional trade unionist. But it does contain their sworn enemy. The new minister for trade and investment, now responsible for much of the policy that will affect union members, was not just the head of the Confederation of British Industry; he was the most Neanderthal boss the CBI has ever had. Digby Jones campaigned to freeze the minimum wage, neuter the EU's working time directive, block corporate killing laws, promote privatisation, cripple environmental rules, curtail maternity leave. Of the unions he said, 'they are an irrelevance. They are backward-looking and not on today's agenda.'[1] As if to show who the boss is, Comrade Digby refuses to join the Labour Party: he has been permitted to enter the government on his own terms.

To test the unions further, Brown has appointed Damon Buffini to two of the bodies which will help the government reshape the workforce: the Business Council and the National Council for Educational Excellence. Buffini is the target of the General, Municipal, Boilermakers and Allied Trade Union's (GMB) most vocal anti-corporate campaign: his private equity company sacked one-third of the Automobile Association's workforce.[2]

The ragged-trousered philanthropists who subsidise this bosses' party mumble and fumble but they will not strike back. Desperate to believe, union leaders cling to broken promises. They refuse to utter the only threat which Brown will heed: disaffiliation.

It is true that some important victories have been won since 1997. We have a minimum wage, better pension protection, improvements in parental leave, better conditions for part-time workers. The list of defeats is much longer. There is the private finance initiative, doggedly promoted by Gordon Brown, which now dominates the provision of most public services. There is the creeping marketisation of health and education. The government promised the unions that it would give employment protection to temporary and agency workers.[3] Instead, it has obstructed the European directive which would have introduced it; when a backbencher proposed a private members' bill, a government minister talked it out.[4] Tony Blair preserved the opt-out clause in the EU's working time directive that allows bosses to blackmail their workers. The government has refused to repeal Thatcher's draconian union laws. After ten years of broken promises we still don't have a corporate killing act. Inequality has reached scarcely imaginable levels, tax evasion is rampant, the railways are still in private hands, council housing remains moribund, companies don't have to publish operating and financial reviews, the minimum wage is far from being a living wage. And there is the small matter of an illegal war in which hundreds of thousands of people have died.

Amicus, one half of Unite, the super-union it recently formed with the Transport and General Workers' Union (TGWU), dismisses such complaints as 'the hard left . . . kick[ing] up a fuss over minor areas of difficulty'.[5] What, I wonder, would be a major area of difficulty? When you challenge the unions, they rattle a yellowed parchment and proclaim, 'But we have the Warwick agreement!' This is the pact they signed with the government in 2004, which persuaded them not to break with the party. But it must now be obvious to anyone who isn't singing loudly while stuffing their fingers in their ears that the government intends only to honour the easy bits. It has punted the more difficult promises – like fair conditions for agency workers – into the indeterminate future.

Of course there is the perpetual fear of something worse. No trade union, quite rightly, wants to let the Tories back in. But if the unions won't use their power, the contest between the two parties will be scarcely worth fighting. Perhaps they don't realise how much the government now needs them. The cash-for-honours scandal has frightened off almost all the major private donors, leaving the party largely dependent on union funds. So what do they intend to do with this power? To judge by their recent statements, nothing.

In his speech to the annual conference in June 2007, the leader of the GMB, Paul Kenny, begged, 'Listen to us. Please listen to us . . . I say to Gordon, please follow your instincts, not the spin doctors of the CBI.'[6] But he threatened nothing. Two weeks later, Dave Prentis, the leader of Unison, told the government that it was 'drinking in the last chance saloon'. But he too imagines that Brown might be sweetly persuaded to 'usher in a new era that sees the restoration of real Labour values'.[7] Last week Tony Woodley, head of the TGWU, railed against the 'outrage' and 'disgrace' of Labour's policies.[8] But it was hot air, and the government knows it. I phoned the TGWU and asked its spokesman what might persuade the union to disaffiliate. 'Nothing', he told me. So if the Labour Party adopted the swastika as its logo and started holding torchlit rallies in Parliament Square, it could still count on the TGWU's support? 'That's an extreme example', he replied. But he did not say 'no'.[9]

Knowing that it can take the support of the affiliated unions for granted, the government can concentrate on appeasing the bosses. The unions' involvement with the Labour Party is rather like the government's special relationship with George Bush: their response to being used as a doormat is to become just a little more bristly.

The affiliated unions still rage about the class war, but keep funding their class enemies. When he crossed the floor and was given the safe seat of St Helen's South, then took his butler on the campaign trail, the multi-millionaire Shaun Woodward represented everything they hated about New Labour. But last year the philanthropists in Amicus helped to fund his constituency office.[10] The GMB denounces Blair's war crimes from the conference stage, but gives money to his office in Sedgefield.[11] None of the bigger unions will contemplate forming or funding another party.

Two trade unions – the National Union of Rail, Maritime and Transport Workers (RMT) and the Fire Brigades Union (FBU) – walked out before the last election. Bob Crow, the leader of the RMT, recently told the other unions, 'Any hope of the Labour Party working for workers is dead, finished, over. I think all you who are staying in the Labour Party are just giving credibility to it.'[12] In 2004, Kevin Curran, then the leader of the GMB, warned that if Labour did not change, 'we would have to look for a political partner that would advance the interests of people we represent'.[13] His timing was bad: the Warwick agreement, gravid with promise, had just been signed. But as the agreement bursts, the necessary threats have not materialised.

Brown has called their bluff, and they have flinched. He now knows that, out of fear and out of sentiment, the unions will stick with him. He can do whatever it takes to keep big business, Rupert Murdoch and the *Daily Mail* onside. The way things are going, the unions might as well cut out the middleman and give their money to the CBI.

10 July 2007

Part 10
Finding Our Place

48

Someone Else's Story

Imagine that the question was posed the other way round. An independent nation is asked to decide whether to surrender its sovereignty to a larger union. It would be allowed a measure of autonomy, but key aspects of its governance would be handed to another nation. It would be used as a military base by the dominant power and yoked to an economy over which it had no control.

It would have to be bloody desperate. Only a nation in which the institutions of governance had collapsed, which had been ruined economically, which was threatened by invasion or civil war or famine might contemplate this drastic step. Most nations faced with such catastrophes choose to retain their independence – in fact will fight to preserve it – rather than surrender to a dominant foreign power.

So what would you say about a country that sacrificed its sovereignty without collapse or compulsion? That had no obvious enemies, a basically sound economy and a broadly functional democracy, yet chose to swap it for remote governance by the hereditary elite of another nation, beholden to a corrupt financial centre?[1]

What would you say about a country that exchanged an economy based on enterprise and distribution for one based on speculation and rent?[2] That chose obeisance to a government which spies on its own citizens, uses the planet as its dustbin, governs on behalf of a transnational elite which owes loyalty to no nation, cedes public services to corporations, forces terminally ill people to work and can't be trusted with a box of fireworks, let alone a fleet of nuclear submarines?[3] You would conclude that it had lost its senses.

So what's the difference? How is the argument altered by the fact that Scotland is considering whether to gain independence, rather than whether to lose it? It's not. Those who would vote no – now, a new poll suggests, a rapidly diminishing majority[4] – could be suffering from system justification.

System justification is defined as the 'process by which existing social arrangements are legitimised, even at the expense of personal and group interest'.[5] It consists of a desire to defend the status quo, regardless of its impacts. It has been demonstrated in a large body of experimental work, which has produced the following surprising results.

System justification becomes stronger when social and economic inequality are more extreme. This is because people try to rationalise their disadvantage by seeking legitimate reasons for their position.[6] In some cases disadvantaged people are more likely than the privileged to support the status quo. One study found that US citizens on low incomes were more likely than those on high incomes to believe that economic inequality is legitimate and necessary.[7]

It explains why women in experimental studies pay

themselves less than men; why people in low-status jobs believe their work is worth less than those in high-status jobs, even when they're performing the same task; and why people accept domination by another group.[8] It might help to explain why so many people in Scotland are inclined to vote no.

The fears the no campaigners have worked so hard to stoke are – by comparison to what the Scots are being asked to lose – mere shadows. As Adam Ramsay points out in his treatise *Forty-Two Reasons to Support Scottish Independence*, there are plenty of nations smaller than Scotland which possess their own currencies and thrive.[9] Most of the world's prosperous nations are small: there are no inherent disadvantages to downsizing.[10]

Remaining in the UK carries as much risk and uncertainty as leaving. England's housing bubble could blow at any time. We might leave the EU. Some of the most determined no campaigners would take us out: witness UKIP's intention to stage a 'pro-Union rally' in Glasgow in September 2014.[11] The Union in question, of course, is the UK, not Europe. This reminds us of a crashing contradiction in the politics of such groups: if our membership of the EU represents an appalling and intolerable loss of sovereignty, why is the far greater loss Scotland is being asked to accept deemed tolerable and necessary?

The Scots are told they will have no control over their own currency if they leave the UK. But they have none today. The monetary policy committee is based in London and bows to the banks. The pound's strength, which damages the manufacturing Scotland seeks to promote, reflects the interests of the City.[12]

To vote no is to choose to live under a political system that sustains one of the rich world's highest levels of inequality and deprivation. This is a system in which all major parties are complicit, which offers no obvious exit from a model that privileges neoliberal economics over other aspirations.[13] It treats the natural world, civic life, equality, public health and effective public services as dispensable luxuries, and the freedom of the rich to exploit the poor as non-negotiable.

Its lack of a codified constitution permits numberless abuses of power. It has failed to reform the House of Lords, royal prerogative, campaign finance and first-past-the-post voting (another triumph for the no brigade).[14] It is dominated by a media owned by tax exiles, who, instructing their editors from their distant chateaux, play the patriotism card at every opportunity. The concerns of swing voters in marginal constituencies outweigh those of the majority; the concerns of corporations with no lasting stake in the country outweigh everything. Broken, corrupt, dysfunctional, retentive: you want to be part of this?

Independence, as more Scots are beginning to see, offers people an opportunity to rewrite the political rules. To create a written constitution, the very process of which is engaging and transformative. To build an economy of benefit to everyone. To promote cohesion, social justice, the defence of the living planet and an end to wars of choice.[15]

To deny this to yourself; to remain subject to the whims of a distant and uncaring elite; to succumb to the bleak, deferential negativity of the no campaign; to accept other people's myths in place of your own story: that would be an astonishing act of self-repudiation and self-harm. Consider yourselves independent and work backwards from there, then ask why you would sacrifice that freedom.

2 September 2014

49

Highland Spring

Bring out the violins. The land reform programme announced by the Scottish government is the end of civilised life on earth, if you believe the corporate press. In a country where 432 people own half the private rural land, all change is Stalinism.[1] The *Daily Telegraph* has published a string of dire warnings, insisting, for example, that deer stalking and grouse shooting could come to an end if business rates are introduced for sporting estates.[2] Moved to tears yet?

Yes, sporting estates – where the richest people in Britain, or oil sheikhs and oligarchs from elsewhere, shoot grouse and stags – are exempt from business rates: a present from John Major's government in 1994.[3] David Cameron has been just as generous with our money: as he cuts essential services for the poor, he has almost doubled the public subsidy for English grouse moors,[4] and frozen the price of shotgun licences,[5] at a public cost of £17 million a year.

But this is small change. Let's talk about the real money. It's no coincidence that the two most regressive forms of taxation in the UK – council tax banding and the payment of farm subsidies – both favour major owners of property. The capping of council tax bands ensures that the owners of £100 million flats in London pay less than the owners of £200,000 houses in Blackburn.[6] Farm subsidies, which remain limitless as a result of the Westminster government's lobbying,[7] ensure that every household in Britain hands £245 a year to the richest people in the land.[8] The single farm payment system – under which landowners are paid by the hectare – is a reinstatement of a mediaeval levy called feudal aid: a tax the vassals had to pay to their lords.[9]

The Westminster government claims to champion an entrepreneurial society, of wealth creators and hard-working families, but the real rewards and incentives are for rent. The power and majesty of the state protects the patrimonial class. A looped and windowed democratic cloak barely covers the corrupt old body of the nation. Here peaceful protesters can still be arrested under the 1361 Justices of the Peace Act. Here, the Royal Mines Act 1424 gives the Crown the right to all the gold and silver in Scotland.[10] Here the Remembrancer of the City of London sits behind the Speaker's chair in the House of Commons, to protect the entitlements of a Corporation that pre-dates the Norman Conquest.[11] This is an essentially feudal nation.

If this is the government of enterprise, not rent, ask yourself why capital gains tax (at 28 per cent) is lower than the top rate of income tax. Ask yourself why principal residences, though their value may rise by millions, are altogether exempt.[12] Ask yourself why rural landowners are typically excused capital gains tax, inheritance tax and the first five years of income tax.[13] The enterprise society? It's a con, designed to create an illusion of social mobility.

The Scottish programme for government is the first serious attempt to address the nature of landholding in Britain since David Lloyd George's budget of 1909.[14] Some of its aims hardly sound radical until you understand the context. For example, it will seek to discover who owns the land. Big deal. Yes, in fact, it is. At the moment the owners of only 26 per cent of the land in Scotland have been identified.[15]

Walk into any *mairie* in France or *ayuntamiento* in Spain and you will be shown the cadastral registers on request, on which all the land and its owners are named. When *The Land* magazine tried to do the same in Britain, it found that there was a full cadastral map available at the local library, which could be photocopied for 70 pence. But it was made in 1840. Even with expert help, it took the magazine several weeks of fighting official obstruction and obfuscation and cost nearly £1,000 to find out who owns the 1.4 square kilometres around its offices in Dorset. It discovered that the old registers had been closed and removed from public view, at the behest of a landed class that wishes to remain as exempt from public scrutiny as it is from taxes. (The landowners are rather more forthcoming when applying for subsidies from the Rural Payments Agency, which possesses a full, though unobtainable, register of their agricultural holdings.) What sort of nation is this, in which you cannot discover who owns the ground beneath your feet?

The Scottish government will consider breaking up large landholdings when they impede the prospects of local people.[16] It will provide further help to communities to buy the land that surrounds them. Compare its promise of 'a fairer, wider and more equitable distribution of land' to the Westminster government's vision of 'greater competitiveness, including by consolidation':[17] which means a continued increase in the size of landholdings. The number of holdings in England is now falling by 2 per cent a year,[18] which is possibly the fastest concentration of ownership since the Acts of enclosure.

Consider Scotland's determination to open up the question of property taxes, which might lead to the only system that is fair and comprehensive: land value taxation.[19] Compare it to the fleabite of a mansion tax proposed by Ed Miliband, which, though it recoups only a tiny percentage of the unearned income of the richest owners, has so outraged the proprietorial class that some of them (yes, Griff Rhys Jones, I'm thinking of you[20]) have threatened to leave the country. Good riddance.

The Scottish government might address the speculative chaos which mangles the countryside while failing to build the houses people need. It might challenge a system in which terrible homes are built at great expense.[21] It might take land into public ownership to ensure that new developments are built by and for those who will live there, rather than for the benefit of volume house-builders. It might prevent mountains from being burnt and overgrazed[22] by a landowning class that cares only about the numbers of deer and grouse it can bag and the bragging rights this earns in London clubs. As Scotland, where feudalism was not legally abolished until 2000,[23] becomes a progressive, modern nation, it leaves England stuck in the pre-democratic past.

Scotland is rudely interrupting the constructed silences that stifle political thought in the United Kingdom. This is why the oligarchs who own the media hate everything that is happening there: their interests are being exposed in a way that is currently impossible south of the border.

For centuries, Britain has been a welfare state for patrimonial capital. It's time we broke it open, and broke the culture of deference that keeps us in our place. Let's bring the Highland Spring south, and start discussing some dangerous subjects.

2 December 2014

50

A Telling Silence

You can learn as much about a country from its silences as you can from its obsessions. The issues politicians do not discuss are as telling and decisive as those they do. While the coalition government's cuts beggar the vulnerable and gut public services, it's time to talk about the turns not taken, the opportunities foregone: the taxes which could have spared us every turn of the screw.

The extent of the forgetting is extraordinary. Take, for example, capital gains tax. Before the 2010 election, the Liberal Democrats promised to raise it from 18 per cent to 'the same rates as income' (in other words a top rate of 50 per cent), to ensure that private equity bosses were no longer paying lower rates of tax than their office cleaners.[1] It made sense, as it would have removed the bosses' incentive to collect their earnings as capital. Despite a powerful economic case, the government refused to raise the top rate above 28 per cent. The Lib Dems protested for a day or two, and have remained silent ever since.[2] In the parliamentary debate about cuts to social security, this missed opportunity wasn't mentioned once.[3]

But at least that tax has risen. In just two and half years, the government has cut corporation tax three times. It will fall from 28 per cent in 2010 to 2 per cent in 2014.[4] George Osborne, the Chancellor, boasted in December 2012 that this 'is the lowest rate of any major western economy'. He is consciously setting up a destructive competition with other nations, creating new excuses further to reduce the UK rate.[5]

Labour's near silence on this issue is easily explained. Under Tony Blair and Gordon Brown, who were often as keen as the Conservatives to appease corporate power, the rate was reduced from 33 per cent to 28 per cent. Prefiguring Osborne's boast, in 1999, Brown bragged that the rate he had set was 'the lowest rate of any major industrialised country anywhere, including Japan and the United States'.[6] What a legacy for a Labour government.

As for a Robin Hood tax on financial transactions, after an initial flutter of interest you are now more likely to hear the call of the jubjub bird in the House of Commons. According to the Institute for Public Policy Research, a tax rate of just 0.01 per cent would raise £25 billion a year, rendering many of the chamber's earnest debates about the devastating cuts void.[7] Silence also surrounds the notion of a windfall tax on extreme wealth. And to say that Professor Greg Philo's arresting idea of transferring the national debt to those who possess assets worth £1 million or more has failed to ignite the flame of passion in Parliament would not overstate the case.[8]

But the loudest silence surrounds the issue of property taxes. The most expensive flat in that favourite haunt of the international super-rich, One Hyde Park, cost £135 million. The owner pays £1,369 in council tax, or 0.001 per cent of its value.[9] Last year the *Independent* revealed that the Sultan of Brunei pays only £32 a month more for his pleasure dome in Kensington Palace Gardens than some of the poorest people in the same borough.[10] A mansion tax – slapped down by David Cameron in October[11] – is only the beginning of what the owners of such places should pay. For the simplest, fairest and least avoidable levy is one which the major parties simply will not contemplate. It's called land value tax.

The term is a misnomer. It's not really a tax. It's a return to the public of the benefits we have donated to the landlords. When land rises in value, the government and the people deliver a great unearned gift to those who happen to own it.

In 1909 a dangerous subversive explained the issue thus:

Roads are made, streets are made, services are improved, electric light turns night into day, water is brought from reservoirs a hundred miles off in the mountains – and all the while the landlord sits still. Every one of those improvements is effected by the labor and cost of other people and the taxpayers. To not one of those improvements does the land monopolist, as a land monopolist, contribute, and yet by every one of them the value of his land is enhanced. He renders no service to the community, he contributes nothing to the general welfare, he contributes nothing to the process from which his own enrichment is derived ... the unearned increment on the land is reaped by the land monopolist in exact proportion, not to the service, but to the disservice done.[12]

Who was this firebrand? Winston Churchill. As Churchill, Adam Smith and many others have pointed out,[13] those who own the land skim wealth from everyone else, without exertion or enterprise. They 'levy a toll upon all other forms of wealth and every form of industry'.[14] Land value tax recoups this toll.

It has a number of other benefits.[15] It stops the speculative land hoarding that prevents homes from being built. It ensures that the most valuable real estate – in city centres – is developed first, discouraging urban sprawl. It prevents speculative property bubbles, of the kind that have recently trashed the economies of Ireland, Spain and other nations and which make rents and first homes so hard to afford. Because it does not affect the supply of land (they stopped making it some time ago), it cannot cause the rents that people must pay to the landlords to be raised. It is easy to calculate and hard to avoid: you can't hide your land in London in a secret account in the Cayman Islands. And it could probably discharge the entire deficit.

It is altogether remarkable, in these straitened and inequitable times, that land value tax is not at the heart of the current political debate. Perhaps it is a sign of how powerful the rent-seeking class in Britain has become. While the silence surrounding this obvious solution exposes Labour's limitations, it also exposes the contradiction at heart of the Conservative Party. The Conservatives claim, in David Cameron's words, to be 'the party of enterprise'.[16] But those who benefit most from its policies are those who are rich already. It is, in reality, the party of rent.

This is where the debate about workers and shirkers, strivers and skivers should have led. The skivers and shirkers sucking the money out of your pockets are not the recipients of social security demonised by the *Daily Mail* and the Conservative Party, the overwhelming majority of whom are honest claimants. We are being parasitised from above, not below, and the tax system should reflect this.

21 January 2013

51

The Values of Everything

So here we are, forming an orderly queue at the slaughter-house gate. The punishment of the poor for the errors of the rich, the abandonment of universalism, the dismantling of the shelter the state provides: apart from a few small protests, none of this has yet brought us out fighting.

The acceptance of policies which counteract our interests is the pervasive mystery of the twenty-first century. In the United States, blue-collar workers angrily demand that they be left without health care, and insist that millionaires should pay less tax. In the UK we appear ready to abandon the social progress for which our ancestors risked their lives with barely a mutter of protest. What has happened to us?

The answer, I think, is provided by the most interesting report I have read this year. 'Common Cause', written by Tom Crompton of the environmental conservation group the World Wildlife Fund for Nature (WWF), examines a series of fascinating recent advances in the field of psychology.[1] It offers, I believe, a remedy to the blight which now afflicts every good cause from welfare to climate change.

Progressives, he shows, have been suckers for a myth of human cognition he labels the Enlightenment model. This holds that people make rational decisions by assessing facts. All that has to be done to persuade people is to lay out the data: they will then use it to decide which options best support their interests and desires.

A host of psychological experiments demonstrates that it doesn't work like this. Instead of performing a rational cost–benefit analysis, we accept information which confirms our identity and values, and we reject information that conflicts with them. We mould our thinking around our social identity, protecting it from serious challenge. Confronting people with inconvenient facts is likely only to harden their resistance to change.

Our social identity is shaped by values which psychologists classify as either extrinsic or intrinsic. Extrinsic values concern status and self-advancement. People with a strong set of extrinsic values fixate on how others see them. They cherish financial success, image and fame. Intrinsic values concern relationships with friends, family and community, and self-acceptance. Those who have a strong set of intrinsic values are not dependent on praise or rewards from other people. They have beliefs which transcend their self-interest.

Few people are all-extrinsic or all-intrinsic. Our social identity is formed by a mixture of values. But psychological tests in nearly seventy countries show that values cluster together in remarkably consistent patterns. Those who strongly value financial success, for example, have less empathy, stronger manipulative tendencies, a stronger attraction to hierarchy and inequality, stronger prejudices towards strangers and less concern about human rights and the environment. Those who have a strong sense of self-acceptance have more empathy and a greater concern about human rights, social justice and the environment. These values suppress each other: the stronger someone's extrinsic aspirations, the weaker his or her intrinsic goals.

We are not born with our values. They are shaped by the social environment around us. By changing our perception of what is normal and acceptable, politics alters our minds as much as our circumstances. Free, universal health provision, for example, tends to reinforce intrinsic values. Shutting the poor out of health care normalises inequality, reinforcing extrinsic values. The sharp rightward shift which began with Margaret Thatcher and persisted under Blair and Brown, all of whose governments emphasised the virtues of competition, the market and financial success, has changed our values. The British Social Attitudes survey, for example, shows a sharp fall over this period in public support for policies which redistribute wealth and opportunity.[2]

This shift has been reinforced by advertising and the media. The media's fascination with power politics; its rich lists; its catalogues of the hundred most powerful, influential, intelligent or beautiful people; its obsessive promotion of celebrity, fashion, fast cars, expensive holidays: all these inculcate extrinsic values. By generating feelings of insecurity and inadequacy – which means reducing self-acceptance – they also suppress intrinsic goals.

Advertisers, who employ large numbers of psychologists, are well aware of this. Crompton quotes Guy Murphy, global planning director for the marketing company JWT. Marketers,

Murphy says, 'should see themselves as trying to manipulate culture; being social engineers, not brand managers; manipulating cultural forces, not brand impressions'.[3] The more they foster extrinsic values, the easier it is to sell their products.

Rightwing politicians have also, instinctively, understood the importance of values in changing the political map. Margaret Thatcher famously remarked that, 'Economics are the method; the object is to change the heart and soul.'[4] Conservatives in the United States generally avoid debating facts and figures. Instead they frame issues in ways that both appeal to and reinforce extrinsic values. Every year, through mechanisms that are rarely visible and seldom discussed, the space in which progressive ideas can flourish shrinks a little more. The progressive response to this trend has been disastrous.

Instead of confronting the shift in values, we have sought to adapt to it. Once-progressive political parties have tried to appease altered public attitudes: think of all those New Labour appeals to Middle England, which was often just a code for self-interest. In doing so they endorse and legitimise extrinsic values. Many Greens and social-justice campaigners have also tried to reach people by appealing to self-interest: explaining how, for example, relieving poverty in the developing world will build a market for British products, or suggesting that, by buying a hybrid car, you can impress your friends and enhance your social status. This tactic also strengthens extrinsic values, making future campaigns even less likely to succeed. Green consumerism has been a catastrophic mistake.

'Common Cause' proposes a simple remedy: that we stop seeking to bury our values and instead explain and champion them. Progressive campaigners, it suggests, should help to foster an understanding of the psychology which informs political change and show how it has been manipulated. They should also come together to challenge forces – particularly the advertising industry – which make us insecure and selfish.

Ed Miliband appears to understand this need. He told the Labour conference that he 'wants to change our society so that it values community and family, not just work', and 'wants to change our foreign policy so that it's always based on values, not just alliances . . . We must shed old thinking and stand up for those who believe there is more to life than the bottom line.'[5] But there's a paradox here, which means that we cannot rely on politicians to drive these changes. Those who succeed in politics are, by definition, people who prioritise extrinsic values. Their ambition must supplant peace of mind, family life, friendship – even brotherly love.

So we must lead this shift ourselves. People with strong intrinsic values must cease to be embarrassed by them. We should argue for the policies we want not on the grounds of expediency but on the grounds that they are empathetic and kind; and against others on the grounds that they are selfish and cruel. In asserting our values we become the change we want to see.

11 October 2010

Acknowledgements

Were it not for the *Guardian*, I would probably be unemployable; so hostile has most of the media become to the voices of those on the left (and in particular, it sometimes seems, to those seeking to defend the living world). My editors, past and present, have given me freedom of the kind I would find scarcely anywhere else. They never seek to stop me writing about uncomfortable and disturbing topics, never seek to dilute my message or hamper my style, suggesting only such changes as might enhance and strengthen my work. So my great thanks go to Becky Gardiner, Katherine Butler and their wonderful teams; Adam Vaughan and James Randerson; as well as the senior editors, sub-editors and many others who have created an inviolable space for free expression, and make publication possible. Thank you too to my assistant Ketty Hughes; my agents James Macdonald Lockhart and Antony Harwood; the editor and commissioner of this book, Leo Hollis, whose idea it was; and the many friends (and opponents) with whom I have debated the issues it contains.

September 2015

Notes

Introduction

1   Thomas Piketty, 2014, *Capital in the Twenty-First Century*, Harvard University Press, Cambridge, MA.

2   Susan Jacoby, 2008, *The Age of American Unreason: Dumbing Down and the Future of Democracy*, Old Street Publishing, London.

3   David Harvey, 2005, *A Brief History of Neoliberalism*, Oxford University Press, Oxford; Naomi Klein, 2007, *The Shock Doctrine: The Rise of Disaster Capitalism*, Penguin Books, London.

4   Isaiah Berlin, 1958, *Two Concepts of Liberty*, published in Isaiah Berlin, 1969, *Four Essays on Liberty*, Oxford University Press, Oxford.

5   Fred Block and Margaret Somers, 2014, *The Power of Market Fundamentalism: Karl Polanyi's Critique*, Harvard University Press, Cambridge, MA.

6   Amartya Sen, 1981, *Poverty and Famines: An Essay on Entitlement and Deprivation*, Oxford University Press, Oxford.

1. Falling Apart

1   Natalie Gil, 20 July 2014, 'Loneliness: A Silent Plague That Is Hurting Young People Most', theguardian.com.

2   International Longevity Centre and Independent Age, 2013, *Isolation: A Growing Issue Among Older Men*, independentage.org.

3   Ibid; Gil, 'Loneliness'.

4   Ian Sample, 16 February 2014, 'Loneliness Twice as Unhealthy as Obesity for Older People, Study Finds', theguardian.com; Gill, 'Loneliness'.

5   Keith Perry, 5 August 2014, 'One in Five Children Just Want to Be Rich When They Grow Up', telegraph.co.uk.

6   John Bingham, 18 June 2014, 'Britain the Loneliness Capital of Europe', telegraph.co.uk.

7   The Campaign to End Loneliness, 'A Million Lonely Older People Spell Public Health Disaster', campaigntoendloneliness.org.

8   The Campaign to End Loneliness, 'Loneliness Research', campaign-toendloneliness.org.

9   Luca Stanca and Luigino Bruni, June 2005, 'Income Aspirations, Television and Happiness: Evidence from the World Values Surveys', boa.unimib.it.

10 Kathryn Hopkins, 13 October 2014, 'FTSE Bosses Earn 120 Times More Than Average Worker', thetimes.co.uk.

11 Jill Treanor, 14 October 2014, 'Richest 1% of People Own Nearly Half of Global Wealth, Says Report', theguardian.com.

12 Graeme Wood, April 2011, 'Secret Fears of the Super-Rich', theatlantic.com.

13 International Longevity Centre, *Isolation*.

2. Deviant and Proud

1   Paul Verhaeghe, 2014, *What about Me? The Struggle for Identity in a Market-Based Society*, Scribe: Melbourne and London.

2   Simon Rogers, 22 May 2012, 'Social Mobility: The Charts That Shame Britain', theguardian.com.

3. Work-Force

1   Peter Wilby, 28 February 2011, 'The Awful Truth: Education Won't Stop the Poor Getting Poorer', theguardian.com.

2   Daniel Huang, 3 June 2015, 'The Ten Commandments for Wall Street Interns', wsj.com.

3   Emma Jacobs, 8 August 2013, 'The Serious Side of Child's Play', ft.com.

4   Greg Hurst, 9 June 2015, 'School Defends Setting Brightest Four-Year-Olds Apart from Rest', times.co.uk.

5   The increase in beds for child mental health patients increased from 844 in 1999 to 1,264 in January 2014. When this was found to be insufficient,

another fifty beds were announced; 10 July 2014, 'NHS England Takes Action to Improve Access to Specialised Mental Health Services for Children and Young People', England.nhs.uk.

6　Children's Rights Alliance for England, *Health: State of Children's Rights in England 2014*, crae.org.uk.

7　Ally Lee, 3 June 2015, 'Large Rise in UK Admissions for Teenage Eating Disorders', youngminds.org.uk.

8　Ally Lee, 14 May 2015, 'English Children Facing Low Self-Esteem and Exam Stress Battles', youngminds.org.uk.

9　Izaak Walton, 1915 (1653), *The Compleat Angler*, Oxford University Press, London, p. 22.

4. Addicted to Comfort

1　Jean-Jacques Rousseau's unanswered question, at the start of *The Social Contract*, published in 1762, concerns the mystery of our submission to captivity.

2　Gloria De Piero, 9 May 2013, 'Instead of Supporting People Suffering from the Blight of ASB the Government Is Proposing to Weaken Powers', labour.org.uk; a speech by Yvette Cooper, 9 May 2013, *Hansard* (column 176), parliament.uk.

3　Press Association, January 2014, 'Lords Reject Government's Antisocial, Crime and Policing Bill', theguardian.com.

4　Russ Choma, 9 January 2014, 'Millionaires' Club: For First Time, Most Lawmakers are Worth $1 Million-Plus', opensecrets.org.

5　Ibid.

6　Alexis de Tocqueville, 2004 (1835), *Democracy in America*, trans. Arthur Goldhammer, The Library of America, New York, p. 587.

5. Dead Zone

1　Anna Minton, 2006, *What Kind of World Are We Building? The Privatization of Public Space*, RICS, rics.org.

2　Alex Gask, 2004, *Anti-Social Behaviour Orders and Human Rights*, Liberty, liberty-human-rights.org.uk.

3　Liberty, 2013, *Liberty's Briefing on the Draft Anti-Social Behaviour Bill*, liberty-human-rights.org.uk.

4　Peter Walker, 17 April 2012, 'Protester Receives Olympics ASBO', theguardian.com.

5   Liberty, *Liberty's Briefing on the Draft Anti-Social Behaviour Bill*.

6   Ibid.

7   Anti-Social Behaviour, Crime and Policing Act 2014, parliament.uk.

8   Ibid.

9   Following the publication of this article, the House of Lords struck down some of the draconian aspects of IPNAs, and the government did not attempt to reinstate them.

10 Lord Macdonald et al., 29 October 2013, *The Anti-Social Behaviour, Crime and Policing Bill: Opinion*, reformclause1.org.uk.

11 Alan Travis, 18 December 2013, 'Right to Protest Protected in Amendments to Bill', theguardian.com.

12 By phone, 6 January 2013.

6. Help Addicts, but Lock Up the Casual Users of Cocaine

1   Antonio Maria Costa, 2009, preface to the *World Drug Report 2009*, United Nations Office on Drugs and Crime, unodc.org.

2   Antony Barnett, 13 February 2005, 'Price of Cocaine Paid with Blood', guardian.com; Andrés Schipani et al., 8 March 2009, 'Spreading Fear: How the New Cartels Deliver Chaos to Four Continents', guardian.com.

3   *Independent*, 19 November 2008, 'This Is Our Problem Too', independent.co.uk.

4   Ian Sample, 23 October 2005, 'Health Timebomb as Rising Cocaine Use Threatens Heart Problems in Young', theguardian.com.

5   Nick Davies, 15 June 2001, 'Demonising Druggies Wins Votes, That's All That Counts', theguardian.com.

6   Nick Davies, 23 May 2003, 'National Plan That Only Fuels the Fire', theguardian.com.

7   Costa, *World Drug Report 2009*.

8   Ibid.

9   Ben Goldacre, 12 June 2009, 'Cocaine Study That Got up the Nose of the US', theguardian.com.

10 World Health Organization, 2005, 'Cocaine Project: Summary Papers', tdpf.org.uk.

11 Cited by Nick Davies, 12 June 2001, 'Make Heroin Legal', theguardian.com.

12 Costa, *World Drug Report 2009*.

13 Transform Drug Policy Foundation, April 2009, 'A Comparison of the Cost-Effectiveness of the Prohibition and Regulation of Drugs', tdpf.org.uk.

7. Rewild the Child

1   Kings College London, April 2011, *Understanding the Diverse Benefits of Learning in Natural Environments*, webarchive,nationalarchives.gov.uk.

2   Stuart Nundy, 2001, *Raising Achievement through the Environment: The Case for Fieldwork and Field Centres*, National Association of Field Studies Officers, as quoted in *Understanding the Diverse Benefits of Learning in Natural Environments*.

3   As listed in William Bird, 2007, *Natural Thinking: Investigating the Links Between the Natural Environment, Biodiversity and Mental Health*, Royal Society for the Protection of Birds, rspb.org.uk.

4   'Executive Summary', *TurnAround* (addendum to both reports), Wilderness Foundation, UK, wildernessfoudnation.org.uk; Jo Peacock, Jules Petty and Rachel Hine, 2007, *Wilderness Therapy: The TurnAround 2007*, Wilderness Foundation, UK, wildernessfoudnation.org.uk; 'Executive Summary', *TurnAround* (addendum to first report), Wilderness Foundation, UK, wildernessfoudnation.org.uk.

5   Ofsted, November 2012, *Learning Outside the Classroom: How Far Should You Go?*, Ofsted, Manchester, nationalarchives.gov.uk.

6   'LotC Manifesto', lotc.org.uk; 'View the Signatories', lotc.org.uk.

7   Defra, 7 June 2011, 'The Natural Choice: Securing the Value of Nature', White Paper, gov.uk.

8   Andrew Bomford, 9 June 2011, 'Cuts May Deny Poorer Children Outdoor School Trips', bbc.com.

9   20 March 2013, 'The Dangers of the New National Curriculum Proposals: Michael Gove Has Prioritised Facts over Creativity', telegraph.co.uk; Greg Hurst, 1 October 2013, 'Narrow Test-Based Education "Harms Children"', thetimes.co.uk.

10   'Our Vision', widehorizons.org.uk.

8. The Child Inside

1   Jay Griffiths, 2013, *Kith: The Riddle of the Childscape*, Penguin Books, London.

2   Stephen Moss, 2012, *Natural Childhood*, nationaltrust.org.uk.

3   Department for Communities and Local Government, 27 March 2012, *National Planning Policy Framework*, gov.uk.

4   Communities and Local Government Committee, 9 December 2014, *Fourth Report*, parliament.uk.

5   Please see the 1997 report *Child's Play: Facilitating Play on Housing Estates* by the Chartered Institute of Housing and the Joseph Rowntree Foundation for an excellent summary of what child-centred design might involve, at jrf.org.uk.

6   Scottish Government, December 2014, *A Consultation on the Future of Land Reform in Scotland: Annex A*, gov.scot; Land Reform Review Group, 2014, 'The Land of Scotland and the Common Good', scotland.gov.uk.

7   Department for Communities and Local Government, 8 May 2015, *2010 to 2015 Government Policy: Localism*, gov.scot.

8   See Stuart Gulliver and Steven Tolson, 2013, *Delivering Great Places to Live: 10 Propositions Aimed at Transforming Placemaking in Scotland*, University of Glasgow, RICS, lanscapeinstitute.org.

9. Amputating Life Close to Its Base

1   Tableau, *What Have UG and PG Leavers Done 6 Months after Oxford?*, tableau.com; Careers Service, *Annual Report 2015*, careers.cam.ac.uk; LSE, *Overview of LSE Graduate Destinations*, lse.ac.uk; London Business School, *MBA Employment Report*, london.edu.

2   Dina Medland, 5 June 2013, 'Whistleblowing Almost Killed Me', ft.com.

10. 'Bug Splats'

1   Barack Obama, 16 December 2012, 'Obama's Newton Speech: Full Text', theguardian.com.

2   Michael Hastings, 16 April 2012, 'The Rise of the Killer Drones: How America Goes to War in Secret', *Rolling Stone*.

3   Greg Miller, 23 October 2012, 'Plan for Hunting Terrorists Signals U.S. Intent to Keep Adding Names to Kill Lists', washingtonpost.com.

4   International Human Rights and Conflict Resolution Clinic, Stanford Law School and Global Justice Clinic, NYU School of Law, September 2012, *Living under Drones: Death, Injury and Trauma to Civilians from US Drone Practices in Pakistan*, livingunderdrones.org.

5   For example: Yousaf Ali, 5 November 2006, 'Most Bajaur Victims Were under 20', thenews.com.pk.

6   International Human Rights and Conflict Resolution Clinic at Stanford Law School and Global Justice Clinic at NYU School of Law, 'Living under Drones'.

7   Jay Carney, 12 December 2012, 'Press Briefing', whitehouse.gov.

8   John Brennan, 30 April 2012, 'The Ethics and Efficacy of the President's Counterterrorism Strategy', wilsoncenter.org.
9   Ibid.
10   International Human Rights and Conflict Resolution Clinic, *Living under Drones*.
11   18 March 2011, 'Rare Condemnation by PN, Army Chief: 40 Killed in Drone Attack', dawn.com.
12   Ibid.
13   Glenn Greenwald, 23 October 2012, 'Joe Klein's Sociopathic Defence of Drone Killings of Children', theguardian.com
14   Ibid.
15   'Obama's Newton Speech', theguardian.com.

11. Kin Hell

1   Coalition for Marriage, c4m.org.uk.
2   William N. Eskridge, 1993, 'A History of Same-Sex Marriage', *Virginia Law Review,* vol. 79, no. 7; Jim Duffy, 11 August 1998, 'When Marriage between Gays Was a Rite', libchrist.com; 'Same-Sex Unions throughout Time: A History of Gay Marriage', randomhistory.com.
3   Luke 14:26.
4   John R. Gillis, 1996, *A World of Their Own Making: Myth, Ritual and the Quest for Family Values*, Basic Books, New York.
5   See George Monbiot, 1994, *No Man's Land: An Investigative Journey through Kenya and Tanzania*, Macmillan, London.
6   Gillis, *A World of Their Own Making.*
7   Ibid.
8   Ibid., p. 148.
9   Colin Heywood, 2001, *A History of Childhood*, Polity, Cambridge.
10   Christina Odone, 14 May 2012, 'Heterosexual Marriage? I'm Sorry, You Can't Discuss That', telegraph.co.uk.

12. The Sacrificial Caste

1   Chris McGreal, 9 January 2012, 'The US Schools with Their Own Police', theguardian.com.
2   Ibid.
3   'Judge William Admas Beats Daughter for Using the Internet (Update)', youtube.com.

4   Giles Termlett, 5 January 2012, 'Spain's "Stolen Babies" Attempt to Blow Lid off Scandal', theguardian.com; Mary Raftery, 8 June 2011, 'Ireland's Magdalene Laundries Scandal Must Be Laid to Rest', theguardian.com; Henry McDonald, 20 May 2009, 'Irish Catholic Church Child Abuse: "A Cruel and Wicked System"', theguardian.com; *Guardian*, 16 February 2000, 'Questions and Answers That Surround a Catalogue of Abuse against Children', theguardian.com; Patrick Barkham, 7 April 2011, 'Child Migrants: "I didn't Belong to Anybody"', theguardian.com; Nick Bryant, 15 November 2009, 'Ordeal of Australia's Child Migrants', bbc.co.uk.

5   Howells School, Denbigh, by phone, 13 January 2012.

6   Joy Schaverien, May 2011, 'Boarding School Syndrome: Broken Attachments – A Hidden Trauma', *British Journal of Psychotherapy*, vol. 27, no. 2.

7   Ibid.

13. A Modest Proposal for Tackling Youth

1   Mark Townsend, 19 June 2010, 'Teenager-Repellent "Mosquito" Must Be Banned, Says Europe', theguardian.com.

2   Amelia Hill, 24 June 2010, 'Mosquito Youth Dispersal Alarms Face Ban', theguardian.com.

3   Townend, 'Teenager-Repellent "Mosquito" Must Be Banned, Says Europe'.

4   Council of Europe, 25 June 2010, 'PACE Calls for Ban on Acoustic "Youth Dispersal" Devices', assembly.coe.int.

5   Children's Rights Alliance of England, 25 June 2010, 'Pressure Mounts on UK to Ban Anti-Child Electronic Devices', crae.org.uk.

6   BBC, 13 March 2010, 'Calls to Raise Age of Criminal Responsibility Rejected', bbc.co.uk.

7   Carolyne Willow, 24 August 2006, 'Treat Children as Humans, Not Nuisances', theguardian.com.

8   Education and Inspections Act 2006, Section 103, legislation.gov.uk.

9   Schedule 10, Serious Organised Crime and Police Act 2005, legislation.gov.uk.

10 Charlotte Walsh, August 2008, 'The Mosquito: A Repellent Response', *Youth Justice*, vol. 8, no. 2, sagepub.com; Tom Whitehead, 13 February 2008, 'Manilow at Full Blast to Blow Street Yobs Away', dailyexpress.co.uk.

11 Crime and Disorder Act 1998, Section 14, legislation.gov.uk.

12 Anti-Social Behaviour Act 2003, Section 30, legislation.gov.uk.

14. Pro-Death

1   Cardinals Cormac Murphy-O'Connor and Keith O'Brien, 22 October 2007, 'Open Letter on the Occasion of the 40th Anniversary of the 1967 Abortion Act from the Presidents of the Catholic Bishops' Conferences of Scotland and England and Wales', christiantoday.com.

2   Riazat Butt, 22 February 2008, 'Archbishop Orders Catholic Hospital Board to Resign in Ethics Dispute', the guardian.com.

3   Ibid.

4   Catholic News Agency, 19 November 2007, 'Defend Marriage and Family Life at All Costs, Benedict XVI Tells Africans', catholicnewsagency.com.

5   Cicely Marston and John Cleland, March 2003, 'Relationships between Contraception and Abortion: A Review of the Evidence', *International Family Planning Perspectives*, vol. 29, no. 1, guttmacher.org.

6   Ibid.

7   Gilda Sedgh et al., 13 October 2007, 'Induced Abortion: Estimated Rates and Trends Worldwide', *Lancet*, vol. 370, pp. 1338–45.

8   Catholic News Agency, 'Defend Marriage'.

9   The Guttmacher Institute, May 1999, 'Abortion in Context: United States and Worldwide', guttmacher.org.

10 Sedgh et al., 'Induced Abortion'.

11 Office of National Statistics and Department of Health, June 2007, 'Abortion Statistics, England and Wales: 2006', webarchive.national-archives.gov.uk.

12 Hannah Brown, 17 November 2007, 'Abortion Round the World', *British Medical Journal*, ncbi.nlm.nih.gov.

13 UNICEF, July 2001, 'A League Table of Teenage Births in Rich Nations', UNICEF Innocenti Research Centre, Florence. unicef-irc.org.

14 Ibid.

15 Alba DiCenso et al., 15 June 2002, 'Interventions to Reduce Unintended Pregnancies among Adolescents: Systematic Review of Randomised Controlled Trials', *British Medical Journal*, vol. 324, no. 1426, bmj.com

16 World Health Organisation, 2007, *Unsafe Abortion: Global and Regional Estimates of the Incidence of Unsafe Abortion and Associated Mortality in 2003*, fifth edition, who.int.

17 Andy Coghlan, 21 October 2007, 'Family Planning Lowers Abortion Rates', *New Scientist*.

18 WHO, *Unsafe Abortion*.

19 Ibid.

20   James Chapman, 25 February 2008, 'Cameron: Cut the Abortion Limit to 21 Weeks', *Daily Mail*.
21   Catholic News Agency, 'Defend Marriage'.
22   Tegan Fleming, 21 June 2007, 'Contraception Spree: Brazilian Government Lowers Birth Control Costs for the Poor', *Pharmacy News*.
23   See globalgagrule.org.

15. Everything Is Connected

1   Nacy Sisinyark, August 2006, 'The Biggest Bear . . . Ever', Alaska Department of Fish and Game, adfg.alaska.gov.
2   George Monbiot, 3 April 2014, '"Like a Demon in a Medieval Book": Is This How the Marsupial Lion Killed Its Prey?', theguardian.com.
3   S. Rule et al., 23 March 2012, 'The Aftermath of Megafaunal Extinction: Ecosystem Transformation in Pleistocene Australia', ncbi.nlm.hih.gov.
4   C. J. Sandom et al., 18 March 2014, 'High Herbivore Density Associated with Vegetation Diversity in Interglacial Ecosystems', ncbi.nlm.hih.gov.
5   Trish J. Lavery et al., July 2014, 'Whales Sustain Fisheries: Blue Whales Stimulate Primary Production in the Southern Ocean', *Marine Mammal Science*, vol. 30, no. 3.
6   Joe Roman et al., September 2014, 'Whales as Marine Ecosystem Engineers', *Frontiers in Ecology and the Environment*, vol. 12, no. 7.
7   V. Smetacek, 10 October 2006, 'Are Declining Antarctic Krill Stocks a Result of Global Warming or Decimation of the Whales?', epic.awi.de.
8   Laura V. Smith et al., August 2013, 'Preliminary Investigation into the Stimulation of Phytoplankton Photophysiology and Growth by Whale Faeces', *Journal of Experimental Marine Biology and Ecology*.
9   Joe Roman and James J. McCarthy, 11 October 2010, 'The Whale Pump: Marine Mammals Enhance Primary Productivity in a Coastal Basin', *Plus One*.
10   Steve Nichol, 12 July 2011, 'Vital Giants: Why Living Seas Need Whales', New Scientist, no. 2820.
11   Joe Roman et al., 'Whales as Marine Ecosystem Engineers'.
12   Sustainable Human, 30 November 2014, 'How Whales Change Climate', YouTube.com.
13   Sustainable Human, 13 February 2014, 'How Wolves Change Rivers', YouTube.com.
14   Joe Roman et al., 'Whales as Marine Ecosystem Engineers'.
15   Christopher C. Wilmers et al., October 2012, 'Do Trophic Cascades Affect the Storage and Flux of Atmospheric Carbon?: An Analysis of Sea Otters and Kelp Forests', *Frontiers in Ecology and the Environment*, vol. 10, no. 8.

16   Matthew S. Savoca and Gabrielle A. Nevitt, 18 March 2014, 'Evidence
     That Dimethyl Sulfide Facilitates a Tritrophic Mutualism between Marine
     Primary Producers and Top Predators', PNAS, vol. 111, no. 11.
17   Oswarlk J. Schmitz, 19 September 2013, 'Animating the Carbon Cycle',
     Ecosystems, vol. 17, no. 2.
18   Ibid.
19   Ibid.

16. Civilisation Is Boring

1   Aldo Leopold, 1949, *A Sand County Almanac*, Oxford University Press,
    Oxford, p. 197.
2   Damian Carrington, 30 September 2014, 'Earth Has Lost Half of Its
    Wildlife in the Past 40 Years, Says WWF', theguardian.com.
3   Blaire van Valkenburgh, 'Predator–Prey Dynamics in Late Pleistocene
    North America', University of California, Los Angeles, eci.ox.ac.uk.
4   W. H. Auden, 1967, *Collected Poems*, Random House, New York, p. 723.
5   rewildingeurope.com/assets/uploads/Downloads/Rewilding-Europe-
    Brochure-2012.pdf.
6   Elizabeth Taylor, 16 November 2012, 'Heeding the Coyote's Call: Jim
    Sterba on the Fight with Wildlife over Space in the Sprawl', chicagotrib-
    une.com.

17. End of an Era

1   *The Future We Want*, Rio+20, slideshare.net.
2   Ozone Secretariat, United Nations Environment Programme, *The
    Montreal Protocol on Substances That Deplete the Ozone Layer*, unep.ch.
3   *Guardian*, 24 July 2012, 'Name a Species: A Competition to Invent
    Common Names for 10 Threatened UK Species', theguardian.com.

18. The Population Myth

1   Optimum Population Trust, 26th August 2009, 'Gaia Scientist to be OPT
    Patron', populationmatters.com.
2   David Satterthwaite, September 2009, 'The Implications of Population
    Growth and Urbanization for Climate Change', *Environment and
    Urbanization*, vol. 21, no. 2, eausagepub.com.

3   Friends of the Earth International, June 2005, *Gas Flaring in Nigeria: A Human Rights, Environmental and Economic Monstrosity*, maanystavat.fi.

4   For example, Satterthwaite cites the study by Gerald Leach and Robin Mearns, 1989, *Beyond the Woodfuel Crisis: People, Land and Trees in Africa*, Earthscan Publications, London.

5   John Harlow, 24 May 2009, 'Billionaire Club in Bid to Curb Overpopulation', *The Sunday Times*.

6   Wolfgang Lutz, Warren Sanderson and Sergei Scherbov, 20 January 2008, 'The Coming Acceleration of Global Population Ageing', *Nature*, vol. 451, pp. 716–19, nature.com.

7   United Nations Department of Economic and Social Affairs, 2005, 'World Population Prospects: The 2004 Revision', un.org.

19. The Dawning

1   R. Evans, June 2004, 'Outdoor Pigs and Flooding: An English Case Study', *Soil Use and Management*, vol. 20, no. 2.

2   Friends of the Earth, December 2008, *What's Feeding Our Food?: The Environmental and Social Impacts of the Livestock Sector*, foe.co.uk.

3   Brian Machovina et al., 1 December 2015, 'Biodiversity Conservation: The Key Is Reducing Meat Consumption', *Science of the Total Environment*, vol. 536.

4   Roger Harrabin, 26 March 2015, 'River Health Revealed in "Shocking" Figures', bbc.com.

5   Lee Brown et al., 1 October 2014, 'Grouse Moor Burning Causes Widespread Environmental Changes', University of Leeds, leeds.ac.uk.

20. Sheepwrecked

1   Jacobs UK Ltd for Transport Scotland, February 2013, 'A83 Trunk Road Route Study Part A: Rest and Be Thankful', Final Report, transportscotland.gov.uk.

2   Ibid.

3   Ibid.

4   M. G. Winter and A. Corby, 2012, *A83 Rest and Be Thankful: Ecological and Related Landslide Mitigation Options*, Transport Scotland, Published Progress Report PPR 636, transportscotland.gov.uk.

5   Ibid.

6   Jacobs UK Ltd for Transport Scotland, 'A83 Trunk Road Route Study Part A: Rest and Be Thankful'.

7   The National Ecosystem Assessment states that 'agricultural land occupied some 1.64 million ha or 79 per cent of Wales in 2008' and that 'crops now account for only 3 per cent of the agricultural land area'. UK National Ecosystem Assessment, Chapter 20, uknea.unep-wcmc.org.

8   Most of the animals farmed are sheep, whose major product is meat. There are also over a million cattle (see ibid). These are split almost evenly between dairy and beef, but the male calves from both industries are reared for beef.

9   UK National Ecosystem Assessment, Chapter 20, Figure 20.39, uknea. unep-wcmc.org.

21. Ripping Apart the Fabric of the Nation

1   R. C. Palmer and R. P. Smith, December 2013, 'Soil Structural Degradation in SW England and Its Impact on Surface-Water Runoff Generation', *Soil Use and Management*, vol. 29, no. 4.

2   Miles King, 6 February 2014, 'Lost in the Drainage Maize', anewnature-blog.wordpress.com.

3   NFU, 3 January 2014, 'Briefing: AD on Track for 1,000 Plants?', nfuonline.com.

4   John Boardman and Karel Vandaele, 18 January 2010, 'Soil Erosion, Muddy Floods and the Need for Institutional Memory', *Area*, vol. 42, no. 4.

5   The Rivers Trust, 2011, 'Defra Strategic Evidence and Partnership Project', theriverstrust.org.

6   Discussion in 'Agricultural Matters' started by Banana Bar, 30 December 2013, thefarmingforum.co.uk.

7   Farming Regulation Task Force, May 2011, *Striking a Balance: Reducing Burdens; Increasing Responsibility; Earning Recognition*, gov.uk.

8   Ibid.

9   George Eustice, 25 February 2014, speech to the National Farmers Union Conference, 'Backing the Business of British Farming', gov.uk.

10   Commission of the European Communities, 22 September 2006, *Proposal for a Directive of the European Parliament and of the Council Establishing a Framework for the Protection of Soil*, eur-lex.europa.eu.

11   NFU, 22 May 2014, 'Withdrawal of Soil Framework Directives Welcomed', nfuonline.com.

22. Drowning in Money

1　Guy Shrubsole, 6 January 2014, 'Cameron's Claims on Flood Defences Don't Stack Up', Friends of the Earth, foe.co.uk.

2　Coed Cadw and Coed Cymru, no date given, 'The Pontbren Project: A Farmer-Led Approach to Sustainable Land Management in the Uplands', europeanlandowners.org.

3　B. Reynolds et al., February 2014, 'The Impact of Rural Land Management Changes on Soil Hydraulic Properties and Runoff Processes: Results from Experimental Plots in Upland UK', *Hydrological Processes* 28, no. 4, doi: 10.1002/hyp.9826.

4　Howard Wheater et al., 2008, 'Impacts of Upland Land Management on Flood Risk: Multi-scale Modelling Methodology and Results from the Pontbren Experiment', FRMRC Research Report UR 16, nora.nerc. ac.uk.

5　Ibid.

6　See for example Natural England, Environment Agency, Defra, Welsh Government et al., 2010, *Greater Working with Natural Processes in Flood and Coastal Erosion Risk Management,* webarchive.nationalarchives.gov. uk.

7　Natural Resources Wales, 9 January 2014, by email.

8　I talked to one of the employees over the weekend: everyone is being made redundant as all funding has ceased.

9　*Official Journal of the European Union*, 31 January 2009. Council Regulation (EC), no. 73/2009 of 19 January 2009, establishing common rules for direct support schemes for farmers under the Common Agricultural Policy and establishing certain support schemes for farmers, amending Regulations (EC) no. 1290/2005, (EC) no. 247/2006, (EC) no 378/2007 and repealing Regulation (EC) no. 1782/2003, Annex III, eur-lex.europa. eu. This rule remains unchanged in the current round.

10　A speech by the Department for Environment, Food and Rural Affairs and the Rt Hon Owen Paterson, 7 January 2014, *Opportunity in Agriculture*, gov.uk.

11　European Commission, 26 June 2013, 'CAP Reform: An Explanation of the Main Elements', europa.eu.

12　Natural England, Environment Agency, Defra, Welsh Government et al., 2012, 'Greater Working with Natural Processes in Flood and Coastal Erosion Risk Management', webarchive.nationalarchives.gov.uk.

13　John Boardman and Karel Vandaele, December 2010, 'Soil Erosion, Muddy Floods and the Need for Institutional Memory', *Area*, vol. 42, no. 4, onlinelibrary.wiley.com.

14   R. Evans, April 2010, 'Runoff and Soil Erosion in Arable Britain: Changes in Perception and Policy since 1945', *Environmental Science and Policy*, vol. 13, no. 2, sciencedirect.com.

15   Boardman and Vandaele, 'Soil Erosion'.

16   Speech by Owen Paterson, 10 October 2013, *Hansard* (column 292), publications.parliament.uk.

17   Owen Paterson, 2013, 'In Evidence to the Environment, Food and Rural Affairs Committee', *Managing Flood Risk*, vol. 1, publications.parliament. uk.

18   I am grateful to Dr Richard Hey and to Charles Rangely-Wilson for the discussions we had about these issues; Natural England, Environment Agency, Defra, Welsh Government et al., 'Greater Working with Natural Processes'; Sir Michael Pitt, 2008, 'The Pitt Review: Learning Lessons from the 2007 Floods', webarchive.nationalarchives.gov.uk.

19   See wildennerdale.co.uk; I hope before long to write up the extraordinary story I was told by a representative of United Utilities about the sharply differing responses of the rewilded River Liza in Ennerdale and the still-canalised St John's Beck in Thirlmere to the famous 2009 downpour.

20   Natural England, Environment Agency, Defra, Welsh Government et al., 'Greater Working with Natural Processes'.

21   Miles King, 7 January 2014, 'Have We Reached Peak Paterson?', anewna-tureblog.wordpress.com.

22   Speech by Owen Paterson, 'Improving the Environment and Growing the Economy, Can We Have It All?' A speech by Owen Paterson, 20 November 2013, policyexchange.org.uk.

23   Charles Rangeley-Wilson, 26 April 2013, 'A Storm-Cloud for Rivers?', charlesrangeleywilson.com.

24   Judy England and Lydia Burgess-Gamble, August 2013, 'Evidence: Impacts of Dredging', Environment Agency, wildtrout.org.

25   Environment Agency, 2009, *River Severn Catchment Flood Management Plan*, Summary Report, environment-agency.gov.uk.

26   Pitt, 'The Pitt Review: Lessons Learned from the 2007 Floods'.

27   Department for Environment, Food and Rural Affairs, 14 October 2013, *Press Release: River Maintenance Pilots Begin*, Environment Agency, gov. uk.

28   Damian Carrington, 7 January 2014, 'Massive Cuts Risk England's Ability to Deal with Floods, MPs Say', theguardian.com.

29   Defra and the Environment Agency, 2011, 'Understanding the Risks, Empowering Communities, Building Resilience: The National Flood and Coastal Erosion Risk Management Strategy for England', official-docu-ments.gov.uk.

30   Izaac, Walton, 1915 (1653), *The Compleat Angler*, Oxford University Press, London, pp. 206–7.

31   Animal Aid, 2013, 'Calling the Shots: The Power and Privilege of the Grouse-Shooting Elite', animalaid.org.uk.

32   See also the Upper Calder Valley Ban the Burn Campaign, energyroyd. org.uk.

33   Department for Environment, Food and Rural Affairs, 10 March 2014, 'The Lower Dove Flood Defence Scheme Is a Succesful Tale of Private–Public Partnership', gov.uk.

23. Small Is Bountiful

1   A statement by President Robert Gabriel Mugabe on the occasion of the Food and Agriculture Organisation High Level Summit on World Food Security and the Challenges of Climate Change and Bio-Energy at Rome, June 2008, fao.org.

2   Amartya Sen, February 1962, 'An Aspect of Indian Agriculture', *Economic Weekly*, vol. 14, epw.in.

3   Fatma Gül Ünal, October 2006, 'Small Is Beautiful: Evidence of Inverse Size Yield Relationship in Rural Turkey', *Policy Innovations*, policyinnovations.org.

4   Giovanni Cornia, 1985, 'Farm Size, Land Yields and the Agricultural Production function: An Analysis for Fifteen Developing Countries', *World Development*, vol. 13, researchgate.net.

5   For example, Peter B. R. Hazell, January 2005, 'Is There a Future for Small Farms?', *Agricultural Economics*, vol. 32.

6   Rasmus Heltberg, October 1998, 'Rural Market Imperfections and the Farm Size: Productivity Relationship: Evidence from Pakistan', *World Development*, vol. 26.

7   See Shenggen Fan and Connie Chan-Kang, 2005. 'Is Small Beautiful? Farm Size, Productivity and Poverty in Asian Agriculture', *Agricultural Economics*, vol. 32.

8   Hazell, 'Is There a Future for Small Farms?'

9   'Country Profile: Turkey', new-ag.info, as quoted in Ünal, 'Small Is Beautiful'.

10   *OECD Economic Surveys: Turkey 2006*, oecd.org, p. 18. I was led to references 9 and 10 via Fatma Gül Ünal, 'Small Is Beautiful'.

11   Food and Agriculture Organization of the United Nations, 'Declaration of the High-Level Conference on World Food Security: The Challenges of Climate Change and Bioenergy,' fao.org.

12   International Assessment of Agricultural Knowledge, Science and

Technology for Development (IAASTD), 2008, 'Agriculture at a Crossroads: Global Summary for Decision Makers', unep.org.

13 Ibid., FAQs.

24. Leave It in the Ground

1   Under two schemes: the Coal Investment Aid and the UK Coal Operating Aid Scheme, see Department of Trade and Industry, 2006, *Coal Industry in the UK*, dti.gov.uk; DBERR, 2007, UK Coal Operating Aid Scheme: *Coal Subsidy Programme / 823100 Cops0010 – Expenditure Profile by Tranche*, berr.gov.uk.

2   Department of Trade and Industry, May 2007, 'Meeting the Energy Challenge: A White Paper on Energy', gov.uk, p. 107.

3   Stephen Timms MP, Department of Trade and Industry, 20 January 2004, letter to Rhodri Morgan AM.

4   Mike O'Brien MP, Department of Trade and Industry, 14 December 2004, letter to Rhodri Morgan AM.

5   The scheme will extract 10.8 million tonnes of coal. Average carbon per tonne of coal = 746 kilogrammes (bioenergy.ornl.gov). CO_2 is 3.667 times the weight of carbon. The figure for sustainable emissions – 0.537 tonnes per person per year – is explained in a 4 December 2007 article of mine titled 'What Is Progress?', monbiot.com.

6   This is equal to 3.4 million tonnes of coal.

7   Banks Developments, 29 November 2007, 'Banks Group's Shotton Surface Mine Proposals Approved', banksdevelopments.com.

8   Department of Trade and Industry, 19 December 2006, 'West of Shetland Task Force Forge Ahead into New Year', webarchive.nation-archives.gov.uk.

9   Department of Trade and Industry, 'West of Shetland Task Force Forge Ahead into New Year'.

10 Quoted by Ed Crooks, 7 December 2007, 'Boost for North Sea Companies', *Financial Times*.

11 International Energy Agency, 2007, *World Energy Outlook, 2007*, table 1.9, p. 95. worldenergyoutlook.org.

12 Alastair Darling, 23 May 2007, parliamentary answer, column 1289, parliament.the-stationery-office.co.uk.

13 Ed Crooks, 9 November 2007, 'Pay-off Time for Sasol pioneers?', *Financial Times*.

25. Applauding Themselves to Death

1   United Nations Framework Convention on Climate Change, unfccc.int.
2   See the section titled Key Steps: unfccc.int/2860.php.
3   United Nations Framework Convention on Climate Change, 2 February 2015, *Report of the Conference of the Parties on Its Twentieth Session, Held in Lima from 1 to 14 December 2014*, unfccc.int.
4   See above, Chapter 24, 'Leave It in the Ground'.
5   George Monbiot, 5 December 2007, 'Bear to Hear the Truth You've Spoken', theguardian.com.
6   The Stationery Office, 2015, 'Maximising Economic Recovery of UK Petroleum', *Infrastructure Act 2015*, legislation.gov.uk.
7   'Wood Review Implementation', gov.uk.
8   Emily Gosden, 6 December 2014, 'Energy Secretary Says Action to Tackle Climate Change Could Make Fossil Fuel Companies the "Sub-Prime Assets of the Future"', telegraph.co.uk.
9   'Malcom Webb to Secretary of State', scribd.com.
10 'Secretary of State to Malcom Webb', scribd.com.
11 Thomas L. Friedman, 7 June 2014, 'Obama on Obama on Climate', nytimes.com.
12 Michael Klare, 12 September 2014, 'How Obama Became the Oil President', motherjones.com.
13 Subhanker Banerjee, 3 March 2015, 'Tomgram: Subhankar Banerjee, Arctic Nightmares', tomdispatch.com.
14 Michael Le Page, 30 September 2013, 'IPCC Digested: Just Leave the Fossil Fuels Underground', newscientist.com.
15 'Representative Proposals to Halt the Allocation of New Blocks in the 23rd Licensing Round on the Norwegian Shelf', stortinget.no.
16 Friedman, 'Obama on Obama on Climate'.
17 George Monbiot, 2 August 2012, 'Stop This Culture of Paying Politicians for Denying Climate Change', theguardian.com.
18 15 June 2008, 'Formal End to Oil Companies Proxy Chaco War 1932/35', mercopress.com.
19 See kyoto2.org.

26. The Grime behind the Crime

1   Kevin Drum, January/February 2013, 'America's Real Criminal Element: Lead', motherjones.com.

2   Rick Nevin, May 2000, 'How Lead Exposure Relates to Temporal Changes in IQ, Violent Crime, and Unwed Pregnancy', *Environmental Research*, vol. 83, no. 1, sciencedirect.com; Rick Nevin, 2007. 'Understanding International Crime Trends: The Legacy of Preschool Lead Exposure', *Environmental Research*, vol. 104, no. 3, sciencedirect.com; Jessica Wolpaw Reyes, May 2007, 'Environmental Policy as Social Policy?: The Impact of Childhood Lead Exposure on Crime', National Bureau of Economic Research Working Paper 13097, nber.org.

3   The three papers whose citations I checked were Nevin, 'How Lead Exposure Relates to Temporal Changes in IQ, Violent Crime, and Unwed Pregnancy'; Nevin, 'Understanding International Crime Trends'; and Reyes, 'Environmental Policy as Social Policy?'.

4   Patricia L. McCalla and Kenneth C. Land, 2004, 'Trends in Environmental Lead Exposure and Troubled Youth, 1960–1995: An Age–Period–Cohort–Characteristic Analysis', *Social Science Research*, vol. 33.

5   M. J. Lynch and P. B. Stretesky, May 2001, 'The Relationship between Lead Exposure and Homicide', *Archives of Pediatrics and Adolescent Medicine*, vol. 155, no. 5; M. J. Lynch and P. B. Stretesky, June 2004, 'The Relationship between Lead and Crime', *Journal of Health and Social Behavior*, vol. 45, no. 2, hsb.sagepub.com; Howard W. Mielke and Sammy Zahran, 2012, 'The Urban Rise and Fall of Air Lead (Pb) and the Latent Surge and Retreat of Societal Violence', *Environment International*, vol. 43, sciencedirect.com.

6   Bureau of Justice, no date given, 'Homicide Trends in the US', bjs.ojp.usdoj.gov.

7   Lynch and Stretesky, 'The Relationship between Lead and Crime'.

8   Mielke and Zahran, 'The Urban Rise and Fall of Air Lead (Pb) and the Latent Surge and Retreat of Societal Violence'.

9   Herbert L. Needleman et al., 2002, 'Bone Lead Levels in Adjudicated Delinquents: A Case Control Study', *Neurotoxicology and Teratology*, vol. 24.

10 David K. Marcus, Jessica J. Fulton and Erin J. Clarke, 2010, 'Lead and Conduct Problems: A Meta-Analysis', *Journal of Clinical Child and Adolescent Psychology*, vol.39, no. 2, tandfonline.com.

11 R. K. Byers and E. E. Lord, 1943, 'Late Effects of Lead Poisoning on Mental Development', *American Journal of Diseases of Children*, vol. 66.

12 Kim M. Cecil et al., 2008, 'Decreased Brain Volume in Adults with Childhood Lead Exposure', *Public Library of Science (PLOS) Medicine*, vol. 5, no. 5, journals.plos.org.

13 Joel T. Nigg et al., January 2010, 'Confirmation and Extension of Association of Blood Lead with Attention-Deficit/Hyperactivity

Disorder (ADHD) and ADHD Symptom Domains at Population-Typical Exposure Levels', *Journal of Child Psychology and Psychiatry*, vol. 51, no.1, onlinelibrary.wiley.com; Joe M. Braun et al., 2006, 'Exposures to Environmental Toxicants and Attention Deficit Hyperactivity Disorder in U.S. Children, *Environmental Health Perspectives*, vol. 114, ncbi.nlm.nih.gov; Danielle Boisvert, Jamie Vaske and John Paul Wright, July 2009, 'Blood Lead Levels in Early Childhood Predict Adulthood Psychopathy', *Youth Violence and Juvenile Justice*, vol. 7, no. 3, yvj.sagepub.com.

14   'There is no lower blood lead threshold for IQ losses', according to Nevin, 'Understanding International Crime Trends'; David Bellinger concludes, 'No level of lead exposure appears to be "safe" and even the current "low" levels of exposure in children are associated with neurodevelopmental deficits', April 2008, 'Very Low Lead Exposures and Children's Neurodevelopment', *Current Opinions in Pediatrics*, vol. 20, no. 2, journals.lww.com.

15   Royal Society of Canada, 1986, 'Lead in the Canadian Environment', Science and Regulation, cited by Nevin, 'Understanding International Crime Trends'.

16   Agency for Toxic Substances and Disease Registry, 1988, *The Nature and Extent of Lead Poisoning in Children in the United States. US Department of Health and Human Services*, cited by Nevin, 'Understanding International Crime Trends'.

17   Nevin, 'Understanding International Crime Trends'.

18   Rick Nevin, February 2012, 'Lead Poisoning and *The Bell Curve*', Munich Personal RePEc Archive, MPRA Paper No. 36569, mpra.ub.uni-muenchen.de.

19   Innospec, 'Octane Additives', www,innospecinc,com/our-markets/octane-additives/octane-additives.

20   Ann Wroe, 21 November 2012, 'Obituary: A Toxin in Your Tank', economist.com; Anne Roberts and Elizabeth O'Brien, June 2011, 'Supply Chain for the Lead in Leaded Petrol', *LEAD Action News*, vol. 11, no. 4.

21   Rob Evans, 18 March 2010, 'Chemical Firm Innospec Admits Bribing Foreign Officials', theguardian.com.

22   David Leigh et al., 30 June 2010, 'UK Firm Octel Bribed Iraqis to Keep Buying Toxic Fuel Additive', theguardian.com.

23   I was passed by Defra to the Department for Transport, then by the DfT to the Department for Business, which told me it was all down to the European list. It was clear that none of them was remotely interested in the issue, or had considered it before.

27. Going Critical

1   Suzanne Goldberg, 14 March 2011, 'Japan's Nuclear Crisis: Regulators Warned of Reactor Risks', theguardian.com.
2   Randall Munroe, 'Radiation Dose Chart', xkcd.com/radiation.
3   George Monbiot, 1 March 2010, 'Are We Really Going to Let Ourselves Be Duped into This Solar Panel Rip-off?', theguardian.com; George Monbiot, 11 March 2010, 'Solar PV Has Failed in Germany and It Will Fail in the UK', theguardian.com.
4   Callum Roberts, 2007, *The Unnatural History of the Sea: The Past and Future of Humanity and Fishing (Gaia Thinking)*, Gaia Books, London.
5   E. A. Wrigley, 2010, *Energy and the English Industrial Revolution*, Cambridge University Press, Cambridge, pp. 37 and 39.
6   The UK steel requirement in 2009 was 15.6 million tonnes, eef.org.uk
7   Wrigley, *Energy and the English Industrial Revolution*, pp. 16 and 17.
8   In the case of radioactive pollution, the multiple of 100 is not figurative: according to *Scientific American*, the fly ash produced by a coal-burning power plant 'carries into the surrounding environment 100 times more radiation than a nuclear power plant producing the same amount of energy', scientificamerican.com; Mark Lynas has just produced his first estimates for the amount of extra carbon dioxide which could be released as a result of the international reaction to the Fukushima crisis: see 'Nuclear: Difference between Two and Three Degrees', 21 March 2011, marklynas.org.
9   See gaslandthemovie.com.

28. Power Crazed

1   'China Coal Plant Emissions by Health Impact', http://bit.ly/JoTuPa.
2   Christine Ottery, 12 December 2013, 'Map: Health impact of China's Coal Plants', greenpeace.co.uk.
3   World Health Organisation, 28 February 2013, 'Global Report on Fukushima Nuclear Accident Details Health Risks', who.int.
4   Ibid.
5   Japan has so far commissioned 3.6 GW of coal plants to cover its nuclear shutdown see Martin Creamer; 13 December 2013, 'Global Coal Demand Growth Calls for Intensified Search for Clean Coal Solution', mining-weekly.com.
6   Joseph Mangano and Janette D. Sherman, 10 June 2011, 'Is the Increase in

Baby Deaths in the US a Result of Fukushima Fallout?', counterpunch. org; Anthony Gucciardi, 3 April 2013, 'Report: Third of U.S. West Coast Children Hit with Thyroid Problems Following Fukushima', inforwars. com.

7   Michael Moyer, 21 June 2011, 'Are Babies Dying in the Pacific Northwest Due to Fukushima? A Look at the Numbers', blogs.scientificamerican.com.

8   Michael Snyder, 5 August 2013, 'Radioactive Water from Fukushima Is Systematically Poisoning the Entire Pacific Ocean', thetruthwins.com; Timothy Bancroft-Hinchey, 6 March 2014, 'Fukushima: The Ticking Nuclear Bomb, over 800 Tons of Radioactive Material Pouring into Pacific Ocean', globalresearch.ca; Gary Stamper, August 2013, 'At the Very Least, Your Days of Eating Pacific Ocean Fish Are over: With Updates', collapsingintoconsciousness.com.

9   Woods Hole Oceanographic Institute, 'FAQ: Radiation from Fukushima', whoi.edu; Ivo Vegter, 3 December 2013, 'Fearful Fukushima Fiction Fatigue', dailymaverick.co.za.

10   See D. Mergler et al., 2007, 'Methylmercury Exposure and Health Effects in Humans: A Worldwide Concern'. *Ambio: A Journal of the Human Environment*, vol. 36, no. 1, http://www.bioone.org; Natural Resources Defense Council, 'Mercury Contamination in Fish: A Guide to Staying Healthy and Fighting Back', nrdc.org.

11   International Agency for Research on Cancer, 17 October 2013, 'Outdoor Air Pollution a Leading Environmental Cause of Cancer Deaths', World Health Organization, iarc.fr.

12   Christine Ottery, 6 December 2013, 'Map: Shanghai's Off-the-Charts Air Pollution', energydesk.greenpeace.org.

13   Yuyu Chen et al., 2013, 'Evidence on the Impact of Sustained Exposure to Air Pollution on Life Expectancy from China's Huai River Policy', Proceedings of the National Academy of Sciences, vol. 110, no. 32, pnas. org.

14   The Clean Air Taskforce, September 2010, *The Toll from Coal: An Updated Assessment of Death and Disease from America's Dirtiest Energy Source*, catf.us.

15   The Health and Environment Alliance, March 2013, *The Unpaid Health Bill: How Coal Power Plants Make Us Sick*, The Health and Environment Alliance, env-health.org.

16   M. Bellanger et al., 2013, 'Economic Benefits of Methylmercury Exposure Control in Europe: Monetary Value of Neurotoxicity Prevention', *Environmental Health*, vol. 12, no. 3, ehjournal.net.

17   The Health and Environment Alliance, *The Unpaid Health Bill*, env-health.org.

18 Vicky Ellis, 12 December 2013, 'Lords Vote against Tougher Coal Plants Rule in UK', energylivenews.com; Carbon Brief, 11 November 2013, 'Could Old Coal Threaten the UK's Carbon Budgets?', carbonbrief.org.

19 Ailun Yang, 20 November 2012, 'New Global Assessment Reveals Nearly 1,200 Proposed Coal-Fired Power Plants', World Resources Institute, wri.org.

20 Yemi Assefa et al., International Price Program, February 2013, 'Coal: A Key Player in Expanded U.S. Energy Exports', *Beyond the Numbers*, vol. 2, no. 3, U.S. Bureau of Labor Statistics, bls.gov.

21 Richard Anderson, 22 November 2012, 'Coal Resurgence Calls Undermine Clean Energy Commitments', bbc.com.

22 International Energy Agency, *World Energy Outlook 2011: Executive Summary*, woldenergyoutlook.org.

29. The Impossibility of Growth

1 Jeremy Grantham, 29 April 2011, 'Time to Wake Up: Days of Abundant Resources and Falling Prices Are Over Forever', *GMO Capital Newsletter*, theoildrum.com.

2 Grantham expressed this volume as 1,057 cubic metres. In his paper 'We Need to Talk about Growth (And We Need to Do the Sums as Well)', Michael Rowan translated this as 2.5 billion billion solar systems (persuademe.com.au). This source gives the volume of the solar system (if it is treated as a sphere) at 39,629,013,196,241.7 cubic kilometres, which is roughly 40 × 1,021 cubic metres. Multiplied by 2.5 billion billion, this gives 1,041.

3 E. A. Wrigley, 2010, *Energy and the English Industrial Revolution*, Cambridge University Press, Cambridge.

4 Suzanne Goldenberg, 12 May 2014, 'Western Antarctic Ice Sheet Collapse Has Already Begun, Scientists Warn', theguardian.com.

5 Adam Vaughan, 23 May 2014, 'Ecuador Signs Permits for Oil Drilling in Amazon's Yasuni National Park', theguardian.com.

6 El Universo, 23 May 2014, 'Ecuador: Gobierno Concede Licencia para la Explotación de Dos Campos del ITT', entornointeligente.com.

7 Jonathan Watts, 16 August 2013, 'Ecuador Approves Yasuni National Park Oil Drilling in Amazon Rainforest', theguardian.com.

8 World Wildlife Fund, 'Virunga: Protecting Africa's Oldest National Park', wwf.org.uk.

9 Terry Macalister and Matthew Weaver, 23 May 2014, '"4.4bn Barrels of Oil" in Weald Basin: Report', theguardian.com.

10   Emily Gosden, 26 January 2014, 'Fracking Could Be Allowed under Homes without Owners' Permission', telegraph.co.uk; Weaver and Macalister, '"4.4bn Barrels of Oil" in Weald Basin: Report'.

11   Philippe Sibaud, 2012, *Opening Pandora's Box: The New Wave of Land Grabbing by the Extractive Industries and the Devastating Impact on Earth*, The Gaia Foundation, gaiafoundation.org.

12   Finnish Forest Industries, 10 July 2013, 'Global Paper Consumption Is Growing', forestindustries.fi.

13   Paul Kingsnorth, 'The Space Race Is Over', globalonenessproject.org.

14   Rowan, 2014, 'We Need to Talk about Growth (and We Need to Do the Sums As Well)'.

30. Curb Your Malthusiasm

1   Patrick Butler, 27 January 2015, 'Yes, David Cameron, Cutting the Benefit Cap Tells Us a Lot about Modern Britain', theguardian.com.

2   Fred Block and Margaret R. Somers, April 2014, *The Power of Market Fundamentalism: Karl Polanyi's Critique*, Harvard University Press, Cambridge, MA.

3   Joseph Townsend, 1971, *A Dissertation on the Poor Laws: By a Well-Wisher to Mankind*, University of California Press, Berkeley.

4   Thomas Malthus, 1798, *An Essay on the Principle of Population*.

5   Living Heritage, 'Reforming Society in the Nineteenth Century: Poor Law Reform', parliament.uk.

6   *Report from His Majesty's Commissioners for Inquiring into the Administration and Practical Operation of the Poor Laws, 1834*, William Clowes, London.

7   1834, An Act for the Amendment and Better Administration of the Laws Relating to the Poor in England and Wales, workhouses.org.uk.

8   Philip Inman, 12 June 2015, 'Academics Attack George Osborne Budget Surplus Proposal', theguardian.com.

9   Block and Somers, *The Power of Market Fundamentalism*.

10   George Osborne and Iain Duncan Smith, 21 June 2015, 'Our Fight to Make Work Pay Better Than the Dole Has Only Just Begun', thesunday-times.co.uk.

11   Nicholas Watt, 1 June 2015, 'Downing Street Rejects Iain Duncan Smith Plan for New Limit on Child Benefit', theguardian.com.

12   Jon Stone, 11 June 2015, 'The DWP Is Trying to Psychologically "Reprogramme" the Unemployed, Study Finds', independent.co.uk.

13   Jamie Doward and Toby Helm, 20 June 2015, 'Child Poverty Rise across Britain "Halts Progress Made Since 1990s"', theguardian.com.

31. Kleptoremuneration

1 Laura Gardiner and Dr Shereen Hussein, March 2015, *As If We Cared: The Costs and Benefits of a Living Wage for Social Care Workers*, Resolution Foundation Report, resolutionfoundation.org.

2 Linda Burnham and Nik Theodore, 2012, Home Economics: *The Invisible and Unregulated World of Domestic Work*, National Domestic Workers Alliance, New York, domesticworkers.org.

3 Patrick Hennessy, 8 September 2012, 'Britain Must Champion the Wealth Creators, Say Tories', telegraph.co.uk.

4 Nick Cohen, 21 March 2015, 'Just How Good Are the Odds of a Rich Donor Becoming a Lord?', theguardian.com.

5 Alex Bracetti, 8 July 2011, 'Horrible Bosses: The Worst Tech CEOs of All Time', ukcomplex.com; Steve Tobak, 27 April 2012, 'America's Worst CEOs: Where Are They Now?', CBS Moneywatch, cbsnews.com.

6 BBC, 14 July 2014, 'Executive Pay "180 Times Average", Report Finds', bbc.com.

32. The Self-Attribution Fallacy

1 Daniel Kahneman, 2011, *Thinking, Fast and Slow,* Farrar, Straus and Giroux, New York, p. 216.

2 Belinda Jane Board and Katarina Fritzon, March 2005, 'Disordered Personalities at Work', *Psychology, Crime and Law*, vol. 11, no. 1, tandfonline.com.

3 Paul Babiak and Robert Hare, 2007, *Snakes in Suits: When Psychopaths Go to Work*, HarperBusiness, London.

4 Robert Reich and Bill Marsh, 4 September 2011, figure in 'The Limping Middle Class', nytimes.com.

5 The figures here have been calculated from Dave Gilson, 10 October 2011, 'Charts: Who Are the 1 Percent?', motherjones.com, which shows the average income of the top 1 per cent rising from just over $400,000 in 1980 to $1,138,000 in 2008, measured in 2008 dollars; the income of the bottom 90 per cent flatlined during the same period.

6 The Poverty Site, 2009, 'Income Inequalities', poverty.org.uk

7 Ibid.

8 Branko Milanovic, 2011, *The Haves and the Have-Nots: A Brief and Idiosyncratic History of Global Inequality*, Basic Books, New York.

9 The debate was organised by Reclaim the City: reclaimthecity.org.

33. The Lairds of Learning

1   The data in this essay are from the time of publication. Many of the trends discussed have continued. I sampled costs in the following Elsevier journals: *Journal of Clinical Epidemiology*, *Radiation Physics and Chemistry* and *Crop Protection*, all of which charged $31.50. Papers in a fourth Elsevier publication I checked, the *Journal of Applied Developmental Psychology*, cost $35.95. I sampled the following Springer journals: *Journal of Applied Spectroscopy*, *Kinematics and Physics of Celestial Bodies* and *Ecotoxicology*, all of which charged €34.95. The Wiley-Blackwell journals I sampled, *Plant Biology*, *Respirology* and *Journal of Applied Social Psychology*, all charged $42.

2   I went into the archive of Elsevier's *Applied Catalysis*, and checked the costs of the material published in its first issue: April 1981.

3   Bjorn Brembs, 2011, *What's Wrong with Scholarly Publishing Today? II*, slideshare.net.

4   www.elsevier.com/wps/find/journaldescription.cws_home/506062/bibliographic.

5   *Economist*, 26 May 2011, 'Of Goats and Headaches', economist.com.

6   Ibid.

7   Glenn S. McGuigan and Robert D. Russell, 2008, 'The Business of Academic Publishing: A Strategic Analysis of the Academic Journal Publishing Industry and Its Impact on the Future of Scholarly Publishing', *Electronic Journal of Academic and Special Librarianship*, vol. 9, no. 3, southernlibrarianship.icaap.org.

8   Springer Corporate Communications, 29 August 2011, by email. I spoke to Elsevier and asked them for a comment, but I have not received one.

9   Deutsche Bank AG, 11 January 2005, 'Reed Elsevier: Moving the Supertanker', *Company Focus: Global Equity Research Report*, quoted by McGuigan and Russell, 'The Business of Academic Publishing'.

10 John P. Conley and Myrna Wooders, March 2009, 'But What Have You Done for Me Lately? Commercial Publishing, Scholarly Communication, and Open-Access', *Economic Analysis and Policy*, vol. 39, no. 1, eap-journal.com.

11 Article 27 of the Universal Declaration of Human Rights, 1948, un.org.

12 *Economist*, 22 January 1998, 'Publishing, Perishing, and Peer Review', economist.com.

13 McGuigan and Russell, 'The Business of Academic Publishing'.

14 Ibid.

15 Research Councils, June 2006, 'Research Councils UK Updated Position Statement on Access to Research Outputs', web.archive.org.

16 Danny Kingsley shows how a small change could make a big difference: 'Currently all universities collect information about, and a copy of, every research article written by their academics each year . . . But the version of the papers collected is the Publisher's PDF. And in most cases this is the version we cannot make open-access through digital repositories . . . the infrastructure is there and the processes are already in place. But there is one small change that has to happen before we can enjoy substantive access to Australian research. The Government must specify that they require the Accepted Version (the final peer-reviewed, corrected version) of the papers rather than the Publisher's PDF for reporting'. See theconversation.edu.au.

17 Brembs, *What's Wrong with Scholarly Publishing Today?*

34. The Man Who Wants to Northern Rock the Planet

1 Matt Ridley, 22 July 1996, 'Power to the People: We Can't Do Any Worse Than Government', *Daily Telegraph*.

2 Treasury Select Committee, 2008, Fifth Report, publications.parliament. uk.

3 The agency in question is the Financial Services Authority. Ibid.

4 Ibid.

5 Matt Ridley, 2010, *The Rational Optimist: How Prosperity Evolves*, Fourth Estate, London.

6 Ibid., p. 356.

7 Ibid., p. 46.

8 Ibid., p. 105. Ridley is quoting Eamonn Butler.

9 Ridley uses this term on p. 357.

10 I think the term was coined by Simon Fairlie in his self-published pamphlet *The Prospect of Cornutopia*, released in 2002.

11 Ridley, *The Rational Optimist*, p. 187.

12 Mark Curtis, 2001, *Trade for Life: Making Trade Work for Poor People*, Christian Aid, London; John Brohman, April 1996, 'Postwar Development in the Asian NICs: Does the Neoliberal Model Fit Reality?', *Economic Geography*, vol. 72, no. 2; Graham Dunkley, 2000 (1997), *The Free Trade Adventure: The WTO, the Uruguay Round and Globalism*, Zed Books, London.

13 Ridley, *The Rational Optimist*, p. 111.

14 The reference he gives is http://masterresource.org/?p=3302#more-3302

15 Ridley, *The Rational Optimist*, p. 280.

16 Howard Friel, 2010, *The Lomborg Deception: Setting the Record Straight about Global Warming*, Yale University Press, New Haven and London.

17 Ridley, *The Rational Optimist*, p. 329.

18 You can see the trend here: metoffice.gov.uk/climatechange/science/ monitoring/hadcrut3.html.

19 Ridley, *The Rational Optimist*, p. 339.

20 Polar Bear Specialist Group, March 2010, pbsg.npolar.no/en/status/ status-table.html.

21 Ridley, *The Rational Optimist*, p. 17.

22 Millennium Ecosystem Assessment, 2005, 'Ecosystems and Human Well-Being: Synthesis', see figure 13, p. 16, millenniumassessment.org.

23 Ridley, *The Rational Optimist*, p. 9.

24 Ibid.

35. The Gift of Death

1 *The Story of Stuff*, storyofstuff.org.

2 It's 57 per cent. See George Monbiot, 5 May 2010, 'Carbon Graveyard', monbiot.com.

3 See the film *Blood in the Mobile*, bloodinthemobile.org.

4 Adam Welz, 27 November 2012, 'The Dirty War against Africa's Remaining Rhinos', e360.yale.edu.

5 Phones 4u, 2 November 2012, 'Christmas Gifts for U and U and U: Phones 4u Advert', youtube.com.

6 Emmanuel Saez, 2 March 2012, 'Striking It Richer: The Evolution of Top Incomes in the United States', eml.berkeley.edu.

7 BBC Radio 4, 8 December 2012, 'Ethical Consumerism', *Moral Maʒe*, bbc.co.uk.

36. How the Billionaires Broke the System

1 Barack Obama, 13 April 2011, 'Remarks by the President on Fiscal Policy', whitehouse.gov.

2 Joseph Stiglitz, May 2011, 'Of the 1%, by the 1%, for the 1%', vanityfair.com.

3 Ewen MacAskill, 31 July 2011, 'U.S. Debt Crisis: Worst Off in Ward Eight Face Prospect of Even Harsher Poverty', theguardian.com.

4 Paul Krugman, 31 July 2011, 'The President Surrenders', nytimes.com.

5 Ewen MacAskill, 30 July 2011, 'US Debt Crisis: Tea Party Iintransigeance Takes America to the Brink', theguardian.com.

6   CNBC, 22 February 2009, 'Rick Santelli's Shout Heard "Round the World"', cnbc.com.

7   Larrikin Films, 2010, *(Astro) Turf Wars*.

8   Jane Mayer, 30 August 2010, 'Covert Operations', newyorker.com.

9   Gary Weiss, 15 October 2008, 'The Price of Immortality', upstart.bizjour-nals.com.

10 'Forbes 400', forbes.com.

11 Tony Carrk, April 2011, *The Koch Brothers: What You Need to Know about the Financiers of the Radical Right*, Center for American Progress Action Fund, americanprogressaction.org.

12 Carrk, *The Koch Brothers*.

37. Plutocracy's Boot Boys

1   Martin Bright, 8 January 2005, 'Desperate Lucan Dreamt of Fascist Coup', theguardian.com.

2   David Frum, 20 November 2011, 'When Did the GOP Lose Touch with Reality?', nymag.com.

3   Jeff Judson, 12 April 2011, '21 Reasons Why Free-Market Think Tanks Are More Effective Than Anyone Else in Changing Public Policy (And One Reason Why They Are Not)', scribd.com.

4   Jane Mayer, 30 August 2011, 'Covert Operations', newyorker.com.

5   Madsen Pirie, 2012, *Think Tank: The Story of the Adam Smith Institute*, Biteback, London.

6   Ibid.

7   Ibid., p. 95.

8   Ibid., p. 18.

9   Ibid., p. 44.

10 Ibid., p. 52.

11 Ibid., p. 212.

12 Ibid., p. 19.

13 George Monbiot, 9 December 2012, 'Think of a Tank', monbiot.com; Political Innovation, *Who Funds You*, whofundsyou.org.

14 Pirie, *Think Tank*, p. 106–16.

15 Ibid.

16 Kwasi Kwarteng et al., 2012, *Britannia Unchained: Global Lessons for Growth and Prosperity*, Palgrave Macmillan, Basingstoke.

17 'Britain Unleashed: The Future of Capitalism (Series)', telegraph.co.uk.

18 Ian Cowie, 19 September 2012, 'Is Mitt Romney Right to Question Representation without Taxation?', telegraph.co.uk.

19   Allister Heath, 25 July 2012, 'Britain Unleashed: David Cameron Needs a Change of Heart – and Some Fire in His Belly', telegraph.co.uk.

38. How Did We Get Into This Mess?

1   Larry Elliott, 23 August 2007, 'Consumers' Debt Overtakes Gross Domestic Product', theguardian.com.

2   Ed Pilkington, 24 August 2007, 'Guano Theory in Bridge Collapse', theguardian.co.uk.

3   Anthony Lane, 27 August 2007, 'New Orleans: A National Humiliation', *New Statesman*.

4   David Harvey, 2005, *A Brief History of Neoliberalism*, Oxford University Press, Oxford.

5   Harvey, *A Brief History of Neoliberalism*, p. 17 (see graph).

6   Ibid.

7   For an account of how this happens, see George Lakoff, 2004, *Don't Think of an Elephant!: Know Your Values and Frame the Debate*, Chelsea Green Publishing, Vermont.

39. Going Naked

1   Nick Davies, 2008, *Flat Earth News*, Chatto & Windus, London.

2   Max Hastings, 2002, *Editor: An Inside Story of Newspapers*, Macmillan, London.

3   Howard Kurtz, 26 December 2005, 'Bush Presses Editors on Security', washingtonpost.com.

4   Greg Toppo, 7 January 2005, 'White House Paid Commentator to Promote Law', usatoday.com; David D. Kirkpatrick, 8 January 2005, 'TV Host Says U.S. Paid Him to Back Policy', nytimes.com.

5   Julian Borger and Kevin Maguire, 24 January 2002, 'Scruton in Media Plot to Push the Sale of Cigarettes', theguardian.com.

6   George Monbiot, 2006, *Heat: How to Stop the Planet Burning*, Allen Lane, London.

7   George Monbiot, 9 December 2012, 'Think of a Tank', monbiot.com.

8   George Monbiot, 'Registry of Interests', monbiot.com.

9   House of Commons, *The Register of Members' Financial Interests*, parliament.uk.

40. The Holocaust We Will Not See

1 David E. Stannard, 1992, *American Holocaust*, Oxford University Press. Unless stated otherwise, all the historical events mentioned in this column are sourced to the same book.

2 Steve Chawkins, 28 August 2009, 'Junipero Serra Needs Just One More Miracle', latimes.com.

3 Rory Carroll, 9 December 2009, 'Amazon's "Man of the Hole" Attacked by Unknown Gunmen', theguardian.com.

4 John Podhoretz, 28 December 2009, 'Avatarocious', weeklystandard.com.

5 *Sun*, 'Vatican Hits out at 3D Avatar', thesun.co.uk.

6 Adam Cohen, 25 December 2009, 'Next-Generation 3-D Medium of "Avatar" Underscores Its Message', nytimes.com.

41. The Empire Strikes Back

1 Caroline Elkins, 2005, *Britain's Gulag: The Brutal End of Empire in Kenya*, Random House, London, p. 189.

2 Ian Cobain, 5 October 2012, 'Mau Mau Torture Case: Kenyans Win Ruling Against UK', theguardian.com.

3 Elkins, *Britain's Gulag*.

4 Ibid.

5 Mark Curtis, 2007, 'The Mau Mau War in Kenya, 1952–60', markcurtis. wordpress.com, reprinted from Curtis, 2003, *Web of Deceit: Britain's Real Role in the World*, Vintage Books, London.

6 Ian Cobain, 16 July 2012, 'Mau Mau Veterans Launch Second Round of Legal Action', theguardian.com.

7 Dominic Casciani, 12 April 2011, 'British Mau Mau Abuse Papers Revealed', bbc.co.uk.

8 Elkins, *Britain's Gulag*.

9 Ian Cobain, Richard Norton-Taylor and Clar Ni Chonghaile, 5 October 2012, 'Mau Mau Veterans Win Right to Sue British Government', theguardian.com; Martyn Day and Dan Leader, 5 October 2012, 'The Kenyans Tortured by the British Must Now Be Justly Treated', theguardian.com.

10 Sven Lindqvist, 1997, *'Exterminate All the Brutes'*, The New Press, New York.

11 Charles White, 1728–1813, *An Account of the Regular Graduations in Man*.

12 Knox was disgraced because he was suspected not merely of

grave- robbing but commissioning murders in order to supply the cadavers he wanted.

13   Quoted by Lindqvist, *'Exterminate All the Brutes'*, p. 280.

14   In *The Descent of Man*, Charles Darwin wrote, 'At some future period not very distant as measured in centuries, the civilised races of man will almost certainly exterminate and replace throughout the world the savage races.' Quoted in ibid., p. 261.

15   In his book *Volksdienst*, quoted in ibid., p. 302.

16   Cited in ibid.

17   George Monbiot, 27 December 2005, 'How Britain Denies Its Holocausts', monbiot.com.

18   Max Hastings, 16 July 2012, 'The Folly of Judges, Vulture Lawyers and a Nation Addicted to Masochism', dailymail.co.uk.

42. Unremitting Pain

1   BBC, 6 February 2015, 'US Bank to Axe Somalia Transfers over al-Shabab Fears', bbc.co.uk.

2   Jamila Trindle, 5 February 2015, 'UN Envoy to Somalia Warns against Cutting off Remittances', foreignpolicy.com; BBC, 'US Bank to Axe Somalia Transfers over al-Shabab Fears'.

3   Beechwood International, September 2013, *Safer Corridors Rapid Assessment: Case Study: Somalia and UK Banking*, Her Majesty's Government, gov. co.uk.

4   Ibid.

5   Mattathias Schwartz, 26 January 2015, 'The Whole Haystack', newyorker.com; USA v. Mohamed, 0:09-cr-00352 (Minnesota District Court, 2009).

6   Beechwood International, *Safer Corridors Rapid Assessment*.

7   Food Security and Nutrition Analysis Unit–Somalia, 'Nutrition Update', fsnau.org.

8   Caitlin Chalmers and Mohamed Aden Hassan, May 2008, *UK Somali Remittances Survey*, Department for International Development, diaspora-center.org.

9   Beechwood International, *Safer Corridors Rapid Assessment*.

10   Stewart Maclean, 26 July 2011, 'Islamist Group in Somalia Bans Samosas after Deciding They're Too Western', dailymail.co.uk.

11   *Daily Mail*, 16 October 2009, 'Whipped for Wearing a "Deceptive" Bra: Hardline Islamists in Somalia Publicly Flog Women in Sharia Crackdown', dailymail.co.uk.

12   Dahir Jibril, 4 September 2013, 'Somalia: Polio Widespread in Regions Under Al-Shabaab Control', allafrica.com.

13   Abdi Sheikh and Feisal Omar, 9 February 2015, 'Al Shabaab Militants Kill Another Somali Lawmaker in Mogadishu', reuters.com.

14   Permanent Subcommittee on Investigations, 16 July 2012, 'HSBC Exposed US Financial System to Money Laundering, Drug, Terrorist Financing Risks', hsgac.senate.gov.

15   Ibid.

16   David Leigh et al., 9 February 2015, 'HSBC Files: HMRC Had Data on Misconduct before Bank Boss Made Trade Minister', theguardian.com.

17   David Leigh et al., 8 February 2015, 'HSBC Files Show How Swiss Bank Helped Clients Dodge Taxes and Hide Millions', theguardian.com.

18   Her Majesty's Government, *2010 to 2015 Government Policy: Economic Growth in Developing Countries: Appendix 11: Enabling the Continued Flow of Remittances*, gov.co.uk.

19   Jessica Hatcher, 6 February 2015, 'Ending Somali–US Money Transfers Will Be Devastating, Merchants Bank Warned', theguardian.com.

20   Scott Reckard and Ronald D. White, 5 February 2015, 'Money Transfers Cut off to Somalia', latimes.com.

21   Ibid.

43. Bomb Everyone

1   Jonathan Steele, June 2014, '40 Die in Baghdad Massacre as Shia Militia Go on Rampage', theguardian.com.

2   *Guardian*, 22 August 2014, 'Shia Militia Attack on Sunni Mosque in Iraq Leaves Scores Dead', theguardian.com.

3   Ghaith Abdul-Ahad, 24 August 2014, 'Iraq: On the Frontline with the Shia Fighters Taking the War to Isis', theguardian.com.

4   Ibid.

5   Saeed Kamali Dehghan, 29 September 2014, 'Iran Executes Man for Heresy', theguardian.com.

6   Frankie Boyle, 29 September 2014, 'Blasphemy Laws Are Deadly Serious: We Must Stand Up for Mohammed Asghar', theguardian.com.

7   Amnesty International, 22 September 2014, 'Further information on UA 201/14 Saudi Arabia: Hajras Al-Qurey Executed', amnesty.se.

8   *Guardian*, 5 December 2010, 'US Embassy Cables: Hillary Clinton Says Saudi Arabia "A Critical Source of Terrorist Funding"', theguardian.com.

9   Patrick Cockburn, 13 July 2014, 'Iraq Crisis: How Saudi Arabia Helped Isis Take over the North of the Country', independent.co.uk.

10   Steve Clemons, 23 June 2014, '"Thank God for the Saudis": ISIS, Iraq, and the Lessons of Blowback', theatlantic.com; Patrick Cockburn, 14 September 2014, 'Islamic State: "US Failure to Look into Saudi Role in 9/11 Has Helped Isis"', independent.co.uk.

11   House of Commons, 26 September 2014, 'Iraq: Coalition against ISIL', *Hansard*, publications.parliament.uk.

12   Glenn Greenwald, 23 September 2014, 'Syria Becomes the 7th Predominantly Muslim Country Bombed by 2009 Nobel Peace Laureate', theintercept.com.

13   'Iraq: Coalition against ISIL', *Hansard*.

14   Oliver Miles, 26 September 2014, 'We Must Beware: Isis Wants the West to Conduct a Crusade', theguardian.com.

15   Martin Chulov, 28 September 2014, 'Isis Reconciles with al-Qaida Group as Syria Air Strikes Continue', theguardian.com.

16   *Haaretz*, 19 September 2014, 'Islamic State Recruitment Soaring in Wake of U.S. Bombing', haaretz.com.

17   Paul Sperry, 15 December 2013, 'Inside the Saudi 9/11 Coverup', nypost.com.

18   *Guardian*, 'The BAE Files (series)', theguardian.com.

19   David Leigh and Rob Evans, 5 February 2010, 'BAE and the Saudis: How Secret Cash Payments Oiled £43bn Arms Deal', theguardian.com.

20   Andrew Bousfield and Richard Brooks, 19 September 2014, 'Shady Arabia and the Desert Fix', *Private Eye*.

44. A Global Ban on Leftwing Politics

1   David Cameron, 23 January 2013, 'EU speech at Bloomberg', gov.uk.

2   George Monbiot, 14 October 2013, 'From Obamacare to Trade, Superversion Not Subversion Is the New and Very Real Threat to the State', theguardian.com.

3   McCabe Centre for Law and Cancer, 'Philip Morris Asia Challenge under Australia–Hong Kong Bilateral Investment Treaty', mccabecentre.org.

4   Corporate Europe Observatory, 3 June 2013, 'A Transatlantic Corporate Bill of Rights', corporateeurope.org.

5   Thomas McDonagh, 2013, *Unfair, Unsustainable, and Under the Radar*, The Democracy Center, democracyctr.org.

6   Glyn Moody, 23 July 2013, 'Eli Lilly Raises Stakes: Says Canada Now Owes It $500 Million for Not Granting a Patent It Wanted', techidirt.com.

7   McDonagh, *Unfair, Unsustainable, and Under the Radar*; Public Citizen, March 2013, 'U.S. Pharmaceutical Corporation Uses NAFTA Foreign

Investor Privileges Regime to Attack Canada's Patent Policy, Demand $100 Million for Invalidation of a Patent', citizen.org.

8   Corporate Europe Observatory, 27 November 2012, 'Chapter 4: Who Guards the Guardians? The Conflicting Interests of Investment Arbitrators', corporateeurope.org.

9   McDonagh, *Unfair, Unsustainable, and Under the Radar*.

10   William Greider, 11 November 2001, 'The Right and US Trade Law: Invalidating the 20th Century', thenation.com.

11   Ibid.

45. Innocent until Proved Dead

1   A picture of the head wound has been reproduced here: Richard Luscombe, 30 May 2013, 'Ibragim Todashev's Father: FBI "Bandits" Murdered My Son', theguardian.com.

2   Ellen Barry and Michael S, Schmidt, 30 May 2013, 'Man Tied to Boston Suspect Is Said to Have Attacked Agent Before being Shot', nytimes.com.

3   Wesley Lowery, 1 June 2013, 'Many Questions 10 Days after FBI Killed Fla. Suspect', bostonglobe.com.

4   Desiree Stennett and Jerriann Sullivan, 22 May 2013, 'Who Is Ibragim Todashev?', orlandosentinel.com.

5   Michael S. Schmidt et al., 22 May 2013, 'Deadly End to FBI Queries on Tsarnaev and a Triple Killing', nytimes.com.

6   Conor Friedersdorf, 31 May 2013, 'Yet Another Explanation for the Killing of Ibragim Todashev', theatlantic.com; Barry and Schmidt, 30 May 2013, 'Man Tied to Boston Suspect Is Said to Have Attacked Agent Before Being Shot'; Lowery, 'Many Questions 10 Days after FBI Killed Fla. Suspect'.

7   Barack Obama, 23 May 2013, 'President Barack Obama's Speech at National Defense University: Full Text', theguardian.com.

8   Eric Holder, 5 March 2012, 'Attorney General Eric Holder Speaks at Northwestern University School of Law', justice.gov.

9   Obama, 'President Barack Obama's Speech at National Defense University: Full Text'.

10   International Human Rights and Conflict Resolution Clinic at Stanford Law School and Global Justice Clinic at NYU School Of Law, September 2012, 'Living under Drones: Death, Injury and Trauma to Civilians from US Drone Practices in Pakistan', law.standford.edu; The Bureau of Investigative Journalism, 'The Covert Drone War', thebureauinvestigates.com.

46. The Paranoia Squad

1   See saveradleylakes.org.uk.
2   The High Court of Justice, order arising from Case HQ07X00505, para 6.4, netcu.org.uk.
3   From lawson-cruttenden.co.uk, accessed 22 December 2008 and since become defunct.
4   Sections 125–7, opsi.gov.uk/acts/acts2005/ukpga_20050015_en_12# pt4-pb1-l1g125.
5   Timothy Lawson-Cruttenden, 2007, 'Injunctive Relief against Harassment and Trespass', Case Commentaries, *Environmental Liability*, p. 194, lawson-cruttenden.co.uk (no longer accessible).
6   Ibid.
7   See netcu.org.uk.
8   NETCU, November 2007, 'Policing Protest: Pocket Legislation Guide,' p. 51. See animalrightscambridge.files.wordpress.com.
9   Mark Townsend and Nick Denning, 9 November 2008, 'Police Warn of Growing Threat from Eco-Terrorists', guardian.com.
10 Stephen Pritchard, 23 November 2008, 'Anonymous Sources and Claims of Eco-Terrorism', guardian.com.
11 NETCU, personal communication, 22 December 2008.
12 Townsend and Denning, 'Police Warn of Growing Threat from Eco-Terrorism.'
13 The site this is take from (netcu.org.uk) was accessed at the time of writing and is no longer available.
14 Leading article, 12 March 2006, 'Email Campaigns', *Observer*, theguardian.com; Linda Harrison, 9 July 2001, 'Anti-Abortion Activists Step up UK Net Campaign', theregister.co.uk.
15 Jeremy Laurance, 8 May 2006, 'Anti-Abortionist Jailed for Photo Protest', independent.co.uk.

47. Union with the Devil

1   Larry Elliott, 26 June 2006, 'Sir Digby Rides Off with All Guns Blazing', theguardian.com.
2   GMB, 11th July 2006, 'AA Roadshow Tackles Damon Buffini: Maidstone and Dover', labournet.net.
3   Trade Union and Labour Party Liaison Organisation, 25 July 2004, 'Full Employment and Working in Modern Britain', *The TULO Guide to the*

Warwick Agreement, National Policy Forum.

4   House of Commons, 2 March 2007, Temporary and Agency Workers (Prevention of Less Favourable Treatment) Bill, Second Reading, *Hansard*, publications.parliament.uk.

5   See amicustheunion.org, accessed 9 July 2007.

6   Paul Kenny, 3 June 2007, speech to the GMB conference, gmb.org.uk/shared_asp_files/GFSR.asp?NodeID=95563.

7   Dave Prentis, quoted by David Hencke, 19 June 2007, 'Change Direction or Lose Election, Brown Warned', theguardian.com.

8   Tony Woodley, 2nd July 2007, speech to the T&G section of Unite's conference, tgwu.org.uk/Templates/Internal.asp?NodeID=93490&int 1stParentNodeID=42438&int2ndParentNodeID=90594.

9   Conversation with TGWU spokesman, 5 July 2007.

10 The relevant information on the Electoral Commission website was accessed at time of writing at the following address: electoralcommission. org.uk/regulatory-issues/regdpoliticalparties.cfm?ec=%7Bts%20 %272007%2D07%2D04%2008%3A07%3A49%27%7D.

11 Ibid.

12 Dave Reid, 5 July 2007, 'RMT Conference: Fighting a Thousand Cuts', socialistparty.org.uk.

13 Kevin Curran, quoted by Christine Buckley and Helen Rumbelow, 30 July 2004, 'Go Left Labour, or Face a New Party, Says Union Boss', *The Times*.

48. Someone Else's Story

1   George Monbiot, 31 October 2011, 'The Medieval, Unaccountable Corporation of London Is Ripe for Protest', theguardian.com.

2   George Monbiot, 29 July 2014, 'The Rich Want Us to Believe Their Wealth Is Good for Us All', theguardian.com.

3   Kevin Rawlinson, 28 February 2014, 'Minister Apologises after Woman in Coma Was Told to Find Work', theguardian.com.

4   Libby Brooks, 2 September 2014, 'Scottish Independence: Yes Campaign Gets Poll Boost', theguardian.com.

5   John T. Jost and Mahzarin R. Banaji, March 1994, 'The Role of Stereotyping in System-Justification and the Production of False Consciousness', *British Journal of Social Psychology*, vol. 33, no. 1, onlinelibrary.wiley.com.

6   John T. Jost, Mahzarin R. Banaji and Brian A. Nosek, December 2004, 'A Decade of System Justification Theory: Accumulated Evidence of

Conscious and Unconscious Bolstering of the Status Quo', *Political Psychology*, vol. 25, no. 6, onlinelibrary.wiley.com.

7   John T. Jost et al., January–February 2003, 'Social Inequality and the Reduction of Ideological Dissonance on Behalf of the System: Evidence of Enhanced System Justification among the Disadvantaged', *European Journal of Social Psychology*, vol. 33, no. 1.

8   John T. Jost et al, 'A Decade of System Justification Theory'.

9   Adam Ramsay, 2014, *42 Reasons to Support Scottish Independence*, Commonwealth Publishing, commonwealth-publishing.com.

10   Adam Price et al., *The Flotilla Effect: Europe's Small Economies through the Eye of the Storm*, Plaid Cymru, party.of.wales/flotilla/?force=1.

11   BBC, 31 August 2014, 'Scottish Independence: Nigel Farage to Appear at UKIP Pro-Union Rally', bbc.co.uk.

12   See also, on these questions, *The Common Weal* report by the Jimmy Reid Foundation, reidfoundation.org.

13   George Monbiot, 5 August 2014, 'Sick of This Market-Driven World? You Should Be', theguardian.com.

14   Robert Booth et al., 3 July 2004, 'Tory Summer Party Drew Super-Rich Supporters with Total Wealth of £11bn', theguardian.com.

15   For more on this, see Ramsay, *42 Reasons to Support Scottish Independence*.

49. Highland Spring

1   James Hunter et al., July 2013, *432:50: Towards a Comprehensive Land Reform Agenda for Scotland*, House of Commons Scottish Affairs Committee, parliament.uk.

2   Simon Johnson, 30 November 2014, '"Future bleak" for Grouse Shooting and Deer Stalking', telegraph.co.uk.

3   Andy Wightman, 26 November 2014, 'Land Reform; The Wait Is Over' andywightman.com.

4   Defra has tried to pass this off as payments for 'moorland farmers', but all owners of grazed or managed moorlands, of which grouse moors are a major component, are eligible: see 'CAP Boost for Moorland', 25 April 2014, gov.uk.

5   Rajeev Syal, 22 April 2014, 'David Cameron Blasted over Shotgun Licence Fees Veto', theguardian.com.

6   This assumes that a house in Blackburn valued at £69,000 in 1991 would cost around £200,000 today; see Blackburn with Daren Council, 'Council Tax Charges for 2015–16', blackburn.gov.uk; see also Ian Jack, 29 March 2014, 'Why Do We Pay More Tax than Oligarch in Knightsbridge Palaces?', theguardian.com.

7   George Monbiot, 3 March 2014, 'The Benefits Claimants the Government Loves', monbiot.com.

8   Defra, 31 August 2011, by email.

9   'Feudal Aid', en.wikipedia.org.

10   Land Reform Review, 24 May 2014, *Final Report*, gov.scot.

11   George Monbiot, 31 October 2011, 'Wealth Destroyers', monbiot.com.

12   Larry Elliot, 22 September 2014, 'Charge Capital Gains Tax on Main Residences, Says Property Expert', theguardian.com.

13   Lucy Warick-Ching, 19 February 2010, 'Investors Drawn to Farmland', ft.com.

14   The Scottish Government, 26 November 2014, *One Scotland: Programme for Government 2014–15*, gov.scot.

15   Andy Wightman, 1 August 2014, 'Rethink Required on Ten-Year Land Registration Goal', andywightman.com.

16   The Scottish Government, *One Scotland*.

17   Defra, January 2011, *UK Response to the Commission Communication and Consultation*, webarchive.nationalarchives.gov.uk.

18   Compare figures in Defra, 29 May 2014, *Agriculture in the United Kingdom 2013*, gov.uk, with Defra, 9 July 2012, *Agriculture in the United Kingdom 2011*, gov.uk.

19   George Monbiot, 21 January 2013, 'I Agree with Churchill: Let's Get Stuck into the Real Shirkers', theguardian.com.

20   Andy Wightman, 4 November 2014, 'Listen up, Griff Rhys Jones, the Mansion Tax Is the Soft Option', theguardian.com.

21   The Land Reform Review Group, 23 May 2014, *The Land of Scotland and the Common Good*, gov.scot.

22   George Monbiot, 19 May 2014, 'I'd Vote Yes to Rid Scotland of Its Feudal Landowners', theguardian.com.

23   'Abolition of Feudal Tenure etc. (Scotland) Act 2000', gov.scot.

50. A Telling Silence

1   'Liberal Democrat Manifesto 2010', politicsresources.net.

2   David Teather, 22 June 2010, 'Capital Gains Tax Rises to 28% for Higher Earners', theguardian.com.

3   House of Commons, 8 January 2013, Welfare Benefits Up-Rating Bill, *Hansard*, publications.parliament.uk.

4   HM Revenues and Customs, 14 April 2013, *Rates and Allowances: Corporation Tax*, gov.uk; Dan Milmo, 5 December 2012, 'Corporation Rate Cut to Nearly Half of US Level as Osborne Ignores Tax Row', theguardian.com.

5   Ibid.

6   Gordon Brown, 1 November 1999, Speech to the CBI Conference.

7   Tony Dolphin, 10 June 2010, *Financial Sector Taxes*, Institute for Public Policy Research, ippr.org.

8   Greg Philo, 15 August 2010, 'Deficit Crisis: Let's Really Be in It Together', theguardian.com.

9   Chris Spillane and Neil Callanan, 28 October 2012, 'Sultan's Tax Discount on London House Shows Law Favours Rich', independent.co.uk.

10   Ibid.

11   Hélène Mulholland, 7 October 2012, 'David Cameron Rules out Mansion Tax and Plans Further Welfare Cuts', theguardian.com.

12   Speech delivered by Winston Churchill in King's Theater, Edinburgh, on 17 July *1909*, see *Current Affairs*, 'Winston Churchill Said It All Better Than We Can', landvaluetax.org.

13   'Ground-rents are a still more proper subject of taxation than the rent of houses. A tax upon ground-rents would not raise the rents of houses. It would fall altogether upon the owner of the ground-rent, who acts always as a monopolist, and exacts the greatest rent which can be got for the use of his ground', from Adam Smith, 1776, *An Inquiry into the Nature and Causes of the Wealth of Nations*, Book V, Chapter 2.

14   Winston Churchill, as above.

15   Land Value Taxation Campaign, 'Land Rent for Public Revenue', land-valuetax.org.

16   David Cameron, 6 March 2011, 'Speech to Conservative Spring Conference | Cardiff', newstatesman.com.

51. The Values of Everything

1   Tom Crompton, September 2010, 'Common Cause: The Case for Working with Our Cultural Values', WWF, Oxfam, Friends of the Earth, CPRE, Climate Outreach Information Network, wwf.org.uk.

2   J. Curtice, 2010, 'Thermostat or Weathervane? Public Reactions to Spending and Redistribution under New Labour', in Alison Park et al. (eds), *British Social Attitudes 2009–2010: The 26th Report*, Sage, London, srmo.sagepub.com. Cited in Crompton, 'Common Cause'.

3   Guy Murphy, 2005, 'Influencing the Size of Your Market', Institute of Practitioners in Advertising, cited in Crompton, 'Common Cause'.

4   Margaret Thatcher, 3 May 1981, interview with *The Sunday Times*, cited in Crompton, 'Common Cause'.

5   Ed Miliband, 28 September 2010, 'Labour Conference: Ed Miliband Speech in Full', theguardian.com.

Index

A

A83, disasters on, 119
abiotic factors, 79
abortion, 72–6, 261
Abramoff, Jack, 223
academic publishing, 193–7
acoustic dispersal devices / acoustic deterrence, 67–8
Adams, William, 63
Adam Smith Institute, 214, 215, 219
Africa
    abortion rate, 74, 75–6
    greenhouse gas emissions in, 104
    population growth in, 103
    Virunga national park, 177
    xawala system in, 237, 238
Age of Loneliness, 9
air pollution, 169, 171
al-Shabaab, 236, 238
ambient energy, 166
ambition, 10, 21, 180, 289
American Enterprise Institute, 213, 219
American Holocaust (Stannard), 227
Americans for Prosperity (AFP), 210–11
Amicus, 265
Amir-Aslani, Mohsen, 242
Animal Aid, 137
animal rights movement, 261
Anti-Social Behaviour Act (2003), 70
Anti-Social Behaviour Bill, 23
anti-social behaviour orders (ASBOs), 28–9, 69
anti-social toddlers, fines for parents of, 69
apparatus of justification, 1, 6
Argentina, sued by international utility companies, 250
Argentine roc (*Argentavis magnificens*), 85
Arjuna, 90
arxiv.org, 196
Asghar, Mohammed, 242
Aspinall, John, 213

aspiration, 11, 12, 19, 21, 183, 274, 287
Associated Octel, 163
astroturfing, 224
Astro Turf Wars (film), 211
atomic energy, 168, 172. *See also* nuclear power
Attenborough, David, 106
Auden, W. H., 94
Auschwitz, 232
Australia
    acoustic dispersal devices / acoustic deterrence, 69
    coal exports from, 172
    destruction of rainforest in, 86
    disappearance of predators in, 81
    trade agreement with Hong Kong, 250
Avatar (film), 227, 230, 231

B

Babiak, Paul, 190
BAE, 244
bail outs, 102, 198, 199, 202, 210
Baker, Norman, 30
Bandar bin Sultan, 242, 244
Bandow, Doug, 223
Bank of England, 156
Barclays Global Power and Utilities, 20
BBC, 41, 90
bears, return of to former ranges, 97
The Bell Curve (Murray and Herrnstein), 163
Bellway Homes, 45, 46
Beowulf, 90
Berlin, Isaiah, 4
Bialowieza Forest (Poland), 96
billionaires
    Charles and David Koch, 211, 214
    freedom of not to pay taxes, 24
    Ian Wood, 155
    negative freedom enjoyed by, 4

political involvement of, 209–12
on population growth, 106
Biochimica et Biophysica Acta, 194
Biological Weapons Convention, 153
Blair, Tony, 219, 244, 264, 266, 281, 287
Blears, Hazel, 149
Block, Fred, 180, 182
Board, Belinda, 189
boarding schools, 64
Boarding Schools Association, 65
Boarding School Syndrome, 64
bosses
  as allowed to blackmail their workers, 264
  and capital gains tax, 280
  Carly Fiorina on list of worst, 186
  as consuming utility their workers provide, 187
  income of as compared to average full-time
    worker, 12
  psychopathic traits of as being rewarded, 189–90
  self-attribution of, 191
Boston College, 12
BP, 151
Brazil
  farming in, 140
  genocide in, 230
  government's contraceptive programme, 76
Brembs, Bjorn, 196
Brennan, John, 55
A Brief History of Neoliberalism (Harvey), 218
Britain Unleashed (article series), 216
Britannia Unchained, 216
British Journal of Psychotherapy, 64
British Medical Journal, 75
British Social Attitudes, 287
Brown, Gordon, 219, 263, 264, 267, 281, 287
Buffini, Damon, 264
Bush, George, 76, 266
Bush, George W., 54, 209, 223
Business Council, 264

C
Californian condor, decline of, 84–5
Cambridge University, 20, 49, 50, 51
Cameron, David, 76, 275, 282, 283
Cameron, James, 227
Canada
  greenhouse gas emissions in, 87
  revocation of patents by, 251
  rise in moose numbers, 86
Canadian tar sands, 151
capital gains tax, 276, 280
Capital in the Twenty-First Century (Piketty), 1
capitalism, 176, 187, 195. *See also* consumer capitalism
capitalists, 193
carbon, governments in rich world exhorting citizens
  to use less, 148
carbon capture and storage, 147, 150
carbon-cutting programmes, 151
carbon dioxide
  catching and burying of, 150
  contributions of whales in removal of, 83
  production of, 86, 148, 204
  rise in, 84, 103–4
carbon-fuelled expansion, 176
Carbon Tracker Initiative, 156
Cardigan Bay, 95
care workers, 184–6

Carnegie, Andrew, 1, 191
carnivores, impact of large carnivores, 80
Catholic church, on abortion and contraception, 72–6
CBI (Confederation of British Industry), 263, 267
Center for Responsive Politics, 24
Centre for Policy Studies, 219
chastity, 59
Cherry Orchard estate, 45
Chesterman, Gordon, 51
child prisoners, 69
children. *See also* youth
  education of in natural environments, 39–42
  play of, 43–7
  sacrificial caste of, 63
  systematic injustice towards, 63
Children's Rights Alliance for England, 68
China
  age of criminal responsibility in, 69
  air pollution in, 171
  coal import projection, 172
  land reform programmes in, 141
  premature deaths caused by coal plants in, 169, 170
Christensen, John, 192
Chuckchi Sea, 157
Churchill, Winston, 282
churnalism, 222
Cincinnati, Ohio (US), 162
city space, 27–8
Class A drugs trade, 35
Clean Air Task Force, 171
climate change
  absence of official recognition of role of fossil fuels
    in causing, 155
  demand-side policy for tackling, 148
  government as ruthlessly interventionist when
    promoting of but not when retraining of, 149,
    156
  government policy in tackling, 149
  governments as refusing to take necessary action,
    217
  groups demanding governments take no action on,
    223
  Norway's policies about, 157
  and population growth, 103
  supply-side policy for tackling, 148, 151
  technology that will save us from, 147
Climate Outreach and Information Network, 158
Clinton, Bill, 219
Clinton, Hillary, 242
CNBC, 210
coal burning, health costs inflicted by, 170, 171, 172
coal extraction/use, 147, 148, 149, 151, 153, 167, 169,
  170, 172, 175–6
Coalition for Marriage, 58
cocaine use, 32, 33, 34, 35, 222
Cohen, Adam, 231
college graduates, recruitment of, 49–52, 187
Columbus, 228
Common Agricultural Policy, 132–3
'Common Cause' (Crompton), 285, 288
compartmentalisation, as human ability, 91, 92, 93, 94
compassionate conservatism, 179
competition
  as driving growth, 12, 15
  emphasis of virtues of, 287
  as religion of our time, 10
The Compleat Angler (Walton), 137

compound growth, 175, 177, 178
Confederation of British Industry (CBI), 263, 267
connectedness, as destroyed, 13
Conrad Black, 222
Conservatives
    in general, 61
    in UK, 41, 187, 253, 281, 283, 284
    in US, 288
constitutional rights, 256
consumer boom, 205
consumer capitalism, 99, 100
consumer debt, 217
consumer economy, 203
consumption. *See also* drug consumption; global
        consumption; pathological consumption;
        pointless consumption
    assault on the biosphere by consumption machine,
        101
    as associated with prosperity and happiness, 206
    diminishing satisfactions of, 100
    of fossil fuels, 87, 153, 204
    of paper, 177
    rise of, 107, 200
contraception, 73, 74, 75
Coors, Adolph, 16, 219
corporate lobbyists, 26
corporate power
    appeasing of, 281
    media as instrument of, 212
    neoliberal think thanks and, 213
    politics as operated by, 23
    promotion of, 4
Corporation of the City of London, 192
corporation tax, 281
Costa, Antonio Maria, 32, 34, 35
Cotton, Charles, 137
council tax, 282
counter-cultural association, 33
counter life, 24
Cowie, Ian, 216
crime, rise and fall of violent crime, 160–3
Crime and Disorder Act (1998), 28, 70
criminal responsibility, age of, 69
Crompton, Tom, 285, 287
cross compliance, 125
Crow, Bob, 267
Cú Chulainn, 90
cultural diversity, loss of, 97
Curran, Kevin, 267

D

Daily Mail, 214, 215, 235, 267, 284
Daily Telegraph, 198, 214, 216, 275
Darling, Alistair, 150
Darwin, Charles, 3, 234
Davey, Ed, 156
Davies, Nick, 33
Dearlove, Richard, 242
Deepwater Horizon disaster, 201
Defending the Dream Summit (2009), 211
dehumanisation, 235
dematerialisation, 177
Democracy Centre, 252
Democrats, in US, 56, 220
demographic transition, 73, 106
Department for Environment, Food and Rural Affairs
        (Defra), 125, 126, 127, 129

depression, rise in, 17
deregulation, 15, 186, 205, 218, 219
Der Lebensraum (Ratzel), 234
Deutsche Bank, 195
dimethyl sulphide, 85
dispersal orders, 30, 70
dispersal powers, 29
Dissertation on the Poor Laws (Townsend), 180
divorce, 60
domestic extremism/domestic extremist, 258, 260, 261
dominant ideology, 3
dominant narratives, 14–15
Drax (England), 172
dredging, 136
drone strikes, 53–7, 255, 256
drug addiction, 33, 35
drug consumption, 34
drugs, legalisation and regulation of, 33–4
drugs policy, 32, 33
drug use
    as elective, 33
    prohibition vs. legalisation of, 35–6
due process, 255, 256

E

Eagle, Angela, 149
early boarding, 64–6
Earth First! 260
Earth Summit (Rio de Janeiro 2012), 99, 100
eating disorders, 17, 22
eco-extremism, 261
economic elite, 19, 100
economic growth, 15, 107, 175
economic parasitism, 195
Economist, 196
ecosystems, 82, 97, 102
eco-terrorists, 260
Edinburgh University, 49, 50
Edison, Thomas, 1
education
    of children in natural environments, 39–42
    early boarding, 64–6
Education and Adoption Bill, 21
elective impotence, 26
Eli Lilly, 251
Elizabethans, 120
Ellesmere Port (Britain), 163
El Salvador, gold mine in, 250–1
Elsevier, 194, 196
empire, brutalisation of, 234–5
employers
    nature and purpose of, 51
    recruitment by, 49–52, 187
energy
    ambient energy, 166
    atomic energy, 168, 172. *See also* nuclear power
    green energy production, 167
    new energy infrastructure, 150
    renewable energy, 158, 165, 166
    technology, costs associated with all kinds of, 168
Energy and the English Industrial Revolution (Wrigley),
        167
English, David, 215
Environment Agency, 136
environmental racism, 163
Environment and Urbanization, 103
Essay on the Principle of Population (Malthus), 180

Ethyl Corporation, 161
'Et in Arcadia' Ego (Auden), 94
Europe
    abortion rate, 74
    acreage being vacated by farmers in, 97
    ecosystems as shaped by elephants, rhinos, hippos
        and other great beasts, 82
    lead withdrawn from petrol, 161
    as massively enriched by genocides in Americas, 227
    premature deaths caused by coal power in, 171
European Commission, 252
European Union, 124, 128, 249
Eustice, George, 127, 128
exploitation (of the planet), 102
Exterminate All the Brutes (Lindqvist), 233

F

Fairtrade movement, 143
family, meaning of prior to nineteenth century, 59
family lives, as invented by nostalgia, 61
family values campaigners, 58
farm animals, treatment of, 113
Farmers' Weekly, 123, 128
farming. *See also* hill farming; pig farming
    big business as killing small farming, 142–3
    in Brazil, 140
    impact of development of, 92, 97
    inspections of, 127
    prejudice against small farmers, 141–2
    and soil. *See* soil
    subsidies for, 121, 122, 124, 125, 127, 128, 133, 276
    in Turkey, 140, 142
    in Wales, 121
    yields from, 140–1
    in Zimbabwe, 139
The Farming Forum, 126
Farming Regulation Task Force, 127
Farrar, Frederick, 234
Ffos-y-fran (South Wales), 147, 148
finance, jobs in, 48, 49
financial sector, and the illusion of skill, 189
Financial Times, 20, 223
Fiorina, Carly, 186
Fire Brigades Union (FBU), 267
flood defence, 130, 132–8
Food and Agriculture Organisation (UN), 142
food security, 139
Food Summit (2008), 139, 142
Forest Industries, 177
Forsyth, Michael, 215
Forty-Two Reasons to Support Scottish Independence
        (Ramsay), 273
fossil fuels
    absence of official recognition of role of in causing
        climate change, 155
    economic growth as artefact of use of, 175
    exploration and extraction of, 153, 157
    impact of unchecked consumption of, 87
    lack of talk about constraining production of, 153
    leaving them in the ground, 147–51
    silence about, 154–6, 158
Four Lions (film), 238
Fox News, 212
Fraser, Stuart, 192
freedom
    acting as if we don't enjoy greater freedom than
        preceding generations, 23

    as championed by neoliberals, 4
    deprivation of, 26
    market freedom, 45, 198, 218
    negative freedom, 4
    political freedom, 5
    surrender of, 12
    think tank freedoms, 24
    as use it or lose it, 26
Free Enterprise Group, 215
free market, 3, 198, 199–200, 213, 224
free-range production, 114
Friedman, Milton, 220
Friel, Howard, 200
Fritzon, Katarina, 189
Frum, David, 213
Fukushima nuclear catastrophe, 164, 168, 169–70

G

Galton, Francis, 234
General, Municipal, Boilermakers and Allied Trade
        Union (GMB), 264, 266
genocide, 227–31
ghost psyche, 89, 111
Gillis, John, 59, 60, 61
Gini coefficient, 191
global agreements, 102
global consumption, 177
global economy, 177
global food market, 143
global growth rate, 178
global warming, 86, 101, 104, 105–6, 155, 159
global wealth, 12, 176
Glooskap, 90
Gloucester, 132
Godhaven, Merrick, 261
godly household, 59
Goldsmith, James, 213, 214
Google, 205
Grantham, Jeremy, 175
Great Leap Backwards, 141
green consumerism, 288
green energy production, 167
greenhouse gases
    attention paid to, 153
    emissions of, 87, 104, 159
    grazing animals as increasing production of, 86
    impact of wildlife protection on, 87
    as topic of official interest in global meetings, 154
Greenpeace, 169, 171, 260
Green Revolution, 140
Greenwald, Glenn, 56
Griffiths, Jay, 43
grouse estates, subsidies for, 137, 275
Guantanamo Bay, detainees in, 256
Guardian, 33, 62, 68, 224, 230, 250
guiding intelligence, belief in, 19
Guttmacher Institute, 74

H

Harbin, particulate concentrations in, 171
Harbour, Peter, 258, 260
hard work, outcomes as based on (or not based on),
        16, 188
Hare, Robert, 190
Harvey, David, 218, 220
Hastings, Max, 222, 235
The Haves and the Have-Nots (Milanovic), 191

Hayek, Friedrich von, 218, 220
Health and Environment Alliance, 171
heating fuel, 165, 167
Heritage Foundation, 219
heroin use, 33, 34–5
Hewlett-Packard, 186
Heywood, Colin, 60
hill farming, 121, 122, 131, 133, 134
Hispaniola, 228
A History of Childhood (Heywood), 60
Hitler, Adolph, 234
Hobbes, Thomas, 9, 13
Holder, Eric, 255
Holocaust, 230, 233
homosexuality, 59
Hoover Institute, 219
Household, Geoffrey, 211
housing estates, play spaces for children in, 44–5
HSBC, 238
Human Plant (BBC series), 90
humans
    ability of to compartmentalise, 91, 92, 93, 94
    hunting/gathering of early humans, 91
    impact of development of farming on, 92
    as wired to respond to nature, 89
Humphreys, Margaret, 64
Hunger Games (film), 90
Hunter's Pride, 110
hunting/gathering, of early humans, 91

I

I=CAT, 104
I=PAT, 104
imperialism, 233, 235
Imperial University, 50
income inequality, 191, 205, 209–10
incomes, rise and fall of, 191
Independent, 282
Independent Age, 10
individual effort, 16
individualism, 10
Infrastructure Act, 155
infrastructure of persuasion, 1, 2
Injunctions to Prevent Nuisance and Annoyance
    (IPNAs), 29–30
Innospec, 163
Institute of Economic Affairs, 214
Institute for Public Policy Research, 281
Intergovernmental Panel on Climate Change, 148
International Assessment of Agriculture Knowledge,
    142
international conferences, 154, 158. *See also specific
    conferences*
International Energy Agency, 149, 172
International Family Planning Perspectives, 73
International Institute for Environment and
    Development, 104
International Monetary Fund, 220
investor-state dispute settlement, 250, 251, 252, 253
Ishiguro, Kazuo, 63
ISIS, 242, 243
Islamic State, 241

J

Jabhat al-Nusra, 243
Japan Tobacco International, 223
Jefferson, Thomas, 230

Jesus, 58–9
Joint Congressional Inquiry into 9/11, 244
Jones, Digby, 263
Jones, Griff Rhys, 278
Joseph, Keith, 220
journals/journalists, 2, 6, 194–6, 214, 222–4
Judson, Jeff, 214
junk, festival of, 205
Justices of the Peace Act (1361), 276
JWT, 287

K

Kahneman, Daniel, 188–9
Kenny, Paul, 266
Kensington Palace Gardens, 282
Keynes, John Maynard, 219
Kidd, Benjamin, 234
Kikuyu, 232, 233, 235
killer whales, change of diet of, 84
King's College London, 39
Kingsnorth climate camp, 260
Kith (Griffiths), 43
Klein, Joe, 56
knowledge monopoly, 197
Knox, Robert, 233
Koch, Charles, 211, 212, 214
Koch, David, 211, 212, 214
Koch Industries, 211

L

Labour Party, 23, 129, 183, 263, 264, 266, 267, 281, 283,
    289
Lac Long Quân, 90
laissez-faire economics, 3, 182
Lake District, 135
Lancet, 73, 75
land-clearing grants, 133
land reform programmes
    in China, 141
    in Scotland, 275, 277–9
    in South Korea, Taiwan and Japan, 141
landscape pornographers, 109
The Land magazine, 277
land value taxation, 278, 282, 283
Latin America, abortion rate, 75–6
law enforcement, in schools in Texas, 62, 66
Lawson-Cruttenden, Timothy, 269
lead poisoning, and crime rates, 161–2
lead pollution, 161, 163
Leahy, Terry, 216
Leonard, Annie, 203
Leopold, Aldo, 88
Liberal Democrats, 280
Liberty, 29, 30
Lilley, Peter, 215
limited liability, 5
Lindqvist, Sven, 233
linearity, 91, 92, 98
livestock production, 113, 114
living systems, impacts of, 80
Lloyd George, David, 277
Lomborg, Bjorn, 200
The Lomborg Deception (Friel), 200
London Business School, 49, 50
London School of Economics (LSE), 49, 50
loneliness, 10, 11, 16
Longannet (Scotland), 172

Lord of the Rings, the Two Towers (film), 90
L'Osservatore Romano, 231
Lovelock, James, 103, 106, 107
Lucan, Lord, 213
lung cancer, as caused by air pollution, 171
lynx, return of to former ranges, 97

M

Macdonald, Lord, 30
Main Kampf (Hitler), 234
maize cultivation, impact of, 124–5
Major, John, 215, 275
Malthus, Thomas, 180, 181, 182
management consultancy, jobs in, 48, 49, 187
Mandelson, Lord, 105
Manilow, Barry, 69
mansion tax, 278, 282
manure production, 114
Marcus Crassus, 191
marine faecal plumes, 79, 82
marine parks, 98
market economy, 5, 16
market freedom, 45, 198, 218
market fundamentalism, 3, 15, 16, 17
Marlowe, Christopher, 120
marriage
    same-sex marriage, 58
    sex outside of, 60
Marshall, George, 158
mass mobilisation, 6
Mau Mau rebellion, 233
Maxwell, Robert, 196, 195195
meat production, 113, 114
media
    accountability of journalists, 222, 224
    as bullying, 23
    on drone strikes, 56
    fascination with power politics, 287
    as instrument of corporate power, 212
    payola scandals, 223
    role of as promoter of neoliberal programme,
        220–1
    think tanks and, 214–16
Men in Sheds, 13
mental health crises, 21–2
mercury pollution, 170
merit, 15, 16
meritocracy, 186
mesopredators, 80–1
methylmercury, 171
micro-hydropower, 166
migratory fish, 167
Milanovic, Branko, 191
Miliband, Ed, 278, 289
military intervention, vs. political solutions, 244
Millennium Ecosystem Assessment, 201
millionaires
    as funders, 23
    media as owned by, 220
    political parties as in the clutches of, 26
    Shaun Woodward, 266
    tax rate, 285
    as on top of *scala natura*, 1–2
    in US Congress, 24
mineral exhaustion, 150
money transfers, 236–9
monsters, human encounters with, 90, 91, 98

Mont Pelerin Society, 218, 220
Montreal Protocol, 100
moose, return of to former ranges, 97
Moral Maze (BBC programme), 206
Morgan, Rhodri, 148
Morris, Chris, 238
Mosquito youth dispersal device, 67, 68, 69, 71
Mother Jones, 160
MSNBC, 56
Mugabe, Robert, 139, 142
multilateralism, 101
Murdoch, Rupert, 193, 194, 212, 267
Murphy, Guy, 287, 288
Murphy-O'Connor, Cormac (Cardinal), 72–3
Muslim world, bombing of, 241, 243, 244–5

N

National Council for Educational Excellence, 264
National Ecosystem Assessment (UK), 121
National Extremism Tactical Co-ordination Unit
        (NETCU), 260, 261, 262
National Farmers' Union (NFU), 124, 127, 128, 129
National Institutes of Health (US), 196
National Union of Rail, Maritime and Transport
        Workers (RMT), 267
Natural Resources Wales, 132
natural gas, impacts of, 167
natural world
    creating refuges for, 102
    deterioration of, 19, 24
Nature, 106
nature programmes, popularity of, 92
negative freedom, 4
neoliberalism, 3, 4, 5, 15, 16, 17, 190, 191, 213, 215,
        216, 218, 219, 220, 221
Netherlands, abortion rate, 75
Never Let Me Go (Ishiguro), 63–4
New Labour, 288
New Testament, pastoral tradition as depicted in, 120
Newtown, Connecticut, 53, 55, 56
New York Times, 231
New York University, 54
Nexus 7, 205
NFU (National Farmers' Union), 124, 127, 128, 129
Ngena detention camp, 232
NHS, 72, 253
Nigeria, greenhouse gas emissions in, 87
1950s, as golden age, 61
Nixon, Richard, 219
North American Free Trade Agreement, 252
North American roc (*Aiolornis incredibilis*), 85
Northern Rock, 198–9, 201
North Sea, 149, 156
Northumberland County Council, 149
Norway, climate change policies, 157
No Turning Back (Pirie), 215, 216
No Turning Back group, 215
nuclear family, 58, 59, 60
nuclear power, 150, 164–72
nursery consultant, 20

O

Obama, Barack, 53, 54, 55, 56, 157, 209, 210, 243, 255,
        256
O'Brien, Mike, 148
Observer, 210, 260, 261
occupations, pointless and destructive jobs, 48

Occupy London, 192
Odone, Cristina, 61
OECD, 142
Office of the Comptroller of the Currency (US), 235, 240
Ofsted, 40
oil and gas prospecting/drilling, 149, 151, 156, 157, 159, 176–7
Oil and Gas UK, 156
Oldham, Taki, 211
Old Poor Law (England), 179
oligarchs, 2, 3, 15, 121, 219, 275, 279
Olin, John M., 16, 219
One Hyde Park, 282
opencast coal mines, 147, 149, 155
opiate use, 34–5
Optimum Population Trust (OPT), 106
Osborne, George, 181, 182, 281
outdoor learning, 39–42
Oxfam, 187
Oxford Farming Conference, 133
Oxford University, 49, 50, 51

P

particulates, 171
pastoral tradition, impact of, 120–1
Paterson, Owen, 133, 134, 135, 136, 137
pathological consumption, 204
pay gap, 187
Peak District National Park, 137
peak oil, 150
Pearl, Steve, 260
performance anxiety, 17
Perrara, Peter, 223
personality disorders, 17, 189
Petroamazonas, 176
Pew, Joseph N., Jr., 16, 219
Philadelphia General Hospital, 34
Philip Morris, 250
Philo, Greg, 281
pig farming, 114
Piketty, Thomas, 1
Pinochet, Augusto, 3
Pirie, Madsen, 214, 215
Pitt Review, 136
planet-eating machine, 102
plant plankton, 82, 83, 85, 86, 87
play, in children, 43–7
playdate coaches, 20–1
plutocratic power, 2, 6, 24, 213
Podhoretz, John, 230
pointless consumption, 205
political constraint, 24
political elite, 100
political freedom, 5
politics, as bankrolled by big oil and big coal, 157
poll tax, 215
pollution
    air pollution, 169, 171
    from coal, 167, 170
    lead pollution, 161, 163
    mercury pollution, 170
    radioactive pollution, 164
pollution permits, 158
Pontbren, 131, 132
poor
    blaming of for excesses of the rich, 107
    characterised as unthinking beasts, 180

cutting essential services for, 275
    effect of raising taxes on, 209
    freedom of the rich to exploit the poor, 274
    misery inflicted on, 75
    as new deviants, 16
    power over, 24
    punishment of for errors of the rich, 285
    shutting of out of healthcare, 287
    as trapped in culture of dependency, 179
    ultra-rich as deciding very poor are trashing the planet, 106
Poor Law Amendment Act (1834), 181
poor relief, 180, 181, 182
poor-rich men, 22
Pope Benedict XVI, 73, 74, 76
population growth, 103–4, 106
Porritt, Jonathan, 106
Portillo, Michael, 215
possessions, 175
poverty, 179–83
The Power of Market Fundamentalism (Block and Somers), 180
predators, 80–1, 89
pregnancy
    premarital pregnancy, 60
    relationship between sex education and falling rates of unintended pregnancy, 74–5
pre-marital sex, 75
Prentis, Dave, 266
Press Complaints Commission, 224
Private Eye, 244
Proceedings of the National Academy of Sciences, 171
Progressives, 286, 289
property taxes, 278, 281
Protection from Harassment Act (1997), 269
protests
    injunctions against, 269
    as muted, 24
    suppression of, 3, 4, 28, 257, 259, 260, 262, 276
proxy life, 24
psychology, applications of advances in, 285–7, 289
Psychology, Crime and Law (journal), 189
public advocacy, 223
Public Library of Science, 196
public places, keeping children and teenagers out of, 67–71
public services, 4, 15, 24, 215, 218, 219, 220, 264, 272, 274, 280
Public Space Protection Orders, 29
public spending, 15, 130

Q

Quantock Hills, 107, 109

R

The Races of Man (Knox), 234
racism, 163, 234, 239
radioactive pollution, 164
Ramsay, Adam, 273
The Rational Optimist (Ridley), 199, 200
Ratzel, Friedrich, 234
Reader, W. Winwood, 234
Reagan, Ronald, 15, 100, 191
Rebel Clown Army, 260
Red Tape Challenge on Agriculture, 127
reforestation, 132, 133, 134
Reformation, 59–60

regulation
and Deepwater Horizon disaster, 201
elite as released from, 21
failure of in Northern Rock issue, 199
failure of in soil issues, 125
groups fighting regulation of tobacco, 223
investor-state dispute settlement and, 250
Koch brothers lobbying against, 211
legalisation and regulation of drugs, 33–4
promotion of less regulation for business, 216
and Red Tape Challenge on Agriculture, 127
as restraint on market freedom, 198
unregulated lending, 217
religion, primary purpose of, 73
religious conviction, impact of on abortion rate, 74
remittance system, 237, 239
renewable energy, 158, 165, 166
Republicans, in US, 186, 210, 219, 220
Research Councils UK, 196
Resolution Foundation, 185
reward, inverse relationship of utility with, 184
rewilding, 97, 98, 102, 135
Ricardo, David, 181, 182
rich. *See also* billionaires; millionaires; super-rich;
super-wealthy; ultra-rich; undeserving rich
benefits from apparatus of justification for, 1
blaming of poor for excesses of, 107
freeing of from constraints of democracy, 216
less power over, 24
as new righteous, 16
punishment of the poor for errors of, 285
raising taxes as taking money from, 209
as wealth creators, 190
Ridley, Matt, 198, 199, 200, 201, 202
Riedel, Bruce, 54
River Dove, 137
rivers, damming and weiring of, 166–7
Rivers Trust, 126
RMT (National Union of Rail, Maritime and Trans-
port Workers), 267
roadkill, 111
The Road (film), 227
roc, Argentine (*Argentavis magnificens*), 85
roc, North American (*Aiolornis incredibilis*), 85
Rockefeller, John D., 1, 191
Rogue Male (Household), 211
Rolling Stone magazine, 54
Romney, Mitt, 186
Rousseau, Jean-Jacques, 23
Rowan, Michael, 178
Royal Commission into the Operation of the Poor
Laws, 181
Royal Mines Act (1424), 276
Rural Payments Agency, 125
RWE npower, 258–9, 260

S

same-sex marriage, 58
Sand Creek Massacre (1864), 230
Santelli, Rick, 210
Sasol, 151
Satterhwaite, David, 104
Scaife, Richard Mellon, 16, 219
scala natura, 2
The Sceptical Environmentalist (Lomborg), 200
Schaverien, Joy, 64
Science of the Total Environment, 114

Scotland
compulsory sale orders in, 46
consideration of independence of, 272–4
land reform programmes in, 275, 277–9
Scruton, Roger, 223
sea, restoration of, 97–8
self-advancement, 22, 286
self-attribution fallacy, 17, 188, 191–2
self-harm, 17, 22, 274
self-interest, 15, 200, 286, 288
Sen, Amartya, 139, 140
Serengeti, 86
Serious Fraud Office (UK), 244
Serious Organised Crime and Police Act, 269
Serra, Junipero, 229
Severn River, 131, 132
sex education, relationship of with rates of unintended
pregnancy, 74–5
sex outside marriage, 60
shale gas production, 167
Shanghai, particulate concentrations in, 171
sheep ranching, 114, 119–22
Sheffield University, 50
Sheil, John, 49, 50
Shell, 157
shopping, value of, 25
Shrewsbury, 132
signature strike doctrine, 56
Sigurd, 90
silence
about fossil fuels, 154–6, 158
on corporation tax, 281
pattern of that surrounds our lives, 154
on property tax, 281–2
that stifles political thought in UK, 278
on windfall tax, 281
Simpson, Alan, 210
Sinbad, 90
Slim, Carlos, 191
Smith, Adam, 282
Smith, Iain Duncan, 182
Snakes in Suits (Babiak and Hare), 190
social immobility, 19
social isolation, 10
social mobility, 16, 216, 277
social phobia, 17
social security, 125, 179, 182, 218, 281, 284
Soco, 177
soil
as being torn apart for no good reason,
125
compaction of, 121, 125, 128, 133
destablising of, 119
erosion of, 80, 114, 120, 123, 125, 126,
128
loss of, 124
management of, 126
protection of, 123, 125, 127, 128, 129
soil slumping, 114
Soil Framework Directive, 128
Soil Management Review, 126
Soil Protection Review (SPR), 125, 126, 127
solar power, 166
Solovetsky camp, 232
Somalis, 235–40
Somers, Margaret, 180, 182
South Down, 134

Soviet Union
    abortion rate, 74
    oligarchs after break up of, 15
space, colonisation of, 178
Spencer, Herbert, 1, 234
Spenser, Edmund, 120
spillover effect, 98
spontaneous gatherings, banning of, 28
Springer, 194, 195
Stanford University, 54
Stannard, David, 227
Stapleton, Howard, 67
St George, 90
Stiglitz, Joseph, 210
St John and St Elizabeth's, 72
The Story of Stuff (film), 203
street life, 28
sub-Saharan Africa
    greenhouses gas emissions in, 104
    population growth in, 103
subsidies
    for business, 220
    to farmers, 121, 122, 124, 125, 127, 128, 133, 276
    to grouse estates, 137, 275
Suffolk, 134
Suharto, 3
Sultan of Brunei, 282
The Sunday Times, 106, 182, 193
superhuman passivity, 24
super-rich, 107, 137, 177, 281–2
super-wealthy, 105
Sustainable Human team, 84
sustained growth, 99, 176
systematic injustice/abuse, 63–4
system justification, 272

T

talent, outcomes as based on, 16
taxation
    according to Matt Ridley, 198
    according to neoliberalism, 15, 218
    break from for companies working in North Sea, 149
    capital gains tax, 276, 280
    on Class A drug trade, 35
    corporation tax, 281
    council tax, 282
    elite as released from, 21
    land value tax, 278, 282, 283
    mansion tax, 278, 282
    no representation without, 216
    poll tax, 215
    property taxes, 278, 281
    in UK, 276–7
    in US, 209–12
    windfall tax, 281
tax evasion, 265
tax exiles, 274
Tax Justice Network, 192
Taylor, Alison, 64
Taylor, Frederick, 19
Taylor, William (Father), 192
Tea Party movement, 210–12
Telegraph (Odone), 61
television, as source of consolation, 11–12, 24, 25
Tesco, 216
tetraethyl lead, 161, 163

Texas (USA)
    age of criminal responsibility in, 69
    law enforcement in schools in, 62
TGWU (Transport and General Workers' Union), 265, 266
Thatcher, Margaret, 15, 100, 191, 214, 215, 219, 220, 264, 287, 288
Thatcherism, 215
Theocritus, 120
think tanks, 1, 2, 16, 24, 213, 214, 216, 219, 224
Think Tank: The Story of the Adam Smith Institute (Pirie), 214
Thomas, Lord Justice, 163
Three-Mile Island disaster, 164
three Rs, renovation, recipes and resorts, 25
Thrupp Lake, 258
Tille, Alexander, 234
The Times, 193, 214
Timms, Stephen, 148
Tocqueville, Alexis de, 26
Todashev, Ibragim, 254, 255
Tories, 265
torture, 232–3
Townsend, Joseph, 180
trade rules, 205
Transatlantic Trade and Investment Partnership (TTIP), 4, 250
Transform, 36
Transport and General Workers' Union (TGWU), 265, 266
tree-planting grants, 132, 133
trophic cascades, 80, 81, 84, 87
tufta, 17
Turkey, farming in, 140, 142
Two Concepts of Liberty (Berlin), 4

U

UK Boarding Schools, 64
UKIP, 273
UK Life League, 261
ultra-rich, 106, 188, 218
Ulysses, 90
unconventional oil, 151
undeserving rich, 187, 192
unemployment, 17, 179, 180, 182, 238
Unicef, 75
unions. *See also* Fire Brigades Union (FBU); General, Municipal, Boilermakers and Allied Trade Union (GMB); National Farmers' Union (NFU); National Union of Rail, Maritime and Transport Workers (RMT); Transport and General Workers' Union (TGWU)
    breaking of/smashing of, 218, 220
    Gordon Brown government and, 263–7
    shaking off of, 190
    subsidies and, 121
    testing of, 264
    and Tories, 265
Unison, 266
Unite, 265
United Kingdom (UK)
    abortion rate, 74
    and age of criminal responsibility, 69
    children's well-being in, 22
    consumer debt in, 217
    income in, 191
    market fundamentalism in, 16

neoliberalism in, 15
pay gap in, 187
taxation in, 276–7
teenage pregnancy rate, 75
wage of care workers in, 185
United States (US)
    abortion rate, 74
    bridge inspections in, 217
    cocaine use in, 33
    Conservatives in, 288
    crime rates in, 161
    deaths caused by pollution from coal plants in, 170, 171
    demands of blue-collar workers in, 285
    and drone strikes. *See* drone strikes
    and illegal money transfers, 239
    income in, 191, 205, 272
    lead withdrawn from petrol, 161
    market fundamentalism in, 16
    neoliberalism in, 15
    productivity in, 191
    reforestation in, 97
    shift of wealth in, 218
    taxation in, 209–12
    teenage pregnancy rate, 75
    wage of care workers in, 185
Universal Declaration of Human Rights, 196
universalism, 285
University of Milan, 11
University of Tasmania, 83
UN Office on Drugs and Crime, 32, 34
upland grazing, 121–2
US Congress, millionaires in, 24
utility, inverse relationship of with reward, 184

V
values, importance of in changing political map, 288
van Valkenburgh, Blaire, 89
Verhaeghe, Paul, 14, 15, 17
vertebrate wildlife, loss of, 88
Victorians, 60, 61
Virgil, 120
Virunga national park (Africa), 177

W
wages
    of care workers, 185
    redistribution of, 187
Wales
    coal mining in, 147, 155
    livestock farming in, 121
    tree-planting grants in, 132
Walking Football, 13
Wallace, Alfred Russell, 234
WalMart, 193
Walton, Izaac, 22, 137
war of every man against every man/war of all against all, 9, 10, 12
Warwick agreement, 265, 267
Warwick University, 50
Washington, George, 230
wealth

as ambition, 10–11, 12
    correlation between global warming and, 105–6
    global wealth, 12, 176
    shift of in US, 218
    wealth creators, 190, 221, 276
Weekly Standard, 230
Wellcome Trust, 182
Welz, Adam, 204
West Antarctic ice sheet, 176
whale poo, 79, 82, 83
whale pump, 82, 84
whales, as maintaining populations of animals they eat, 82–3
whaling, impact of on Californian condors, 84–5
What About Me?: The Struggle for Identity in a Market-Based Society (Verhaeghe), 14
White, Charles, 233
WHO (World Health Organization), 34, 75, 76, 169, 171
WideHorizons, 40
wildebeest, 86
Wilderness Foundation UK, 39
wildlife
    encounters with, 107–12, 115
    loss of, 88
Wiley-Blackwell, 194
Williams, Armstrong, 223
windfall tax, 281
windfarms, 165
wind power, 166
wolves
    impact of, 84, 86–7
    return of to former ranges, 97
wonder, value of, 97, 98
Wood, Ian, 155–6
Wood Group, 155
Woodley, Tony, 266
Woodward, Shaun, 266
World Bank, 220
World Health Organization (WHO), 34, 75, 76, 169, 171
A World of Their Own Making (Gillis), 59
World Wildlife Fund for Nature (WWF), 285
Wrigley, EA, 167

X
xawala system, 237–8

Y
yachts, fuel use of, 105
Yasuni national park (Ecuador), 176
Yellowstone National Park, 84
You and Yours (radio programme), 184
YoungMinds, 22
youth. *See also* children
    curfews for, 70
    on the streets, dispersal of, 67–71

Z
zero-hour contracts, 24
Zimbabwe, farming in, 139

May 14